AMAZING NORTHEAST

NAGALAND

AMAZING NORTHEAST

NAGALAND

Edited & Compiled by
Aribam Indubala Devi

Vij Books India Pvt. Ltd.
(Publishers, Dustributors & Importers)
4675-A, 21, Ansari Road, Darya Ganj,
New Delhi-110002

Published by
Vij Books India Pvt. Ltd.
(Publishers, Distributors & Importers)
4675-A, 21, Ansari Road, Darya Ganj,
New Delhi-110002
Phone: 91-11-65449971, 91-11-43596460
Fax: 91-11-47340674
E-mail: vijbooks@rediffmail.com

Copyright © Publishers

First Edition: 2010

ISBN: 978-93-80177-29-8

Contents

Preface

In India, the Northeastern region is quite charming and interesting enough to be known about. Among the eight Northeastern States, Nagaland is mostly mountainous, except those areas, bordering Assam valley. Mount Saramati is the highest peak in Nagaland with a height of 3,840 metre and its range forms a natural barrier between Nagaland and Myanmar. Naga people belong to Indo-Mongoloid group of people, living in contiguous areas of the northeastern hills of India and the upper portion of Western Myanmar. Major recognised tribes of Nagaland are Angami, Ao, Chakhesang, Chang, Khiamniungan, Kuki, Konyak, Lotha, Phom, Pochury, Rengma, Sangtam, Sumi, Yimchungru and Zeliang.

Nagaland, as a State of the Indian Union, was established in 1963. It is bound by Myanmar on east, Arunachal on north, Assam on west and Manipur on south. It lies between the parallels of 98 degree and 96 degree E longitude and 26.6 degree and 27.4 degree N latitude. The State of Nagaland has an area of 16.579 sq km with a population of 19,88,636 as per the 2001 census. Naga languages differ from tribe to tribe and sometimes even from one village to another. They all are, however, under the Tibeto-Burma family. In 12th and 13th centuries, gradual contacts with Ahoms of present day Assam were established but this did not have any significant impact on traditional Naga way of life. However, in 19th Century the British appeared on the scene and ultimately the area was brought under British Administration. After independence, this territory was made a centrally administered area in 1957, administered by the Governor of Assam. It was known as the Naga Hills Tuensang Area. This failed to quell popular aspirations and unrest began. Hence, in 1961, the area was renamed as Nagaland and given the status of a State of the Indian Union, which was formally inaugurated on 1 December 1963.

This small but comprehensive and compact book on this northeastern state, offers all information, within one cover. Hopefully, it would serve all those working on or interested in knowing about northeastern India, be they scholars, researchers, journalists, students or general readers. This is in fact, 'Knowledge in Nutshell'.

— *Editor*

Nagaland
An Overview

Governor	:	Nikhil Kumar
Chief Minister	:	Neiphiu Rio
Speaker	:	Kiyanilie Peseyie
Chief Secretary	:	Lalthara
Capital	:	Kohima
High Court	:	Guwahati (Bench at Kohima)

Brief Description

Nagaland or the land of the Nagas is located between 93.20° to 95.15° East longitude and 25.60° to 26.40° North latitude in the extreme northeastern end of India. It is bounded by Myanmar in the east, Assam in the west, Arunachal Pradesh and a part of Assam in the north and Manipur in the south. Nagaland shares a 258 km long international border with Myanmar.

Nagaland is spread over a total area of 16,579 sq km comprising 6.32 per cent of the whole of North-East and 0.5 per cent of the total area of India. Nagaland became the 16th State of the Indian union on 1 December 1963. The state capital Kohima is

Facts and Figures

- *Area:* 16,527 sq km (6.3% of total area of North-East)
- *Geographical Location:* Situated between 25°6' N to 27°4'N latitude & 93°20'E to 95°15'E longitude
- *Capital:* Kohima
- *Population:* 19,88,636 (2001 Census) (5% of population of North-East)
- *Principal Languages*: Angami, Ao, Chang, Konyak, Lotha, Sangtam, Sema and Chakhesang
- *Male:* 10,41,686
- *Female:* 9,46,950

Contd...

located at 1,444.12 m above the sea level. The state is currently divided into 11 districts.

The people of Nagaland though commonly known as the Nagas, actually comprise 16 tribes (Konyak, Lotha, Phom, Pochury, Rengma, Sumi, Sangtam, Yimchungru, Zeliang) and many more subtribes belonging to the mongoloid stock. According to Census 2001, Nagaland has a total population of 1,988,636 and a density of 120 persons per sq km. It constitutes 0.19 per cent of the total population of India and 5.09 per cent of the entire North-East.

The economy of the state is predominantly based on agriculture. The major land use pattern is slash and burn cultivation locally known as *jhum*. About 1,01,400 hectare of land is under *jhum* cultivation. 68.03 per cent of the working population pursue agriculture and other allied activities as their chief means of livelihood. The per capita Gross State Domestic Product (GSDP) in 2004-05 is rupees 26,129. Nagaland ranks 11th in the human resource development index and 22nd in the poverty index in India. The rate of literacy of the state is 67.11 per cent.

According to an estimate in 2003, 52 per cent of the total land area of the state is under forests. Nagaland is rich with regard to its mineral wealth. The total deposit of limestone in the state is estimated at 1,000 million tonnes. In addition, there are substantial

- *Density (per sq km):* 120 (National Figure: 324)
- *Per Capita Income (1996-97):* Rs. 11,368
- *Population below Poverty Line:* 32.7% (National Figure: 27.5%)
- *Sex Ratio:* 900 females to 1,000 males (National figure: 933 females to 1,000 males)
- *Literacy Rate (2007):* 72.5% (National Figure: 67.6%)
- *Birth Rate (2006):* 17.3 (National Figure: 23.1)
- *Death Rate (2006):* 4.8 (National Figure: 7.4)
- *Infant Mortality Rate (2007):* 21 (National Figure: 55)
- *No. of Towns (as per 2001 Census):* 9
- *No. of Villages (as per 2001 Census):* 1317
- *Per Capita Income (in Rs.) (2006-07):* 20,998 (National Figure: Rs. 29,901)
- *Net State Domestic Product (NSDP) (Rs. in crore) (2005-06):* 5,255 (National Figure: 29,02,074)
- *Per Capita NSDP (2005-06):* Rs. 21,083 (National Figure: Rs. 26,003)
- *Per Capita GSDP (2004-05):* Rs. 26,129 (National Figure: Rs. 25,944)
- *State Bird:* Blyth 's Tragopan
- *State Animal:* Mithun
- *State Flower:* Rhododendron
- *Language:* Nagamese, English, Hindi & local dialects

Contd...

reserves of marble and decorative stone reserves, petroleum and natural gas. But due to lack of modern industries, proper utilisation of these resources has been rather restricted. The process of industrialisation in the state is in its infancy.

The six-decade long insurgency has been a major impediment for the development in the state. Insurgent violence has impacted on all sectors of governance and lives of the common people. Although the major outfits are under ceasefire with the government, effective peace is yet to return to the state. In addition, illegal migration of Bangladeshis is emerging as a potential area of future conflict in the state.

- *No. of Districts:* (11) Dimapur, Kiphire, Kohima, Longleng, Mokokchung, Mon, Peren, Phek, Tuensang, Wokha, Zunheboto
- *Major Towns:* Dimapur, Kohima, Mokokchung, Tuensang, Wokha, Mon, Zunheboto
- *Major Crops:* Rice, Maize, Wheat, Grams, Mustard, Cotton, Jute, Sugarcane
- *Major Plantations:* Tea, Rubber, Coffee
- *Major Fruits, Vegetables & Spices:* Banana, Pineapple, Jackfruit, Potato, Sweet, potato, Tapioca, Chillies, Ginger, Garlic
- *Major Minerals:* Coal, Limestone, Petroleum, Slate
- *Airport:* Dimapur

Area, Population and Headquarters of Districts

S.No.	District	Area (sq km)	Population	Headquarters
1	Kohima	3,144	3,14,366	Kohima
2.	Mokokchung	1,615	2,27,320	Mokokchung
3.	Mon 1,876	2,59,604		Mon
4.	Tuensang	4,228	4,14,801	Phek
5.	Zunheboto	1,255	1,54,909	Tuensang
6.	Wokha	1,628	1,61,098	Wokha
7.	Dimapur	927	3,08,382	Dimapur
8.	Phek	2,026	1,48,246	Phek
9.	Kiphire	1,255	1,06,136	Kiphire
10.	Longleng	885	1,58,300	Longleng
11.	Peren	2,300	96,825	Peren Town

[Based on Latest Official Data Available]

Nagaland

Outline Map

Geographical Map

Tourist Map

Districts of the State

$$\boxed{1}$$

Introduction

Nagaland is a hill state located in the far northeastern part of India. It borders the state of Assam to the west, Arunachal Pradesh and part of Assam to the north, Myanmar to the east and Manipur to the south. The state capital is Kohima, and the largest city is Dimapur. With a population of nearly two million people, it has a total area of 16,527 sq km — making it one of the smallest states of India.

Nagaland offers rich incomparable traditional and cultural heritage. The State of Nagaland was formally inaugurated on December 1st, 1963, as the 16th State of the Indian Union. The State consists of eight Administrative Districts, inhabited by 16 major tribes along with other subtribes. The terrain is hilly, rugged and mountainous. The highest peak is Saramati in the Twensang District which is 3,840 metres above sea level. The average height of the peaks is between 900 and 1,200 metres. The main rivers that flow through the state are Dhansiri, Doyang, Dikhu, Tizu and Melak.

There is no waterfall in Nagaland. The only lake well known is Lacham to the east of Mehiri. The hill sides are covered with green forests. In the Angami region, the terraced fields are a feast to the eyes. Nagaland has a single-chamber Legislative Assembly with 60 seats. The state sends two members to the Indian National Parliament: one to the Rajya Sabha (upper house) and one to the Lok Sabha (lower house).

If one is looking for a quiet getaway, from the hustle and bustle of city life, it provides the right ambience; as life here is laidback and slow — providing a tension free life. For the adventurous and the intrepid, Nagaland is an ideal place for trekking, rock climbing, jungle camping and offers limitless exploration possibilities in its lush and verdant subtropical rain forests which are also a treasure trove of a plethora of medicinal plants.

Historical Aspects

The early history of Nagaland is the customs, economic activities of the Naga tribes. The people were originally referred to as Chingmee (Hill People) or Hao (Tribes) in the history of Manipur. The Naga tribes had socio-economic and political links with tribes in Assam and Burma (Myanmar) Even today a large population of Naga inhabits Assam. Following an invasion in 1816, the area along with Assam came under direct rule of Burma. This period was noted for the oppressive rule and turmoil in Assam and Nagaland. When the British East India Company took control of Assam in 1826, they steadily expanded their domain over modern Nagaland. By 1892, all of modern Nagaland except the Tuensang area in the North-East was governed by the British. It was politically amalgamated into Assam. The Christian missionaries played an important part in converting Nagaland's Naga tribes in Christianity.

After the independence of India in 1947, the area remained a part of the province of Assam. Nationalist activities arose amongst Naga tribes, who demanded a political union of their ancestral and native groups, damaged government and civil infrastructure, and attacked government officials and civilians from other states of India. The Union government sent the Indian Army in 1955, to restore order.

In 1957, the government began diplomatic talks with representatives of Naga tribes, and the Naga Hills District of Assam and the Tuensang frontier were united in a single political entity that became a Union territory — directly administered by the Central government with a large degree of autonomy. This was not satisfactory to the tribes, however, and soon agitation and violence increased across the state — included attacks on Army and government institutions, as well as civil disobedience and non-payment of taxes.

In July 1960, a further political accord was reached at the Naga People's Convention that Nagaland should become a constituent and self-governing state in the Indian union. Statehood was officially granted in 1963 and the first state-level democratic elections were held in 1964. Insurgencies were quelled in the early-1980s. Violence had re-erupted and there was conflict between rebel group factions till the late-1990s. On 25 July, 1997, Prime Minister Inder Kumar Gujral announced that the government after talks with Isaac group of the Nationalist Socialist Council of Nagaland (NSCN) declared a ceasefire or cessation of operations with effect from 1st August, 1997 for a period of three months. The ceasefire has since been extended.

Geographical Aspects

Nagaland is largely a mountainous state. The Naga Hills rise from the Brahmaputra Valley in Assam to about 2,000 feet and rise further to the southeast, as high as 6,000 feet. Mount Saramati at an elevation of 12,598 feet is the state's highest peak — this is where the Naga Hills merge with the Patkai Range in Myanmar. Rivers such as the Doyang and Diphu to the north, the Barak River in the southwest and the Chindwin River of Myanmar in the southeast, dissect the entire state.

Nagaland is rich in flora and fauna. About one-sixth of Nagaland is under the cover of tropical and subtropical evergreen forests — including palms, bamboo and rattan as well as timber and mahogany forests. While some forest areas have been cleared for *jhum* — cultivation — many scrub forests, high grass, reeds and secondary dogs, pangolins, porcupines, elephants, leopards, bears, many species of monkeys, sambar, deers, oxen and buffaloes thrive across the state's forests. The Great Indian Hornbill is one of the most famous birds found in the state.

Nagaland has a largely monsoon climate with high humidity levels. Annual rainfall averages around 70-100 inches — concentrated in the months of May to September. Temperatures range from 70 to 104°F. In winter, temperatures don't generally drop below 39°F, but frost is common at high elevations.

Climate

The salubrious mountain climate of Nagaland is responsible for the health and well-being of the citizens of the state and its visitors. The climate is an important component in the study of the geography of state. Various factors like the altitude, geographical coordinates, distance from the sea and the wind direction influence the climate in Nagaland.

The hilly terrains of the state is instrumental in shaping the cool and pleasant climatic conditions. Summer is the shortest season in the state that lasts for only a few months. The temperature during the summer season remains between the 16 and 31°C. The torrential monsoon downpours continues non-stop during the months of June, July, August and September.

Heavy rainfall occurs between the months of May and August. September and October months influence occasional showers. The recorded average annual rainfall of the state ranges from 2,000-2,500 mm. Winter makes an early arrival. The temperature drops as low as of 4°C in winter. Bitter cold and dry weather strikes certain regions of the state. The maximum average temperature recorded in the winter season is 24°C. The higher altitudes are enveloped in snow. Strong northwest winds blow across Nagaland during the months of February and March.

Rivers

The proximity to the Himalayan foothills and the torrential monsoon rains has resulted in the prosperity of the mighty rivers in Nagaland. The rivers form an integral part of the geography of Nagaland. The mountain region is the source of several streams and rivulets. The tributaries of the great Brahmaputra River flow through the state to join the main river before reaching its mouth in the Bay of Bengal.

The state is drained by four main rivers. One of the chief tributaries of the Brahmaputra River is Dhansiri which originates in the mountainous Laisang peak. The districts of Nagaland receives water from the Dhansiri River prior to its confluence with the Brahmaputra River.

Three other rivers are the Dikhu, Doyang and the Jhanji. The four chief rivers form huge catchment areas. The rich alluvial deposit of the rivers facilitates crop cultivation in the state. The government has also set up power stations in order to generate hydroelectricity from these rivers. Fishes breed in the fresh mountain waters of the rivers.

Vegetation

The lush green vegetation depicts the natural and the cultivated growth in the state. The lush foliage is dependent on the geography of Nagaland. The economy of the state is dependent on agriculture which forms the chief occupation of the tribal inhabitants. The people practice terrace farming in the hilly regions of the state. Drained by four rivers, the alluvial deposits of the rivers facilitate the growth of various agricultural food products.

The mountainous slopes of the state is rich in the growth of natural vegetation. 8,62,930 hectares of land or 20 per cent of the total land area of the state is covered with the evergreen tropical and subtropical forest that are endowed with rich flora and fauna. The forests of Nagaland are enveloped in a dense growth of timber, palms, mahogany, rattan and bamboos trees. Some parts of the forest regions are accessible to the people of the state while the interiors are impenetrable and home to wild animals.

The crop cultivation is practised by the tribal people of Nagaland. The major crops cultivated in the state are rice, millet, grams, rubber, maize and tea. The state is also reputed for the production of fruits. Banana, orange, fruit, pineapple, pear, jack fruit and plums are cultivated in the state. Garlic, chilli, cabbage, tomato, potato and ginger are some of the main vegetables that account for the cultivation in Nagaland. The agro-based industries like that of edible oils and species facilitate from the cultivation of these products.

The forest regions of the state are being cleared to practice Jhum cultivation. This has caused the depletion of the natural vegetation of Nagaland.

Soil

A survey conducted on the soil of Nagaland has revealed that the soil can be categorised into 10 major groups, 14 subgroups, 4 orders, 7 suborders and 72 soil families. The soils are an important part of the topography and the geography of Nagaland. The classification of the soils into groups and orders have aided the management of the land use planning which is of primary significance in the agricultural sector. The systematic survey and classification of soils in Nagaland has facilitated extensive crop cultivation in the state.

The following are the four orders of soil in Nagaland that constitute the 16.6 million hectares of geographical land of the state:

- Inceptisols,
- Entisols,
- Alfisols,
- Ultisols.

The most important type of soil that covers about 66 per cent of the land area of Nagaland are the Inceptisols. The soil textures consists of fine clay, clay loamy and the fine loamy clay. These soil types are predominant near the river beds.

About 23.8 per cent of the land area is enveloped by the Utisols. The soil is characterised by its low base saturation feature. This soil type is found in different regions of the state and is prevalent mostly in the forested regions of the state which receive a high amount of rainfall. The texture of the soil remains clayey.

Entisols cover 7.3 per cent of the land area and is found mainly in the north and the Northeastern parts of the state. This nascent category of soil comprises fine loamy and the fine categories of soil textures.

The light coloured and mineral rich, Alfisols cover a meagre 2.9 per cent of the land area. The fine loamy and the fine drained class of soil texture occur in the western extremity of the state near its border with Assam.

Flora and Fauna

The variations in the altitude, latitude, climate and soil have given rise to a diversity of forest types, ranging from tropical evergreen to temperate evergreen and the coniferous.

Bamboo groves are extensive everywhere. Among the common species, mention may be made of the Naga Bhe and plants such as Mesuaferrea, Careyaarbotrea and Fiscus electica. On the hill slopes are found oak, chestnut, birch, magnolia, cherry, maple, laurel and fig. Pine trees are found at high altitude areas, varying from 3,000 to 4,000 ft. Wild vegetables, roots, fruits and tubers are found in abundance throughout Nagaland.

Nagaland constitutes a meeting ground for the sub-Himalayan, Indian, Chinese and Burmese type of fauna. Elephants, tigers, barking deer and sambar are found in different places of the state. Monkeys, jackals, wild buffaloes, wild pigs, bear and wild dogs are sparsely distributed through the Naga Hills. Among the ritually most valued species is Mithun. Other common species are lizards, toads, monitors.

Social Aspects

Nagaland society and culture comprises the tribal and subtribal communities, their living patterns, festivals and beliefs. The people of Nagaland are divided into several tribes. These tribes have again many subsections. Commonly known as Naga people, the local inhabitants of Nagaland are said to belong to the Indo-Mongoloid clan. Most of the tribal groups earn their livelihood from agriculture.

The ethnicity is a medley of many tribes and subtribes that have been living in the state, since time immemorial. Christianity is the widely followed religion of the various Naga ethnic groups. Besides, the communities other than Nagas living in the state are followers of Hinduism and Islam.

The social structure of each and every Naga tribe is different from the other. The rituals, festivals and beliefs of each of the Naga tribes differentiate it from another tribe or subtribe. The cultural heritage of Nagas is quite rich. Living in the state harmoniously from many ancient decades, the ethnic communities of Nagaland have developed a vibrant platform of cultural dynamism.

The tribes dwelling in the rural pockets preserve their own age-old customs and rituals. Known for their friendly demeanour and hardworking nature, the people have a significant contribution towards the sociocultural development of the state.

Today, Nagaland houses many a socioethnic communities within its geographical premises all of which have their own distinct array of cultural and social identity.

Demographics

Nagas speak 60 different dialects belonging to the Sino-Tibetan family of languages. Nagamese, a variant language form of Assamese and local dialects is the most widely spoken market language. Every tribe has their own mother tongue language but communicate with each other in Nagamese. As such Nagamese is neither a mother tongue of any of the tribes nor it is a written language. English, the official state language is widely spoken in official circles and is the medium for education in Nagaland.

Christianity is the predominant religion of Nagaland. The census of 2001 recorded the state's Christian population at 1,790,349 (90.02 per cent of the state's population), making it (with Meghalaya and Mizoram) one of the three Christian-majority states in India, and the only state where Christians form 90 per cent of the population. The state has a very high church attendance rate in both urban and rural areas. The largest of Asia's churches dominate the skylines of Kohima, Dimapur and Mokokchung. Among Christians, Baptists are the predominant group constituting more than 75 per cent of the state's population.

Nagaland is known as "The most populated Baptist state in the world". The state's population is 1.988 million, out of which 90.02 per cent are Christians. Seventy-five per cent of the state's population profess the Baptist faith, thus making it more Baptist than Mississippi (in the southern United States), where 52 per cent of its population is Baptist. Catholics, Revivalists, and Pentecostals are the other Christian denomination numbers.

Catholics are found in significant numbers in parts of Wokha District as also in the urban areas of Kohima and Dimapur. Hinduism and Islam are minority religions in state, at 7.7 per cent and 1.8 per cent of the population respectively. A small minority, less than 0.3 per cent, still practise the traditional religions and are mainly concentrated in Peren and the Eastern districts.

Marriage

Marriage in Nagaland is centred around many interesting beliefs, facts and principles that are rooted deep within the tribal people of the state. They strictly follow a set of traditional morals of marriage. As far as the marriages are concerned, the different tribes have different beliefs and morals, which they maintain with dedication and commitment.

As far as marriage is concerned, the Naga tribes follow the exogamous principles. People of the same clan do not marry each other. The only exception in this case is the Konyak chiefs. They are considered sacred and their wives can be of the same clan.

Another tribe named Angami follows a ritual like the strangling of a fowl. Here, the girl can reject the suitor if she dreams of anything inauspicious within a prescribed period of time, while the negotiation is still going on.

The members of the Mongsen tribe practise a strange norm. After the engagement, the boy and the girl sent on a trading journey for twenty days. If the expedition is gainful, the preparations are made for the marriage. In case of a loss, the engagement is broken off as it is considered inauspicious.

While the Angamis are monogamous, the Semas choose to be polygamous and marry as many girls as possible. One of the wives is given the place of the head wife, though she may not be the first wife. Four to six wives are permissible to the Changs. As far as the Lothas are concerned, a rich man may marry another time and have a second wife.

All these curious and peculiar facts make the Nagaland marriages very exciting and interesting.

Food

The food of Nagaland comprises plain rice, cooked vegetables and meat. The local indigenous tribal communities are non-vegetarians who savour meats of all the animals. Dogs, spiders, pork, beef, crabs, cats, chicken and even elephants are eaten with great enthusiasm.

The native population of Naga tribes loves to add spices and chillies in their daily diet. The food habits reflect the unique cultural traits and traditional legacy of the local indigenous inhabitants of Nagaland who usually do not throw any part of the animal. The intestines and skins of the animals are considered to be a delicious dish among the native population of the state.

However, owing to their rich religious beliefs and customs, the Naga tribal community is not allowed to eat flesh of some animals lest the qualities of that particular animal are transferred. As per the traditional rituals, the majority of the restrictions are applied to the female folk. In some cases, the old men are not subjected to any kind of social taboo.

Representing the vibrant and dynamic cultural lifestyle, the local indigenous inhabitants of Nagaland prepare several drinks from rice. Some of the varieties of indigenous drinks are:

- Dzutse,
- Zutho,
- Ruhi.

All the inhabitants of Nagaland savour the drinks irrespective of age and sex. The drinks relieve the native population from the stress and strains of daily living and rejuvenate with a fresh bout of energy and vigour.

Economic Aspects

Nagaland is one of the hill states in the North-East, famous for its rich mosaic of numerous tribes with their rich culture. Agriculture and animal husbandry, including poultry, are the main occupations of the Nagas. Bamboo, cane, spears making and weaving are the traditional occupations of these people. The secondary sector is small. Traditional village industries based on local forest product form the backbone of this sector. The state also possesses natural oil reserves.

Macroeconomic Trend

This is a chart of trend of gross state domestic product of Nagaland at market prices estimated by *Ministry of Statistics and Programme Implementation* with figures in millions of Indian Rupees.

Year	Gross State Domestic Product
1980	1,027
1985	2,730
1990	6,550
1995	18,140
2000	36,790

Nagaland's gross state domestic product for 2004 was estimated at $1.4 billion at current prices. Agriculture is the most important economic activity in Nagaland, with more than 90 per cent of the population employed crops include rice, corn, millets, pulses, tobacco, oilseeds, sugarcane, potatoes and fibres. However, state still depends on the import of food supplies from other states. The widespread practice of *jhum* — clearing for cultivation — has led to soil erosion and loss of fertility, particularly in the eastern districts. Only the Angami and Chakesang tribes in the Kohima and Phek districts use terracing techniques. And most of the Aos, Lothas and Zeliangs in Mokokchung, Wokha and Peren districts respectively cultivates in the many valleys of the district. Forestry is also an important source of income. Cottage industries such as weaving, woodwork and pottery are also an important source of revenue. Tourism is important, but largely limited due to insurgency since the last five decades.

Transportation

The railway network in the state is minimal. The length of broad gauge lines is 12.85 km. The length of National Highway roads is 365.38 km and state roads is 1,094 km. There is one airport in Dimapur and another is being planned for Kohima, the state capital.

Livestock

Livestock in Nagaland is considered to be a major sector which contributes significantly towards the rapid economic growth of the state. Animal husbandry is a prime occupation of the local people of Nagaland. Poultry, fishery, piggery, dairy and cattle farming are the areas which are taken care of under the animal husbandry department of Nagaland. The livestock has huge possibilities of further growth. In fact, the livestock of the state plays an important role in enhancing the economy. The local people include a lot of meat items in their daily diet. Hence, it is but natural that the meat products are in high demand. Also, there is a ready market for dairy, poultry and fish products.

The government of Nagaland is planning to widen the scientific scopes in the field of livestock rearing and breeding in the state. Since the angora wool has a high economic value hence the rearing of angora rabbits is another important field where the State Government is taking initiatives.

In order to make livestock a prime facilitator in the economic progress of the state, there is a need for proper infrastructural system. The poultry farms and fishery departments of the state are required to be equipped with all modern-day facilities that can help in the efficient functioning of the same. There are enough opportunities of transforming the livestock into flourishing an economic field of the state through continuous developmental efforts both by the government and the local inhabitants of the place.

Capital of the State: Kohima

Kohima pronunciation is the hilly capital of India's Northeastern border state of Nagaland which shares its borders with Burma. It lies in Kohima District and is also one of the three Nagaland towns with Municipal council status along with Dimapur and Mokokchung.

Kohima is so called because "Kew Hi" is the name of a plant grown on the mountainside. "Kew Hi Ma" means "the men of the land where the flower Kew Hi grows". Earlier, Kohima was known as "Thigoma".

History

The British incursions into the Naga territory, beginning in the 1840s, met with stiff resistance from the independence loving Nagas who had never been conquered by any empire before. The stiffness of the resistance can be gauged by the fact that it took nearly four decades for the British to conquer a territory that is less than 10,000 square kilometres (the eastern region was left free). Kohima was the first seat of modern administration as the Headquarter of Naga Hills District (then under Assam) with the appointment of G. H. Damant as Political Officer in 1879. When Nagaland became a full-fledged state on 1st December 1963, Kohima was christened as the state capital.

In 1944, during World War II the Battle of Kohima along with the simultaneous Battle of Imphal was the turning point in the Burma Campaign. For the first time in South East Asia the Japanese lost the initiative to the Allies which they then retained until the end of the war. This hand-to-hand battle and slaughter prevented the Japanese from gaining a high base from which they might next roll across the extensive flatlands of India like a juggernaut.

Kohima has a large cemetery for the Allied war dead maintained by the Commonwealth Graves Commission. The cemetery lies on the slopes of Garrison Hill, in what was once the Deputy Commissioner's tennis court which was the scene of intense fighting. The epitaph carved on the memorial of the 2nd British Division in the cemetery

> "When You Go Home, Tell Them Of Us And Say, For Your Tomorrow, We Gave Our Today"

has become world-famous as the Kohima poem. The verse is attributed to John Maxwell Edmonds (1875-1958), and is thought to have been inspired by the epitaph written by Simonides to honour the Greek who fell at the Battle of Thermopylae in 480 BC.

Demographics

As of 2001 India census, Kohima had a population of 78,584. Males constitute 53 per cent of the population and females 47 per cent. Kohima has an average literacy rate of 75 per cent, higher than the national average of 64.84 per cent: male literacy is 79 per cent, and female literacy is 70 per cent. In Kohima, 13 per cent of the population is under 6 years of age.

The main indigenous inhabitants of Kohima District are the Angamis, and the Rengma.

Today the town's population compose of all the 16 tribes of Nagaland. The population of the Angamis and Aos are the largest in present-day Kohima urban area.

Greater Kohima which includes Kohima Village, Jakhama and Jotsoma along with Kohima town is the second largest urban area of Nagaland after Dimapur-Chumukedima. It has a population of about 99,795.

Geography and Climate

Kohima has a pleasant and moderate climate — not too cold in winters and pleasant summers. December and January are the coldest months when frost occurs and in the higher altitudes snowfall occurs occasionally. During the height of summers, from July-August, temperature ranges an average of 80-90 Fahrenheit. Heavy rainfall occurs during summer.

Kohima is located at 25°40' N 94°07' E. It has an average elevation of 1,261 metres (4,137 feet).

The town of Kohima is located on the top of a high ridge and the town serpentines all along the top of the surrounding mountain ranges as is typical of most Naga settlements.

'Kohima village' called 'Bara Basti' or 'large village', which is the largest village in Asia forms the northeastern part of Kohima urban area today. The Bara Basti is divided into 'khels' or localities. There are four of them, namely — Tsutuonuomia, Lhisemia, Dapfutsumia and Pfuchatsumia. They are termed shortly as T, L, D, and P Khel, respectively.

The Nagaland State Museum is a one-stop treasure house where one can get a glimpse into Naga culture through history. The main items exhibited are gateposts, statues, pillars, and jewellery. A ceremonial drum which looks like a dugout war canoe is exhibited in a separate shed. The basement of the museum has birds and animals of the Northeastern hill states.

2

Salient Features

- -

The Backdrop

Like other inhabitants of the Northeastern Region, the Nagas too have their share of legend and folklore regarding their origin and evolution through the ages. Nagas are basically tribal people and every tribe had its own effective system of self-governance from time immemorial. In the 12th and 13th centuries, gradual contact with the Ahoms of present-day Assam was established but this did not have any significant impact on the traditional Naga way of Life. However, in the 19th century the British appeared on the scene and ultimately the area was brought under British administration. After Independence this territory was made a Centrally administered area in 1957, administered by the Governor of Assam. It was known as the Naga Hills Tuensang Area. This failed to quell popular aspirations and unrest began. Hence in 1961, this was renamed as Nagaland and given the status of State of the Indian Union which was formally inaugurated on 1 December 1963. Situated in the extreme northeast of the country, Nagaland is bounded by Auranchal Pradesh in the north, Assam in west, Manipur in south and Myanmar in the east.

Cultural Features

The population of Nagaland is entirely tribal. Each tribe is distinct in character from the other in terms of customs, language and dress. Each of the 16 odd tribes and subtribes that dwell in this exotic hill State can easily be distinguished by the colourful and intricately designed costumes, jewellery and beads that they adorn. It could broadly be said that they are straight forward people, honest, hard working, sturdy and with a high standard of integrity. They are lacking in humility and are inclined to equate a kind and sympathetic approach with weakness. Weaving is a traditional art handed down through generations in Nagaland. Each of the major tribes has its own unique designs and colours. Warm and colourful Naga shawls, hand-woven shoulder bags, decorative spears, tablemats, woodcarvings and bamboo works make magnificent souvenirs.

Tribal dances of the Nagas give us an insight into the inborn reticence of these people. War dances and dances belonging to distinctive tribes, form the major art form. In colourful costumes and jewellery, the dancers go through amazing mock war motions, which could prove very dangerous, if one were to be a little careless. Festivals, marriages, harvests, or just the joy of the moment — are occasions for the Nagas to burst into dance. Some of the important festivals are Sekrenyi, Moatsu, Tuluni and Tokhu Emong. Nagaland is a rural state. More than four-fifths of the population lives in small, isolated villages. Built on the most prominent points along the ridges of the hills, these villages were once stockaded, with massive wooden gates approached by narrow, sunken paths. The villages are usually divided into khels, or quarters, each with its own headmen and administration. Dimapur, Kohima, Mokokchung, and Tuensang are the only urban centres with more than 20,000 people.

Museums

Located in the far northeastern part of India, Nagaland is found to have its existence in the ancient Indian epic Mahabharata. Different people of Nagaland like the Lothas, Angami, Ao, Chakhesang and several others incorporate a distinct historical background.

As a result of this, museum has been built in Nagaland to preserve the rich cultural and historical heritage of the past. Today, houses the State Museum located at Kohima displaying various objects of the past that demands a bond with the present.

State Museum, Kohima: The State Museum at Kohima was established in the year 1970 as a multi-purpose museum.

Festivals

Nagaland Festivals add to the colour and the rich cultural heritage of the state. It is a land of many festivals inhabited by 16 main tribes. Some of the tribes that live in the state are the Kukis, the Changs, the Angamis, the Aos, the Konyaks, the Kacharis, the Chakhesangs, the Sumis, the Lothas, the Pochurys, etc. All these tribes have their unique culture, tradition, customs and festivals. Throughout the year state celebrates various tribal festivals. All the tribes have their unique and indigenous festivals.

As agriculture is the main source of income for the people of Naga society, most of the festivals revolve round agriculture. They deeply believe in the blessing of Nature. Some religious and spiritual sentiments are interlinked with the rites and rituals of the festivals. They believe in the Supreme Being who is recognised with a variety of names in different Naga dialects. During these festivals, the Village Shaman sacrifices to appease the Gods. They pray for a bountiful harvest and the happiness of the community. Some famous festivals of Nagaland as follows:

- Horn Bill Festival;
- Moatsu Festival;
- Nazu Festival;
- Nagaland Sekrenyi Festival;
- Tuluni Festival;
- Yemshe Festival;
- Nagaland Sankarni Festival;
- Rengma Ngadah Festival.

Dance

The Nagaland dance represents the vibrant and dynamic cultural traditions of the State. Accompanied with indigenous musical instruments and melodious folk songs, the Naga men perform the group dance with great enthusiasm.

Most of the traditional dances of the aboriginal tribes prefer male performers who dance in closed circle. Dressed in traditional and attractive clothes, the dancers perform with full dedication which is reflected in their flawless performance. The Zeliang dance portrays the unique dancing qualities and artistic skills of the performers.

Almost all the tribal communities have their unique dancing styles. The dances derive their name from the different movements of hands and feet of the performers. One such unique dance is the Cock dance of the Nruirolians which has derived its name because the hand movements bear resemblance to the movements of a cock.

The Fly dance requires the performers to move like the Temangnetin insect, while in the Cricket dance the dancers move their hands and feet in all directions. The valiant men perform the Bear dance which is commonly referred to as Hetateulee after they have successfully defeated their foes.

An integral part of social and cultural lifestyle of the native population the unique dancing styles of the state are performed with proper props of dao, shield or spear. Any religious or social gathering among the local indigenous tribal groups is incomplete without the performance of their traditional folk dances.

Music

Nagaland music represents the rhythmically rich cultural heritage of the state. The tribes living in the remote corners have their inherent tradition of music. Since there are various tribal communities in Nagaland, the music of the state also expresses the melodious diversity of the same.

The themes on which the music is formed centre around either the religious beliefs, romance or bravery. The Heliamleu which is also called by the name of dancing song of Nagaland is one of the popular music forms of the state which is based upon romanticism. Generally both the youth and the aged people create lines for this music.

The Hereileu song is known as the war song of Nagaland. This is because the aged people narrate their achievements in past battles through this form of music. Then there is the Neuleu song which expresses the legendary acts of any particular figure or a significant ancient happening in the state.

Hekialeu is another enticing part of the music which is of two types. The first type of Hekialeu song is composed and sung by the old people to glorify the deeds of their youthful days. The second type of Hekialeu song is created by both the young and old generation.

There are several rhythmic instrument that aptly accompany the music. Trumpet, theku, petu and many other string instruments are commonly used during the music sessions. Apart from creating a melodious effect, these musical instruments also enhances the quality of music.

Heliamleu: Heliamleu is a popular tribal song. The young people as well as the old people of the state involve themselves in the making of the Heliamleu song. Romantic themes are generally selected for the Heliamleu song.

Ever since the tribes started living in the rural parts they developed an array of cultural features. Music is a prime expression of that very cultural base.

During the major festivals, the tribes of Nagaland gather in a place and share the music of Heliamleu. Known as one of the oldest music forms of music Heliamleu boasts of a rich and vibrant heritage. Sometimes the song of Heliamleu is also accompanied by musical instruments. In other cases, the Heliamleu song is sung by the aged and the young with their own melodious vocal chords.

Since Heliamleu song is sung by the tribes of Nagaland from a very long time hence it has become an integral part of the cultural diversity of the state. The lines and lyrics of Heliamleu song are composed with great enthusiasm by both the younger and the older generation.

Nagaland music has always been the centre of attraction for the local tribes and subtribes of the state. The music in fact reflect the lifestyle, customs and beliefs of the local inhabitants.

It can be said that Heliamleu is the perfect manifestation of the music tradition of the state.

Hereileu: Hereileu is a special form of song of Nagaland state which is created and sung mostly by the senior inhabitants of the place. Being a part of the Nagaland music Hereileu song is composed on such themes as the past deeds of the aged people of the state. The older generation narrate their achievements through the Hereileu song.

In the ancient times, the various tribes used to involve in wars. Hereileu song is basically sung by the older generation to refresh their memories about those brave battles fought in the past. This is why Hereileu is also known as war song.

The way aged people once won a battle or lost it are generally included in the Hereileu song. This type of song specially glorify the bravery of the aged people during their youthful days. This is also done to inspire and encourage the younger generation.

Nagaland has always been a vibrant platform of cultural dynamism. Music is an essential component of the culture of Nagaland. The different tribal communities have their own line of music tradition.

Among others the Hereileu song is one such enigmatic part of the music heritage which showcases the golden era of the past ages.

Neuleu: Neuleu song is a special form of Nagaland music which is performed primarily by the older generation of state. Also called as legendary song, Neuleu is composed mainly to narrate a certain happening that took place in Nagaland many years back. The song of Neuleu also describes the achievements of a particular person who has created a mark for himself through his outstanding performance in certain fields.

Neuleu is considered as a prime manifestation of the music. The tribal groups inhabiting the land from many past centuries are quite deft in the Neuleu song. The aged people who have seen the glorious past ages are commonly entrusted with the job of composing the Neuleu song. They, in turn, make the song of Neuleu in such a way that the performance, deeds or a particular historical event gets the prominent focus.

During the tribal festivals the Neuleu song is sung by the old people of the state. The vocal melody of these people are so enigmatic that at times musical instruments become secondary.

It can be said that Neuleu song brings forward the bright bygone days of the state when the gallant tribes of the place have done many a chivalrous deed.

Hekialeu: The song of Hekialeu has two variations. While one type of Hekialeu is sung only by the old people the other one is sung by both the old and young generation of the state. Hekialeu song of old people involves the description of interesting events that took place in their youthful days whereas the Hekialeu song composed by old and young includes various aspects of both the generation.

Nagaland music is one of the most appealing cultural traits of the place. Being populated by various tribes and their subsections, the state presents a diverse range of music forms. Hekialeu is one such type of music which is present in the state from many past decades.

The old people of the state have a storehouse of experience. Hekialeu song is a medium through which these aged inhabitants share their life story with others. Also, when the young girls and boys sing the Hekialeu song during any tribal festival it rejuvenates the entire ambiance of the place.

Hekialeu, in a way, symbolises the apt synchronisation of the various generations of Nagaland that have a treasure house of different types of experiences.

Religious Features

Nagaland used to be an animist region, with the worshipping of ancestors and spirits. With the influence of the British the religion is now predominantly Christian with 90 per cent of the population following the church. The rest of the people are either Hindu, Muslim or still actively follow animistic practices. It is a strange concept but almost every village has its own church.

Dr. E. W. Clark had spread the message of tolerance and love among the native population. Every village has a Church that follows strict religious rituals and customs. The followers of Christianity regularly visit Church and take part in the Services of the religious institution to seek divine blessings of the Supreme Being.

Some population of the local indigenous inhabitants still follows the ancient religion of Animism. According to the principles of animism, the followers worship their ancestors who are believed to help them from any kind of difficult predicament. A little proportion of the native population are ardent followers of Hindu, Islam and Sikh religious community.

The local inhabitants celebrate Christmas with great religious fervour and enthusiasm. The true believers of Christianity, the vast majority of Christian population strictly adhere to the customary rituals of the religion. All the villages wear a decorative look on special festive occasions of Christmas and Easter.

Nagaland boasts of several aboriginal tribes who follow different social rituals and traditional customs. However, keeping in tune with the secular identity of India, all the different tribal communities coexist in a peaceful ambiance.

Lingual and Literary Features

Although maximum people of the state speak Nagamese, several other languages also coexist in the state. The Nagaland languages fall in the Tibetan-Burmese group of languages. They are classified into three divisions:

- *Eastern Subgroup:* The Konyak and Chang languages fall within this division;
- *Central Subgroup:* Languages such as Lotha, Ao, Phom, etc., belong to this division;

- *Western Subgroup:* Sema, Angami, Rengma and Chakhesang are some of the major languages of this division.

One of the interesting aspect of the Naga languages is the use of Sanskrit words. The tribes form the maximum chunk of Nagaland population and these tribal people speak Nagamese, which is a mixture of the basic Naga languages and Assamese. It is popular for its simplicity and there are no written scripts for the Nagamese language. English is the official language of the state and it is quite popular among the educated mass. The national language — Hindi is also not uncommon among the mass and most of the people understand and speak Hindi.

The Ao Naga is one of the languages that have written scripts. The British missionaries introduced the scripts to popularise the practice of the language. The Tenyidie is another language in that has a written script.

Ao

One of the important languages in Nagaland, Ao is spoken by a large number of people in the state. The Ao or Ao-Naga language falls in the Tibetan-Burmese group of languages. Some regional dialects like the Mongsen, Chungli, Chanki, etc., are prominent among the Ao-Naga language family. Among all the dialects, Chungli is the most widely spoken one and efforts are on to make it the standard Ao-Naga language.

The inhabitants of the Mokokchung District mainly converse in this language. It is also quite popular in Southern part of the state of Assam. Ao-Naga has written script that maintains its own codes of grammar. Three types of tones constitute the Ao language of Nagaland — the falling tone, the rising tone and the level tone. Wide use of the Copula is a notable characteristic of the language.

Media

The media of Nagaland, like media in any other place, is an important component of the state. It has a somewhat isolated location but the media makes sure that all kinds of news, both National and International reaches the people.

Media of Nagaland includes, Television, Radio and Newspapers. The state has access to almost all the Indian news, entertainment and sports channels and are therefore well connected to the rest of the Nation.

The newspaper media is the broadest and besides the National newspapers of India, a number of newspapers are published from the state itself. The most popular newspaper media in Nagaland includes:

- Nagaland Post;
- The Eastern Mirror;

- The Morung Express;
- The North-East Herald;
- Nagaland Page.

Nagaland has a considerable tribal population and keeping their need in mind the local Media publishes a number of newspapers in the tribal languages, these are:

- Capi in the Tenyidie language;
- Tir Yimyim in the Ao language;
- Tenyi Ralha in the Tenyidie language;
- Ao Milen in the Ao language.

In the Ramayana and Mahabharata, there are references to the Kiratas who have been identified with the Indo-Mongoloid tribal people of North-East India. (The Puranas and the Epics refer to many Naga dynasties (Naga Vansa). In the Mahabharata, Arjun, the great Pandava is to said to have married Ulupee, a Naga Princess here. Indian scholars have attempted to identify the Nagas of the ancient Sanskrit literature with the Nagas of North-East. This is evidently not correct. The Nagas of the Sanskrit literatures may be identified with the Nagas, who in their climax of glory came to rule in Northern India, after the fall of the great Kushanas before the rise of the imperial Guptas in Northern India, the descendants of whom may be the present Naga Sadhus of central India. Thus it is hard to accept the theory of "Naga" originating from Sanskrit "Nag" meaning serpent. There is no snake worship cult among the Nagas, though the Python is revered sometimes and its killing is done ceremonially and elaborately. Some have connected the "Naga" with Sanskrit "Nag" meaning mountain as the people live mostly in the hills, thus implying "hill men."

Educational Features

The 2001 Census Report on Nagaland education pointed out that only 66.59 per cent of the total population were literate. Such a low education rate is obviously a cause of concern. The Government of Nagaland is working towards increasing the level of elementary education. In order to make sure that education percolates down into the masses, the government has introduced a policy of free and compulsory education for all children below the age of 14.

The schools are the base of education system and there are a number of schools in different parts of the state. The most popular schools in the state includes:

- Jawahar Navodaya Vidyalayas;
- Assam Rifles Training Centre High School;
- Little Flower School;

- Vivekanand Kendra Vidyalaya;
- Assam Rifles High School;
- Kendriya Vidyalaya.

There are a number of colleges in Nagaland and they offer different kinds of courses. These colleges are a major boost to the system of education. The types of colleges include:

- Research Institutes;
- Computer Colleges;
- Engineering Colleges;
- Hotel Management;
- Law Colleges;
- Polytechnic.

The final level education is the Nagaland University which is a Central University. Established by the Government of India in the year 1994, the University of Nagaland has its campuses in Lumami, Medziphema and Kohima. A total of 47 colleges are affiliated to this university and there are almost 18,000 students who study under this university.

Schools

There are a number of schools and all of them maintain a certain level of quality and standard. Most of the schools are affiliated to the NBSE, that is the Nagaland Board of School Education but there are also some schools that follow the Central Board or the CBSE. The Nagaland Board of School Education which was inaugurated in the year 1974 is the nucleus of all Nagaland schools.

The schools usually comprises classes 1 to 10 and some of the schools also have the 11 and 12 classes. Education at the schools are very class room oriented and the teacher tries to provide the students with an all round idea of the subjects. Games and sports are also a part of the curriculum of the schools and the students are often taken out for picnics and excursions. Secondary School Leaving Certificate Examination in class 10 and the Higher Secondary School Leaving Certificate Examination in class 12 are the two most important exams in the Nagaland schools.

Colleges

Nagaland colleges are an integral part of the education system and there are a number of colleges spread all over the state. There are different kinds of colleges and all of them specialise in particular courses. The colleges offer different kinds of courses which includes:

- Research Institutes;
- Computer Colleges;

- Hotel Management;
- Commerce Colleges;
- Law Colleges;
- Engineering Colleges;
- Polytechnic;
- Art Colleges;
- Medical colleges;
- Science Colleges;
- Music Colleges.

The oldest college is the Fazl Ali College in Mokokchung. This college houses a total of 13 departments of Arts and Science subjects. The Patkai Christian College is another premier college and it has been rated as the best in the state by the National Assessment and Accreditation Council.

Besides these two colleges, there are many other colleges that are popular and provide a standard level of education, these include:

- City Law College;
- College of Agriculture Medziphema;
- Dimapur College;
- Science College;
- Selesian College of Higher Education;
- Mountain View Kohima Christian College;
- Nagaland College of Education;
- Oriental College East Ciralare;
- Salt Christian College;
- Regional Institute of *e*-Learning and Information Technology Lerie;
- Dimapur Government College;
- Sao Chang College;
- St. Joseph's College;
- Institute of Communication and Information Technology;
- Government Polytechnic;
- Kheloshe Polytechnic.

University

In the year 1989, the Parliament Act No. 35 passed the Nagaland University Act. However, although the Act was passed in the year 1989 it was only in the year 1994 that the Central Nagaland University was established. The Nagaland University is a teaching cum affiliating university and a number of colleges are affiliated to it.

The headquarter of the Nagaland University is in the city of Lumami and it has a jurisdiction over the entire state of Nagaland. There are a total of 39 colleges that are affiliated to the University of Nagaland and the total student strength of the university is around 18,078. The University of Nagaland has campuses all over the state including, Kohima, Lumami and Medsiphema. The Nagaland University offers different kinds of courses and also has a number of schools of studies. Overall there are a total of 4 schools of studies and 25 departments under the Nagaland University, these include:

- Department of English;
- Department of Geology;
- Department of History and Archaeology;
- Department of Commerce;
- Department of Education;
- School of Agricultural Science and Rural Developments;
- Nagaland College of Teacher Education;
- Department of Linguistics.

Economic Features

Industry

The Process of industrialisation in the state is in infancy but the need to have more industries has been well recognised. The Nagaland Sugar Mill at Dimapur has an installed capacity of 1,000 tonnes per day. There is a pulp and paper mill at Tuli and a plywood factory at Tizit. Handloom and handicrafts are important cottage industries which are mainly being managed by cooperative societies. An industrial growth centre near Dimapur is under construction. The Nagaland Industrial Development Corporation is the premier promotional organisation in providing guidance and capital assistance to entrepreneurs. The mini-cement plant at Wazeho has commenced production. The fruits and vegetables processing and cold storage Plant at Dimapur has an installed capacity of 5 MT per day.

Agriculture

Agriculture is the main occupation of the people in the state. During 1999-2000, the production of rice was 2,20,700 MT, of wheat 12,500 MT, maize 48,000 MT and of pulses, 13,000 MT.

Irrigation and Power

Minor irrigation works are mostly meant to divert small hill streamlets to irrigate valleys used for rice cultivation. Under minor irrigation, surface minor irrigation covered 6,736.76 hectares during 1999-2000. Number of electrified villages stands at 1,196. Nagaland has achieved cent per cent electrification of rural areas. A 24 megawatt hydroelectric project is under erection at Likhimro. Efforts are being made to set up a 24 MW Thermal Power Project at Dimapur.

Transportation

Roads: Total length of roads in Nagaland is 9,860 km.

Railways/Aviation: Dimapur is the only place where rail and air services are available. There is an Indian Airlines service connecting Dimapur with Guwahati and Kolkata.

Festivals: Some of the important festivals are *Sekrenyi, Moatsu, Tuluni* and *Tokhu Emong.* All tribes celebrate their distinct seasonal festivals with a pageantry of colour and a feast of music.

3

History

Ancient Times

The ancient history of Nagas is shrouded in obscurity. On being asked about their history the Naga elders explain the absence of recorded chronicle through a story. They explain that in the beginning God created the Universe and some people to live therein. In order to preserve their history, God imparted the knowledge of reading and writing to the newly-created persons. He gave them the skin of the deer to record their achievements and allotted them different parts for their settlement. The early settlers of Nagaland also got a skin. In due course of time, the Naga Hills were visited by a worst famine. The early settlers of the region fell back upon wild fruits, flowers, leaves, wild beasts and birds. In the end they devoured the deer skin also. Consequently, they say Nagas have no record of their past. Ptolemy has also made a brief mention of Nagas.

About 2000 years before Christ the Mongols started penetrating into India through Burma and Tibet. Some of the Mongols entered India via Tibet and settled in Garo Hills. Kuki and Bodo tribes came to be settled in Cachhar Hills. They were subdivided into many branches which came to acquire different community names. The Cachharis ruled over northern Assam till 16th century. Dimapur is said to be the capital of the Cachharis. The old Dimapur is in ruins, situated to the north of the present town of Dimapur on the bank of Dhansiri river in the dense wood of Nambur. At that time it was probably known as Hidimbapur. The site is now dotted with the ruins of about 50 buildings and affords a peep into the architecture of that period.

According to traditions, Nagaland afforded a land-route to tribes migrating from Burma Via Manipur Hill through a passage was made by tribes are described to have Austric and Kareen affinities. An Angami tradition which gives corroboration states that

Piphema and Kigwema were among the original Karen villages, but possibly the Angami preponderated so that the Karena were diffused elsewhere. But another tradition holds that Angami and Karens were close Kinsmen who lived together. The Karens of Kigwema and Piphema are said to have practised megalithic rituals and made several stone weapons, celts, basins, and grinding stones. Probably Karens who are found scattered near Borpathor and in Sibsagar may have had historical links and Kinship with the parent Karen group who once made their home in Nagaland.

Traditions also clearly indicate that the Semas, the close neighbours of Angami, with whom they were closely allied on the north and east, were not aboriginal till now, the stories told are of the cultivators in the Sema area who came across ornamental beads and conch-shells and at times ruins of dismantled buildings which lay buried inside the earth. It is difficult to identify the preceding tribe in the Sema land but it is possible that it belongs to the same preceding group of people which once made its home in the Angami territory.

The exact date of the migration of these present tribes to Nagaland is not known. A tradition in vogue amongst the Angami, the Rengma, the Lotha and the Sema is that their forefathers came together in one migration and reached their present abode via Manipur from Burma. The Lotha, the first who entered Nagaland via Mao, were followed by the Sema who came by the southern route, but the latter may have halted at Kigwema, whose traditions are still vivid about that place connected with their migration.

Rengama and the Angami were the last. Another common tradition in southern Nagaland associates the Ao with this historic migration who preceded the other four tribes, but it is contradicted by the Aos who uphold that their origin lay in Chungliyimti (in modern Tuensang) before they migrated to Ungma and spread to other places. And the Ao tradition does not go further than chungliyimti. The tribes, although with separate identities from each other, claimed that they have emerged from the four paternal ancestors who were brothers. It was at the foot of Japfu, there tribes, another tradition says, selected the different routes of migration before they ensconced themselves in their present respective homelands. A tradition further refers to a great havoc which occurred in their ancient homeland causing this migration to be undertaken simultaneously and as well the treaties and pledges entered into by the tribes to cling together in the wandering and to live as one people who they came into their new settlement.

There are stories which state how the Nagas came to Nagaland. According to the Rengmas, their forefathers came in search of metals; the Lothas maintain that they selected their present territory because of the availability of crags which were to be extracted in connection with their megalithic erections. The Angamis came in search of terrace fields which were developed along the precipitous slopes. There is a tradition among other Nagas that their forefathers came here in search of plumes for the purpose of ornamentation and decoration.

Many stories regarding the earliest stages of settlement are worthy of notice which connect Khezha-Kenoma towards the south with the migration of the Lotha, Sema, Chakhesang and Rengma tribes. It was here, traditions say, that they split in separate migrations. First, the Lotha went northwardly to Aongsha where they spread and thence broke eastwardly. Then Rengma proceeded as much far as Tseminyu where they established themselves. The Angamis spread the north and north-westward from Khezha-Kenoma whilst Chakhasang selected an eastern terrain. Both went on further.

Chakhasang described to be eastern Angami by the British official not appreciated because Khezha and Chakru (Chokri) stemmed out from the Sema wave of Migration but these groups have adopted customs and cultural practices from Angami and became admixed with them through inter-relations and marriages. Western Chakhasang are bilingual and they knew Sema and Angami but while Chakesang still retain stone culture, it is no longer practised by the Semas. Many place names in proper Chakhezang sound more Sema than Angami. At Chakru area, the first Sema immigrants are believed to have settled before they ensconced in Tuensang and Mokokchung in large swarms. Before Independence, the Chakru, Khezha, Sangtam and Eastern Rengmas groups were merged together for forming the present Chakesang tribe. Sangtam is an offshoot of the parent Sangtam tribe lodged in central Tueusang as Meluri is a branch of Rengma proper located north of Angami. But Sema and Sangtam still live together in many places whilst in eastern Chakezang, the Meluri and Pochuri groups had developed other cultural relations.

It is known that even amongst the Eastern Chakhasangs themselves, there are certain marked difference in respect of dress, language and other cultural factors. For instance Maluri group, hitherto known during the British period as Naked Rengma with the offshoots at Swemi and Laphori, have little affinities with the southern Sangtam group scattered in Temini and Premi although at the latter are found also some Rengmas. The Sangtam is said to have more affinities with the Lothas. The Sangtam unlike their neighbours practised tattooing. But all these tribes call themselves Pochuri since the early times which may suggest that, as previously mentioned, they were processed to a more vigorous integration for a common protection. Meluri group believed that they belonged to Salari, a division of a tribe. The important Rengma dialect is Teburi (Swemi) while Akhegho is the important Sangtam dialect. The Temiri dialect is called *chezorr*. All these groups of tribes are again divided into exogamous subgroups just like Rengma and Angami.

The Rengmas migrated and settled mainly in the southern parts of Nagaland, the Lothas on the north and the Semas on the east but a group long ago went to ensconce in the eastern Chakesang extremities while a group was diverted to Borpathor area in the outlying plains. Intervening tribes are between the Rengma in the northern Kohima and Meluri. According to a tradition, a Rengma batch went eastwardly when chasing a white Muskin which they lost on a trail, but according to another story, they happened to go so far in search of the brine springs for the purpose of salt excavation. Till today the Tezu valley is known for the local manufacture of salt from the brines but monopoly of salt trade from the plains in the west had passed to other tribes.

The Meluri group may have fought with the Sema and the Nagas of the adjoining Burmese highlands but in spite of adversities, they continued to preserve themselves. But a story told is also of the Meluri-Pochuri alliance against their enemy. The Meluri Rengmas started in on eastwardly trail from Kitane in northern Kohima District. Reaching the eastern Chakasang terrain, they found that Pochuri-Santam group had been in possession of the brines but by the treaty which followed the Meluri group was allowed to handle salt trade. One tradition notes that the other branch broke off from Aongsha to the plains and came to inhabit the Regmapani banks where their colonies still survive. Another tradition states that they had migrated to Dimapur through which place from implements were from the hills supplied to the plains.

During an Ahom invasion of Dimapur about the 15th century they had to flee northwardly towards Golaghat. In the last century their settlement was located between Kaliani and Dhansiri scattered in 32 villages. In 1848, the Mikir Hill Rengmas numbered 689 households scattered among 32 villages. Long ago (1855) Butler wrote: "In physiognomy they differ but little from the Cachharea tribes and many had married Cachharee and Assamese wives." A few had adopted a plain-man's dress and ways of life considering the circumstances to which they were placed and the necessary adjustment which they made. These Rengmas are Known as Nzong Teri Phani or Ntenyi Awi Klriya after thee dense cane jungle bordering on the plains.

The Zeliangroung came at a later wave of migration, constituted of Zemi, Liangmai and Roungmai allied to the Kabui Naga tribe who came by the Barail southwardly route; hordes of the first immigrants are said to have traversed through the impassable mountain region along the Barak in avoiding conflicts with the other tribes and ensconced in the western mountain tracts where they made their home. Probably they came in search of brines. Only this tribe came alone, not having joined the other body of migration. Yet many powerful Zeliangroung villages are said to have an admixed Zeliangroung-Angami parentage.

Early History

The early history is hitherto mostly unrecorded. However, more details are available by the close of the 14th century owing to reference into emissaries and evidence of cultural relations which had grown up with the Kacharis whose capital was Dimapur. There is a reference as early as 1375 AD to one Khasi expatriate who fled from the Jaintia Hills, came to Dimapur and later on became admixed with the Angarni.

Sukhpa, the founder of Ahom Kingdom is believed to have entered Assam from Burma through Tirap region of Arunachal Pradesh around 1228 AD. The Ahoms had their first contacts with the tribal communities of Nocte, Konyak and Wancho. With the gradual expansion of the Ahom Kingdom the Aos and Lothas also came into contact with the Ahoms. There were frequent clashes among these tribes and Lothas, but Ahoms somehow managed to keep their control over this region. Nagas used to present gifts and tributes to Ahoms who in return allowed the former to carry on revenue-free cultivation of paddy in the fields and fishing in the bills. So long as Nagas desisted from their predatory raids on the plains man, Ahoms did not interfere at all in the daily chores of the Nagas. Their internal strifes among the different communities were never taken seriously by the Ahoms.

In the year 1536, an Ahom expedition against the Nagas for quelling the Konyak uprising was defeated by the latter who also 'seized four guns from the Ahoms. Subsequently a larger Ahom force was sent to teach a lesson to the Konyaks. The Konyaks were defeated and they were made to return to guns. During this expedition hundreds of Nagas were brutally murdered at Dimapur.

The town was almost razed to the ground. The way Sukhpa carried on discriminate slaughter of the Nagas and destruction of Naga villages is still recounted by the Naga elders by way of tales being told to successive generations. Nagas have also been quite brutal but it is gathered that Ahoms surpassed them. The Ahoms not only killed the Naga youths, their females and children were also not spared. Nonetheless after sometime Sukhpa himself developed a fascination for Naga Hills. Subsequently the Ahoms even picked up Vaishnava Hindu cult from these Hills.

Later on the Mughal General Kala Pahar also smashed the town of Dimapur. In 1650 the Konyaks of Lakma chopped off six human heads during their predatory raid on the plains. Once again the Ahom wrath had its fury on the Nagas, who were made to surrender and apologise. In the times of King Gadadhar Singh (1681-96) the Lothas carried on their raids on the settlements of Doyang valley. Tired of their repeated attacks on the plainsman, Ahom King sent his most capable general, Tamcheng Chinghai Phukan to curb the undesirable element. Surprisingly the Phukan reached the village, he found it deserted. Enraged by this act he set entire village on fire and turned the belongings of the Lothas to ashes. Fearing a still most wrath the Lothas surrendered and offered many gifts including two female slaves. Thus the Ahom rulers succeeded in establishing their authority on the Naga Hills. Resultantly no major untoward incident occurred in these hills in the eighteenth century.

During the 19th century the Ahom Kingdom itself started receiving many threats to its authority. The Momariaa rebellion sufficiently sapped the energy and strength of Ahom Kingdom. The Burmese invasion of 1816 gave it a shattering blow. The Naga tribes took advantage of weakening power of the Ahom rule and political confusion then prevailed in the Ahom hierarchy. The Nagas once again resumed the practice of raiding and plundering the settlements in the plains of Assam. It appears that predating has been a favourite pastime with the Nagas ever since their origin.

The British came into contact with the Nagas during the early period of the Nineteenth century. They found the Nagas, a hard nut to crack. Nevertheless they adopted changing policies to quell and curb the Naga hostilities with a heavy hand. On other occasions they thought it proper not to interfere with the internal warfares of the Nagas while defending their predatory raids on the adjacent plains. Ultimately they decided to extend and establish their authority in the Naga Hills. Broadly speaking, the British Naga relations can be studied under the three phases, viz., military promenades (1832-50), non-intervention (1815-56) and establishment of British authority (1866 onwards) in Naga Hills.

The British made a series of raids in Naga Hills as a part of their reconnaissance of this region between 1832 and 1850. It has been observed by many leading historians that before launching any campaign British made a thorough study of the physical environment of Nagaland. Their success in many a battle was because of their being very serious students of geography.

Thus in the case of Naga Hills, located in harsh and inhospitable environment and inhabited by turbulent tribes they acquired sufficient knowledge about the region before undertaking an expedition.

Nagas came into contact with the British when the latter were making efforts to open lines of communications between Manipur and Assam. Captain Jenkins and captain Pamberton marched from Manipur to Assam through the Naga Hills at the head of a strong force in 1832. The movement of non-tribals through their homeland greatly irritated the Nagas. The Nagas rolled down huge boulders, threw spears (Daps), etc., and created a huge noise though constant yelling.

In the year 1833 Raja Gambhir Singh of Manipur set on a similar march and was accompanied by Lt. Gordon and his soldiers. Raja who is said to have exercised some sort of authority over the Nagas advised the force to follow a slightly eastern route than that followed earlier to avoid any clash. After the death of Cachhar ruler in 1832, Cachhar was annexed by the British. This event brought the British in contact with the Angami Nagas. British desired the rulers of Cachhar and Manipur to keep the turbulent Naga tribes under control, as they thought that both the princely orders enjoyed a sort of control on the parts of Naga Hills.

Cachhar ruler did not have the means to control the Nagas. Manipur, no doubt, was in a position to harass the Nagas off and on but was utterly unable to control the Nagas who have always been very adept in hide and seek as well as guerilla tactics. Notwithstanding the problems of these adjacent princely states the British Government of India "was not prepared itself to take over the Naga territory, and still inclined to regard the Manipuris as the *de facto* masters of the Hills. The Board Directors, however, did not approve of such a policy and pleaded for a practical arrangement. As result, Mr. Grange, a sub-Assistant at Nowgang (Assam) was entrusted with the job of leading an expedition to Naga country in 1838. This expedition did not prove to be successful for want of adequate transport facilities and proper planning. In 1840, Mr. Grange again made an attempt and this time he was fully armed. The five Naga settlements opposing his venture were burnt and eleven of their inhabitants arrested.

Lieutenant Bigge, a person with foresight, planned of developing friendly relations with the Nagas instead of offending them. He got two friendly mission to the Naga Hills in 1840-42. He succeeded in his aim. On the demand of Naga chief, he lost no time in opening a salt depot at Dimapur. This gesture of goodwill made him popular among the tribals. With the help of captain Gordon, Bigge also succeeded in demarcating a boundary, separating the Naga country from Manipur. In 1844 Nagas, however, started raiding the plain areas and also picked up internecine quarrels among themselves. As a result nine persons of the Rengma area and three Shan soldiers on duty in north Cachhar Hills were killed. To curb the nefarious activities of Nagas, the British again sent an armed expedition under the leadership of captain Eld. Including the village of Khonoma, he burnt several Naga villages.

In 1845 John Butler, the new Principal Assistant Commissioner at Nowgong again thought and acted in the lines of Bigge. He toured through the Naga Hills and persuaded the Naga chiefs to desist from provocative acts and led a peaceful life. He negotiated settlement with the chiefs of Khonoma and some other villages. The settlement was accorded recognition in a colourful ceremony held on December 11, 1845. Vide this agreement the Chiefs agreed not to raid any area, to abstain from plundering and off cutting heads of other Nagas. They also agreed to refer their disputes to British authorities for settlement and also pay tributes to British as a token of their recognition of British authority. The British pledged to protect Nagas from aggression and also committed themselves for the general welfare and prosperity of Nagas.

On the contrary, after the British troops left the area, the agreement was followed more by way of violation then adherence to the clauses. The turbulent tribals not only stopped paying tributes to the British but also continued their marauding raids on the adjacent plain habitations. British, then thought of setting of an outpost at Samaguting (Chumukdema) with a hope that it would work as a deterrent. Bhogchand was the first Darogha of the post who was no doubt an honest and efficient officer but not very discreet. In 1949, he had to go to Mozema to investigate a dispute between the Jubili and Nilholi tribes. In this dispute a Jubili had been killed by some Nilholis.

On the basis of the facts and evidence, Bhogchand arrested seven Cachharis owing allegiance to the Jubili Chief besides the culprits. This act enraged both the groups. They forgot their differences and attacked Bhogchand and his party. Fourteen persons, including the Darogha were killed. British were once again upset. In December 1849, Captain Vincent was sent to the Naga Hills to chastise the turbulent Nagas. He led an armed expedition in March 1850 and burnt the village of Mozema and Khonoma. Though he succeeded in establishing his control over Mozema, Khonoma could not be contained by him. In December 1850, Major Foquett came to the Naga Hills to enforce Vincent. The combined forces achieved their aim of capturing Khonoma and destroying its defence.

After this skirmish two young Nagas of Kekrima village entered Vincent's encampment and threw a challenge of a pitched battle on behalf of their village. They asked Vincent to have a hand to hand fight with the help of spears and Daos as they did not possess sophisticated weapons. But to the surprise of Nagas, a strong British contingent armed with muskets, three pounders, mortar and supported by friendly Nagas stormed Kekrima on 11th February, 1851. The villagers put up a heroic fight in the pitched and bloody battle but they were not match for the superior fire power of Vincent. About 250 persons including women, children and old were killed in this battle. The village was totally burnt. "It was one of the rare instances when the Nagas fought an open battle.

After these military expeditions the British felt that their attempt was quite futile and the effort was not worthy the trouble and hardships to which soldiers and officers were put to. Moreover, their attempts had short time effects only. Thus henceforth they decided upon a policy of non-intervention. Thus Dalhousie did not favour to gain effective control over Naga Hills. He opined that such a control was not only unproductive but costly too. Those who pleaded to have control with a view to curb Naga raids and plundering hostilities on the adjoining plains were quietened by him with an argument that it is more fruitful to establish effective means of defence on the frontiers than to administer them. He said, "we should confine ourselves to our own grounds; protect it as it can and must be protected; not meddle in the feuds or fights of these savages; encourage trade with that as long as they are peaceful towards us and rigidly exclude them from all communications either to sell what they have got, or to buy what they want if they should become turbulent or troublesome."

For about a decade and a half, British followed laissez faire policy towards Naga Hills. The British post at Dimapur was abandoned and Borpathor became the forward post. After sometime when it was found that North Cachhar Hills became a scene for tribal hostilities, British thought of abandoning these Hills too. On the other hand, Nagas were very happy by this arrangement. They accelerated their plundering activity. During the year 1851 they carried on twenty-two raids in Assam Valley alone. Besides taking 113 plainsmen as captive they wounded ten and killed fifty-five persons. The position became very embarrassing for the British authorities as the plainsmen started doubting the capacity of the British in protecting their lives and property.

Thus in 1862 the commissioner of Assam recommended to the Lieutenant Governor to do away with the policy of non-intervention and follow practical as well as effective measures to control the turbulent Nagas. He argued that acting as powerless spectators to the scene of brutal murder, loot and arson of their subjects did not be have the British. He said that not doubt the non-interference policy was good in theory, but the detailed probe of the pros and cons of such a policy convinced that it must be abandoned in practice. Lieutenant Governor Sir Cecil Beadon accepted the recommendation and urged upon the Government of India to reorient their policy towards Naga Hills. He found no use in establishing check posts with the purpose of curbing Naga hostilities over plains. He suggested that it was desirable "to reassert our authority and bring them under a system of administration suited to their circumstances and gradually to reclaim them from habits of lawlessness to those of order and civilization." The Government of India had to yield under the recommendations of the involved officers and a policy of effective control over Nagaland was followed.

Medieval Times

Before the arrival of the British Raj, Nagaland was administered as part of Manipur under the Thibomei and Thimbong districts. With the permission of a Manipuri King, the East India Company explored deep inside the naga hills in search of trade routes and other physical resources. In the process, the British brought many Assamese and Bengali traders into the region, from whom the Naga eventually adopted their dialect called Nagamese, which is a mixture of both the Assamese and Bengali dialects.

The early history of Nagaland consists of the customs and economic activities of the various Naga tribes that lived in the region. These Naga tribes had socio-economic and political links with tribes in Assam and Myanmar, and even today a large population of Naga people inhabits Assam. Following an invasion in 1816, the area along with Assam came under the direct rule of Myanmar. This period was noted for its oppressive rule and the turmoil it created, both in Assam and Nagaland. When the British East India Company took control of Assam in 1826, they steadily expanded their domain over modern Nagaland as well. By 1892, all of modern Nagaland except the Tuensang area in the northeast was governed by the British. It was politically assimilated into Assam, which was considered as part of the province of Bengal for a long period of time. The British Christian missionaries that spent time in Nagaland played an important part in transforming the culture of the region. As a result of their missionary work, many Naga tribes embraced Christianity, and especially the Baptist faith, making Nagaland into the largest Baptist state in the world as of today.

Nagaland played a central role in one of the many battles of World War II, as its capital city of Kohima served as one of the final points where the British and Indian forces were able to turn back the Japanese movement into South Asia.

Modern Times

After the independence, Nagaland remained a part of the province of Assam. Nationalist activities arose amongst Naga tribes and they demanded for a political union of their ancestral and native groups. They turned militant and damaged government and civil infrastructure, and attacked government officials and Indians from other states. In order to restore peace, the Union government sent the Indian Army. The Government began diplomatic talks with representatives of Naga tribes, and the Naga Hills district of Assam and the Tuensang frontier were united as a single political entity that became a Union territory (directly administered by the Central government with a large degree of autonomy). This move too was not satisfactory to the tribes and soon they began agitation and violence. This included a series of attacks on Army and government institutions. Further political accord was reached at the Naga People's Convention that Nagaland should become a self-governing state in the Indian union.

In July of 1960, a further political accord was reached at the *Naga People's Convention* which stated that Nagaland should become a constituent and self-governing state in the Indian union. An Interim Body of 42 members was constituted on February 18, 1961. This was to function as the *de facto* legislature. It consisted of a five-member Executive Council whose head was the Chief Executive Councillor. This functioned as *de facto* Council of Ministers. The first Chairman of the Naga People's Convention, Dr. Imkongliba Ao, was appointed as the first Chairman of the Interim Body. P. Shilo was appointed as the Chief Executive Councillor and finally became the first Chief Minister of Nagaland. The late Vishnu Sahay became the first Governor of Nagaland.

Statehood was officially granted to the area in 1963 and the first state-level democratic elections were held in 1964. While resistance still remained at this point, most of the insurgencies were quelled in the early 1980s. However, violence re-erupted in the late 1990s, creating conflict between rebel group factions. On July 25, 1997, the Prime Minister, Mr. I. K. Gujral announced that the national Government had declared a cease-fire after talks with the Nationalist Socialist Council of Nagaland (NSCN). The group had agreed on a cessation of operations starting from August 1, 1997, and lasting for a period of three months. Since that point, the cease-fire has since been extended, but there is still resistance related conflict going on in the region, largely due to the belief by the tribal groups that they are under the dominion of "Indian imperialism."

British Control and Authority

Over the Naga territory the British authority and control began in 1866 in pursuance of the decision taken by the Government of India on the recommendations of the Lieutenant Governor of Assam. Lieutenant Gregory set up his check post at Samaguting. Apart from a strong contingent he was also given discretionary powers to deal with the situation.

The Manipuris were forbidden to embark on any expedition in Naga Hills. Angamis and other Nagas visiting Assam Valley were required to deposit their spears, Daos, etc., at the check post and obtain a permit to visit the plains. Notwithstanding these precautionary measures, the Naga predatory raids were far from being curbed. The Razephema Nagas in their raid in 1866 practically slaughtered each and every inhabitant of Mikil village. The British as a punitive measure turned the Razephema village to dust and dispersed its inhabitants.

In 1869, the British found the situation relatively peaceful and decided to carry on reconnaissance survey of the Naga Hills so as to frame their future policy. For this purpose two parties entered, one each from north and south. The party coming from north was suddenly attacked by the Nagas in 1874. One of the two leaders Holcombe and eight of his men were slaughtered while about fifty including the other leader (Badgdey) were seriously wounded.

The other party led by Butler was ambushed in 1875 in the Lothas region near Pangti village. Butler and some of his men were killed. In their retaliatory step the British burnt the entire village of Pangti. This punitive expedition was led by Lieutenant Woodthrope. Colonel Johnstone gained control of three Naga villages. The villagers agree to pay revenue to the British authorities as a token of their submission. "It has rightly been said that this was the first step towards the formal annexation of the Naga Hills into the British India."

In 1876, the British government in India received the report of the Chief Commissioner. He apprised the government of the constant warfare continuing between different tribes of the Naga Hills and suggested the initiation of early steps to curb their internecine warfare, failing which he faced a major turmoil. The government was still pondering over the report when the Mozema Nagas killed six British subjects of Gumaigaju in North Cachhar Hills. Again the British in their bid to punish the turbulent Nagas got the village of Mozema burnt by an army expedition led by captain Brydon in 1877.

In spite of it, the dwellers of this burnt village continued to harass British with the support of Khonoma and Jotsoma Nagas. After a great difficulty three Nagas were subdued. In fact the customary laws, their independence and the very root of their democratic system were all disturbed when the British government set up the law courts and started trying cases of all sorts according to their law. Thus Nagas started challenging the alien authority.

In June 1877, the then Government of India impressed upon the Secretary of the State that the British should not be content merely with the defence of their own borders and subjects but should bring the Naga Hills under their direct control so that law and order could be fully maintained in the region itself. It further urged upon the measures to be taken to civilize the wild and waring tribes. These recommendations were accepted and in furtherance of the policy adopted well-defined posts were established at Kohima and Wokha in 1878. The tribals resented the move and their reaction was violent. Mr. Henry Damant was appointed the first Deputy Commissioner of Naga Hills. By this time sixteen Naga villages had been brought under the direct control of British authorities.

Henry Damant was another capable and well efficient officer but indiscreet and that proved to be his undoing. While setting ready to visit Ao region, Damant got a news that the Khonoma villagers were busy arming themselves with ammunitions and weapons for questionable purposes. He cancelled his scheduled visit and instead proceeded to Khonoma with a strength of 56 soldiers. On October 13, 1879 it was gathered that an interpreter belonging to Jotsoma village warned Mr. Damant not to proceed towards Khonoma. Mr. Damant totally uncared the warning and reached the gate of Khonoma village, which had been closed by the inmates of the village. Damant demanded entry and in response got a shower of bullets and he died on the spot. This created panic among his escort party, the members of which ran helter-skelter.

Finding confusion the Nagas followed down their village and took a heavy toll of the soldiers. Thirty-five soldiers were killed and nineteen were badly wounded. The news of this disaster reached the Kohima post but the garrison there was quite insufficient. As a result messages for the reinforcement were flashed the same day. On October 19, Hinde reached Kohima with about 60 men. He came from Wokha post. On the other hand thousands of Nagas from the neighbouring villages collected and laid a siege of Kohima on October 21, 1879. They avoided a direct assault. Their strategy was to starve out the garrison. Col. Johnstone arrived at the scene on October 27 with about two thousand Manipuri soldiers and relieved the garrison. The Nagas dispersed away without putting up any fight. The authorities mobilised all the forces available there and a regular attack under Brig. Gen. Nation was launched on November 22.

The tribals, on the other hand, had properly fortified their settlement with indigenous means. The attack lasted the whole day. Three officers and forty-four soldiers were killed. By the evening the commander decided to hold on the captured ground and launch a massive reinforced attack next morning. Next morning dawned with a shocking surprise to the British when they found the village completely deserted. Finding themselves to be the ultimate losers Nagas withdrawn in the darkness of the night to the Chakka Fort on the Brail Range.

The British who found themselves Humbled and humiliated started mopping up operations. All the hostile settlements in the western Angami tract were severely dealt with. The Khonomans continued their guerrilla tactics and raided the areas as far as Baladhan in the North Cachhar Hills. There they killed a British Manager of a tea-estate alongwith his sixteen workers. British got still more enraged and besieged the Chakka Fort to starve out the Nagas. The Nagas who are voracious eaters surrendered on March 28, 1880. The surrendering tribals were fined in cash and kind. Their firearms and terraced fields were confiscated and they were ordered to vacate the village site. This order however, was modified when the British found that the Nagas were reluctant to settle anywhere else and also it was feared that the turbulent people might retaliate. In 1881, a separate Naga Hills District was formed.

About the formation of the District, British followed the policy of consolidating their authority in the region and also pursued steady penetration into the interior. Mozung Jami, then known as "village of wicked men" was occupied by the authorities on January 12, 1889. In 1890, Mokokchung Subdivision with A. W. Davis as subdivisional officer, was also formed. Slowly and gradually the British went on expanding their frontier towards the east in one or the other pretext. In this context the plea of the Chief Commissioner is worthy of note. He wrote, "Where there is an ethnological boundary, it will be said that a further extension is necessary in order to secure a good natural and geographical boundary. When the boundary is a natural one an ethnological frontier is declared to be the best. When the boundary is a stream it is proposed to push it on to the top of the mountain ridge beyond. When the watershed has been reached it will be found that political consideration require an extension to the bed of the next river below and so on ad infinitum.

The local officers recommended time and again to absorb more area gradually till the whole country between Assam and Burma was occupied for maintaining law and order in these Hills. The government was also being pressurised to extend the frontiers eastward and take over the Dikhu coalfield for exploitation. Thus Primi (Akhegwo) and Meloni (Meluri) were annexed to the Naga Hills District in 1922.

Exploratory Expedition

The Survey work to connect Dimapur with Manipur was not very successful. The work touched only parts of Angami and Zeliangroung country. The establishment of British authority on Naga Hills necessitated more exploratory operations to acquire knowledge of the other surrounding tribes and to decide policies in dealing with them. Thereupon in 1871 a regular survey was started by Captain John Butler in Company with Ridgeway, Woodthrope, Ogge. John Butler was the second Deputy Commissioner, son of John Butler who had opened negotiations with several Naga chiefs, fostered trade relations with them, opened the first police outpost at Cumu Kedima and entrusted it to Bhogchand's charge. He had written a book entitled "Travels and Adventures in Assam" (1851) which also set some account about Angami-Zeliangroung and their relations and wars with the East India Company up till 1851.

The report of the exploration expedition in 1873 is interesting and provides another historical background. The survey placed on record the following tribes: Arung, Naia, Kuki, Kacha, Angami, Mao or Sapvomah, Khezha, Zami, Sema, and Rengma who exhibit the southern Naga mountain tract. Arung, a branch of Zeliang, a small and peaceful community was confined to North Cachar. Kuki embracing Thaido, Changsen, and Singphou clans inhabited the head-waters off Dhansiri with 21 villages, 718 houses and a population of 2599 souls but had been pressing westwardly to Dhansiri valley while becoming so sparsely distributed south of Kapa mezu. Zeliang with 23 villages, 1284 houses and an approximate population of 600 souls were found on both sides of Brail water-parting north to the course of Barak river and in close proximity to Leneu Peak, an impassable barrier chain.

Punglwa is described thus, "On walking over the village I found it in a regular state of barricade and palisading thrown up in all direction, with a strong stockade surrounding the upper portion of the village, the sides of the hill cut down right across the ridge of the hill, and the whole places so thickly studded with Panjies. This is all owing to the Sanomah Khel of Khonoma having made raid upon this village." Auganni occupied a most charming country, enjoying a beautiful climate and most fertile soil, well cultivated, drained and manured. The land was more populated than the neighbouring places. For instance Kohima contained 865 homes, Khonoma 545, Viswema 530. There were a total of 46 Angami villages with 6367 houses and population of about 31,835 souls.

Simultaneously another survey was exploring the present Tirap and Tans-Patkoi Naga area under Lt. Holcombe. Up to the close of 1873, there was no Naga opposition to the survey. It was not until 1874 that the survey was confronted with the first opposition in the Rengma territory. Butler had traversed the northern Angani area from Kohima via Nerhema, Chicliarna now known as Chiefhobozou and advanced for Tesopheneyu on January 4. Here the survey was hindered.

The route was thickly panicled at an outer row, while nearly one mile above it, the ditch dung out was come across. The party saw the groups of Rangma warriors on the lower spur of the village shouting and yelling. The messenger engaged by Butler to announce their peaceful intention came back, telling that the village was challenging the survey. The Rengmas operated by casting out rocks and sending hails of spears upon the survey party for which the soldiers were ordered to open fire upon the frenzied mob who soon dispersed. The village was abandoned, a part of it was burnt by Butler and his men.

Meanwhile the survey work was going on. The survey advanced to Wokha but was attacked by the Lothas. A few survey personnel were killed. But the village later on was retaliated.

In 1878 the district headquarters was shifted to Kohima which was acquired without difficulty. The objective of this shift in capital was to keep an effective control over the insurgent tribes, Kohima being more centrally situated. The climate of Chumukedima was moreover insalubrious and therefore unsuitable for the purpose of effective administration.

Nagas during World Wars

During the First World War the British raised as labour force of Nagas. Semas in particular responded well. Others who joined the force were Lothas, Rengmas, Aos and Changs. The Angamis, however, refused to join and cooperate with the British. Apart from it, the Nagas contributed Rs. 26,264 (1917-18) and Rs. 39,000 (1918-19) to the War Fund of the British.

It was however, during the Second World War that the British came to know about the real mettle of the Nagas. The sixty-four-day battle at Kohima was described as one "of the most stubborn, close and bloody fighting in the whole of the Second World War." It is wrong to say that the Kohima battle proved to be a turning point of the war. It is doubtful whether the British would have won the Kohima battle without the active support of the Nagas. "Throughout the fighting the Nagas not only remained loyal to the British but also rendered them valuable assistance. They provided coolies, passed intelligence, escorted patrols, helped in the evacuation of the wounded, and harassed the Japanese in many ways."

In 1944, the Japanese forces baked by Indian National army advanced towards Kohima as well as Imphal from Burma. After capturing Kohima, it was easier for them to annex Imphal. Thereafter they would have captured the railway station of Dimapur, and succeeded in cutting off Assam from the rest of the country. But the Kohima battle would be recalled by the Japanese as the Germans recall the battle of Stalingrad where they were badly defeated.

These in accessible hills located in inhospitable environment were so well known to the Naga tribes that they could trek through these Hills without any difficulty even in the darkness of night. They were so adept that they used to sneak into the Japanese encampments without creating any sound and thus at many an occasion succeeded in spying for the British. British were quite cautious in their relations with the Nagas. They did not interfere with many of their traditions, customs, culture and the religious beliefs. The Christian missionaries had also rendered health and medical aid to these tribals. The Japanese on the other hand, burnt the villages of such Nagas who had refused to cooperate with them. Obviously in this period Nagas were favourably inclined towards the British.

In the initial stage of Kohima battle the British were facing reverses. Half of Kohima had come under the control of the Japanese. The road leading to Imphal had been captured by the Japanese. For about forty days the British suffered heavy loses and their ultimate defeat seemed imminent. Hundreds of British and Indian soldiers were killed and the evacuation of hundreds of wounded personnel posed a serious problem.

In want of roads the wounded persons could not be taken to the hospitals located at Dimapur, Guwahati, and Shillong. At this critical juncture, the Nagas rendered yeoman's service. They carried the wounded persons either on bamboo stretchers or palanquins. They did all this without charging any wages. Nagas also accompanied the forces to the front as porters. They moved with speed along the steep gradients, dense forests, narrow passages and marshy valleys infested with snakes and mosquitoes. Field Marshall William Slim acknowledged in his book 'Defeat into Victory' that the victory of British in Kohima battle was largely the result of Naga's active cooperation. The Marshall described the Nagas as gallant 'whose loyalty, even in the most depressing times of the invasion, never faltered'.

Haimendory described that 'they split through the Japanese lines with valuable intelligences, rescued allied wounded... and at night, often guided the allied air in arms... the Angamis brought on a large number of prisoners. Many Nagas became prisoners and in the most trying times even fought with the enemy single-handed or at the most with their indigenous weapons.

The War Cemetery where the tide of invasion was repulsed from Kohima, tells the grim story of the war with all its pathos and horrors. Shortly after the Japanese had retreated, resettlement of evacuees were made in the Angami-Chakesang area. The Japanese during the siege were considerably assisted by the Indian National Army. A negligible Naga group is said to have joined the Japanese and the National Army during the invasion.

With the war, several calamities visited the country. Many Naga villages in Manipur and Southern Nagaland were affected by epidemics where hundreds of people died of dysentery, typhoid, enteric fever and cholera. Matters became worsened when medical relief failed to reach in night time because of transport difficulties and complicated issues arising of the invasion. Villagers in interior places went on starving owing to a shortage of foodstuffs after their village were cut off by the Japanese, whilst the latter butchered all livestock available and confiscated the agricultural crops wherever found, but a tradition says, the Japanese respected the children and women. Many village around Kohima were evacuated but when the villagers had returned, they found it difficult, owing to the disturbed state, to settle down to their old way of life. It was therefore, at the cost of such difficulties underwent by people who inhabit these eastern frontier mountain tracts that Eastern India was saved, whilst the programmes made by the invaders to reach the impenetrable jungle all the way from Burma remained an act of wonder to many a spectator.

The invasion launched Naga Hills into another transformation of an epoch-making. Heavy mechanisation and mechinisation came with the war. Administrative control became extended. There was an upsurge of the new patterns of business consciousness. The war forged a sense of unity among the different tribes. After the war the Naga Hills District Tribal Council was formed which in 1946 changed itself into the Naga National Council. It was to guide the Naga politics for more than one decade.

Post-independence Period

The Naga disturbances which have disturbed the peace of the nation hundreds of time in the post-independence period are unique in character as much as they are based entirely on political foundations. The Naga politics became more complicated with the advent of Independence and it was only after the inception of Nagaland, nay the resumption of the Agreement for the suspension of operations in 1964, that a definite measures of political settlement was restored. Economically Nagas have never been exploited in the known history. There was totally no interference with their social, cultured and religious life. When viewed in retrospect it appears that the hostile disturbances by the Nagas against the Democratic Government of India were instigated by the foreign powers for their vested interests and also fanned and financed at times by the same powers.

The British administration in this region was mainly confined to the maintenance of law and order and the pursuit of sociological studies. The negative approaches of 'preservation and protection of culture' marked the anxiety. Nothing was done to initiate and stimulate economic progress in the hills. Administrative machinery was always sketchy and the general appearance of the region bore a static and not a dynamic look. A kind of district barrier was maintained between these hills and the plains during the British rule. Non-tribals were not given admittance to these areas without special permission, which was given rather freely to foreign missionaries. Such restrictions deepened isolation of these areas from the rest of the state.

With the Independence of India, the foreign missionaries started a silent revolution among the Nagas, warning them against the forceful conversion of Nagas to Hinduism. The ignorant Naga masses were entrapped in sentimental whirlwind and became the antagonists of the Indian Government. Angami Zaphu Phizo and his followers propagated such views among the Nagas. He pleaded that Naga country was never a part of India, but an independent territory between India and Burma. They impressed upon the people that after the withdrawal of the British Naga had *ipso facto* became independent. Such a vicious propaganda based on facile and distorted facts of history went home with a section of Nagas who rose in arms and led a protracted strife for about a decade that wrought havoc on the Naga country in particular and India at large.

Phizo was born in the historic village of Khomona around 1900 AD. He hailed from the Gwitzantsu clan of the Angami tribe. He is said to have matriculated from missionary school at Shillong. He wanted to take to business as his career. He went to Burma in 1933 to try his hand at business. He pursued the insurance business there and remained in that country till 1946. At one stage he also joined Subhash Chandra Bose's Indian National Army in 1943. After the recapture of Burma by the British he was made prisoner and his property confiscated. On release he found that the situation in Naga country was ripe for him to fulfil his political ambition which he had gathered while being in Indian National Army (INA). Thus he came to India and plunged into politics.

In the year 1918, Naga Club was formed in Kohima with British patronage. Government officials and village chiefs were the main members of this club. In 1929, the club submitted a memorandum to the Simon Commission with the demand that the proposed reforms should not affect the tribal Nagas and their country be placed directly under the British

Government. It is apparent that such a demand was not directly made by the Nagas but some other brain was behind such a move. In the year 1945, when Independence of India became imminent to many of the then British officers in the country they started sowing seeds of discordance under the apparent move for improvement. Charles Pawsey was then the Deputy Commissioner of the Naga Hills District. He formed Naga Hills District Tribal Council with an apparent view of uniting all the Nagas under one banner and taking up post-war reconstruction work. The council became Naga National Council (NCC) in April 1946 and held its first Conference at Wokha. To begin with the NCC decided upon to take the soft line. On 19th June 1946, the NCC submitted a four-point memorandum on the then Governor of Assam, Mr. Robert Reid:

- This Naga Council stands for the solidarity of Naga tribes, including those in the unadministered area;

- This council strongly protested against the grouping of Assam with Bengal;

- The Naga Hills should be constitutionally included in an autonomous Assam, in a free India with local autonomy and due safeguards for the interest of the Nagas; and

- The Naga tribe should have a separate electorate.

While reading in between the lines of this memorandum one is convinced that the Nagas were instigated before India could attain freedom to have a separate political entity. The last British Governor of Assam writes, "... and if control is ever decided upon the future it may will be that a scheme for establishing a number of small states may have to be considered." This narration also lends credence to the view that the foreign ruler desired the country to be parcelled out not only in two main divisions but many more divisions. They instigated the vulnerable elements at an unprecedented speed.

The NCC which had in a soft way presented its four demands rapidly changed its colour and style. On 20th February, 1947 the NCC struck another note in a different tone saying that "a constitution drawn up by the people who have no knowledge of the Naga Hills and the Naga people will be quite unsuitable and unacceptable to the Naga people" and that "thrown among 40 crore of Indians, the one million Nagas with this unique system of life will be wiped out of existence." By this time Phizo had entered the political arena.

The rapidly changing colour of the NCC leaves no doubt about the inference that the tribals were instigated to create problems for the new government. Taking their plea into account, not only India but all the sizeable nations of the world should have been parcelled out into numerous units.

The NCC appealed to the outgoing government and the incoming government to establish an interim government and the incoming government to establish an interim government for the Nagas for a decade at the end of which the Nagas should be free to choose the form of government they liked. Immediately thereafter on May 19, 1947 the NCC submitted another memorandum clarifying the earlier one. They wanted the interim government to clarifying the earlier one. They wanted the interim government to be constituted of Naga people with full powers over executive, judicial and legislative matters and also wanted the defence of their country from other powers. Next day the Bardoloi Committee visited Kohima and had detailed talks with the NCC leaders but with no concrete results.

In June 1947, Sir Akbar Hydri, the then governor of Assam had discussions with the Naga leaders at Kohima. A nine-point understanding was drawn up which was unfortunately termed as nine-point agreement by the mischievous elements. This understanding recognised the right of these tribes to develop themselves in accordance with their wishes.

It also hoped that no Provincial or Central Legislature affecting the religious practices of these tribals would be enforced in the Naga Hills without the consent of Naga Council. Naga Council was to be held responsible for executive matters while the judicial matters had to be referred to duly constituted Naga courts. It was also agreed to that land would not be given or sold to a non-Naga without the consent of the Naga Council. There was disagreement on the clause number 9 which created misunderstanding between the parties and this misunderstanding became a root cause of the unhappy events to come.

The extremist Nagas interpreted the way it suited them. They held that after the expiry of ten years they were free to opt for a sovereign independent state. The government stuck to the letter and spirit of the clause that narrated that after the expiry of the period of the Naga Council would be asked whether they require the continuation of the arrangement or desired new arrangement, of course guaranteeing fullest measure of autonomy within the Union. How could it be expected of a government to allow the separation of its part.

Phizo wanted full control over the NCC and used it as a forum to further his political ambitions. In 1948, however, he resigned from the NCC as his radical outlook was misfit in a body dominated by the moderates. He instead formed Naga Clans Council and demanded complete independence. Such a move on his part resulted in his arrest and detention. In 1949 he was released and now he restarted his agitational activity vigorously. Once again he joined NNC and became its President in 1950. At his behest the Nagas boycotted the elections to District Councils and General Elections of 1952.

Earlier in 1951 Phizo had organised a plebiscite on the issue of complete independence in a unique way. He claimed to have visited every village in the Naga Hills and asserted that 99 per cent of the people voted for his cause. A point to be keenly observed that the Tuensang area, now the part of Naga Hills District was not covered. Moreover, women were not considered politically mature enough to express their opinion on this issue. It is also doubtful whether the issue was properly explained to the people. "At one place,

Phizo asked the villagers if they wanted their lands to remain with them or were willing to surrender than to India.

Such an over simplification can be dangerously misleading and it is no wonder that the villagers who indicated their option voted for 'independence', which alone seemed to guarantee than their land. Phizo played on the psychology of the Naga people — their attachment to land to create unrest where there was peace, to produce discord where there was harmony." On the other hand, Pandit Jawahar Lal Nehru the then Prime Minister, stood for progress and prosperity for the Nagas but not at the cost of national integration as it would have adversely affected the welfare of rest of the country. He is reported to have told Phizo in an interview in July 1952 that 'even if the heavens fell or India went to pieces, Nagas could not be given the sort of independence demanded by a handful of hostiles.'

Frustrated by failure on all sides Phizo managed a show of disobedience in Naga Hills by getting official functions boycotted, returning red blankets (conferred as honour) by some village elders and stopping revenue payments. In 1952, he even addressed a memorandum to the UNO and attempted to crossover to Pakistan via Burma but the Burmese pushed him back. Whereas the Indian Government was firm in not allowing cessation of the Naga Hills, they were also determined to initiate and accelerate economic progress in these Hills to fulfil the cherished dreams of the Nagas.

Phizo arranged and organised an armed rebellion in Nagaland. There were abductions, murders, plunders, arson and loot of worst order. The peaceful Nagas were threatened by the hostiles at every step. In September 1954 Phizo announced about the formation of Khunak Kautang Nageukhum, i.e. Peoples' Sovereign Republic of Free Nagaland headed by Hongkin as President. On March 22, 1956 Hongkin government was replaced by Naga central Government. Naga Home Guards with Thungti as chief were raised. Prior to it Kaito Sema had already organised Naga Safe Guards.

On March 4, 1956 Kaito had also been elected as the Commander-in-Chief. The formation of two parallel armed organisations led to a conflict between the hostiles themselves. Phizo favoured Thungti. When Phizo did not yield on this issue the Semas left hostiles *en masse* on June 22, 1956. The Semas did not cooperate in the attack on Kohima launched on July 22, 1956. Thungi got disappointed and submitted his resignation but Phizo did not accept it. Kaito on the other hand threatened to surrender to Indian Army in case he was not elevated. His threat worked. On November 8, 1957 both the forces were merged to became Naga Country Guard with Kaito as Commander-in-Chief. Naga Central Government was restructured as Naga Federal Government on October 6, 1959 with Scatoswti as its Kedaghe, i.e. President.

The Government of India was doing everything possible to restore peace in the troubled area. Verrier Elwin, a known authority on this North-East States, was appointed

Advisor on Tribal Affairs who was a great friend of Michela Scott, later on Phizo's host in England. It was on his recommendation that the Tuensang area was detached from North Eastern Frontier Agency, NEFA (now Arunachal Pradesh) and merged with Naga Hills District. The new unit was named as NHTA, i.e. Naga Hills Tuensang Area. After about one year the first Naga People's Convention (NPC) was held at Kohima (22 to 26 August 1957) presided over by Dr. Imkongliba.

The convention demanded that NHTA should be made into a separate unit under External Affairs Ministry. Though the demand was anomalous in as much as it demanded an Indian Territory to be placed under not the Home Ministry but External Ministry, but Pandit Nehru accepted it in the interest of peace and harmony. He did not yield 'to violence as propagated by some quarters but he desired peace and prosperity of India without jeopardising the national integration.

Thus a new administrative unit NHTA was ushered on December 1, 1957. The Third Naga People's Conference (October 1959) demanded the formation of separate State to be known as Nagaland within the Indian Union. It presented a sixteen-point charter of demands to the government. There were long discussions on each point between the Naga leaders and the Government of India.

Thus Pandit Nehru agreed to grant 'autonomy' to Nagas within the framework of the Indian Union. As a result he announced the proposal to form Nagaland, in the Lok Sabha on August 1, 1960. This announcement however, did not fulfil the ambitions of the underground Nagas. Thus they stepped up their terrorist activities soon after Nehru's announcement. On August 25, 1960 they attacked Assam Rifles post at Purr in Tuensang. A Dakota aircraft on supply dropping mission was shot and forced to land at Purr.

The government was undeterred by such movements, and it took all steps to curb such activities. It decided to grant statehood to Nagaland with effect from 1st December 1963. As a first step towards it, the Governor of Assam inaugurated the Nagaland Interim Body on February 18, 1961. It consisted of 52 members as Dr. Imkangliba as its elected Chairman. An Executive Council with five members was also constituted. Underground Nagas killed Dr. Imkongliba on August 22, 1961. T. N. Angami became the new Chairman. The state of Nagaland Act, 1962 was passed by both the Houses of Parliament. In accordance with this Act the separate State of Nagaland was inaugurated by Dr. Sarvepalli Radhakrishnan, the then President of India on December 1, 1963 at Kohima. Necessary alterations were made in some points, and noticing the improvement of conditions in the Naga Hills, the then Prime Minister Pandit Nehru on August 10, 1960 announced his Government's final decision for the establishment of the 16th state in the Indian Union to be called Nagaland.

The President of India promulgated the Nagaland (Transitional Provisions) Regulation on January 24, 1961, to bring into operation a new administrative set-up for Nagaland.

It provided for the setting up of a 45-member elected 'Interim Body' to serve as advisory body to the Governor (of Assam and concurrently Governor of Nagaland), and whose members were to be elected from the tribes in Nagaland—the area comprising the Naga Hills and Tuensang Area. The Interim Body was to make necessary separations for the establishment of the state of Nagaland. The Governor inaugurated the first meeting of the Interim Body on February 5, 1960.

The Interim Body was given most of the administrative powers vested in the commissioner did the advisor to the Governor of Assam. It was also empowered to discuss and make recommendations to the Executive council on (a) matters of administration, general policy and schemes of development, (b) any other matter referred to it by the Executive Council (except Tuensang unless the consent of all the members of Tuensang district has been obtained) It was also given powers to make recommendations to the Executive Council 'in regard to the Constitution and composition of the Legislative Assembly of the state of Nagaland'.

The Executive Council was to consist of five members of the Interim Body recommended by it and appointed by the governor. The regulation also said that the 'Council shall as soon as may choose a member of the council to be its Chairman'.

The regulation further laid down that each village was to have a Village Council and each tribe a Tribal Council, to come into being on a date fixed by the commissioner. The term of the Interim Body was three years from the day of its first meeting.

Phizo, who had slipped to Pakistan in December 1957 reached London on June 12, 1960 to seek support of the West. On October 8, 1960 he addressed a memorandum to the UNO alleging with India but they were being invaded and crushed under the instructions of External Affairs Ministry of India. Many underground Nagas slipped to then East Pakistan and there from to China. They were alleged to have been trained by these countries in sophisticated weapons and sent back to Nagaland with arms and ammunitions. These hostile and instigated people did a great harm and loss to the Naga life and property. UNO could not interfere in the internal affairs of a member nation and thus Phizo's hopes were dashed to ground. On February 11, 1962 Phizo submitted a petition to the International Community of Jurists, charging India of Genocide. However, all his attempts to throw dust into the eyes of others turned futile.

Verrier Elwin died soon after Chinese invasion on India. His death created a void. Michael Scott, the host of Phizo in London, was posted in this place by Nehru.

He was permitted to visit India and Nagaland and meet the followers of Phizo and being about a peaceful as well as a lasting settlement by Jaya Prakash Narayan, the veteran national leader also offered his services to bring about peace in Nagaland. He joined Scott and both formed 'peace Mission' in Nagaland. Dr. Aram, a Naga leader, also joined the mission later. As a first step the Mission succeeded in bringing about ceasefire between the hostile Nagas and Indian Security Forces. This ushered peace and the time was utilised for making quick economic development into hitherto war-torn Nagaland. In the meanwhile Scott's moves became questionable. Jaya Prakash Narayan left the Peace Mission. Pandit Nehru died. Lal Bahadur Shastri expelled Michael Scott from India for his anti-Indian activities. He criticised India through his writings and fully supported Phizo's cause for an Independent Nagaland. His protestations did not work. India started new phases in the field of peace in Nagaland. The peace Mission with Dr. Aram as its Chairman continued to bring about an accord between the hostiles and the government.

Ultimately agreement was arrived at through Shillong Accord signed on November 11, 1975 between the representatives of the Government of India and underground Nagas. The underground hostile Nagas accepted the Indian Constitution and agreed to deposit arms and ammunition at the appointed places. Apart from the deposition of these arms the Government of Nagaland succeeded in unearthing arms, ammunition and explosives. Peace camps were organised to accommodate the ex-underground Nagas temporarily to give time to them to adjust to new open life. A general reprieve was announced for the arrested underground Nagas and under trials. Those released or surrendered were given cash grants ranging from Rs. 5,000 to Rs. 20,000 for their rehabilitation. Assistance was also given to families of those who had been killed during the disturbances. Collective fines imposed on villagers after September 1972 for not reporting underground activities were refunded to the villagers.

In 1974, elections no party secured majority in Nagaland. Seven independents joined the United Democratic Front which formed a government in a House of sixty members. But defections reduced the government to minority which had to resign on March 9, 1975. On March 27, 1975, President's Rule imposed in Nagaland. In November 1977, elections were held again.

The National Convention of Nagaland contested 31 seats and the Janata Party supported UDF contested 38 seats. The latter emerged victorious because it had won 35 seats. In November 1977, Vizol, leader of the UDF, formed his twelve-member Cabinet. The Legislature of the state is unicameral.

4

Geography

Inaugurated on December 1, 1963, the state of Nagaland is the third smallest state of the country after Sikkim and Goa. The predominantly tribal, state of Nagaland has a unique geographical personality. Its simmering rivers, evergreen subtropical forests, denuded peaks, invigorating climate and pristine but progressive population are unparalleled in the country.

Nagaland stretches between 26° 6'N and 29° 4'N latitudes, and between 92° 20'E to 95° 15'E longitudes. The state is bounded by Assam in the west, Arunachal Pradesh in the north, Burma in the east and Manipur in south. Sprawling over 16,579 sq km, Nagaland as per the census of 1981 had a population of 774,930 with an average density of 47 persons per sq km. The state comprises of seven administrative districts. The area, population and administrative headquarters of the constituent districts has been given in the following: As stated in the preceding para Nagaland is predominantly a tribal state. The entire tribal population is divisible into twenty major tribal groups. The dominant tribes which have their well-defined territorial jurisdiction are — Aos, Angamis, Changs, Chakhesang, Kabuis, Kacharis, Khein Mangas, Konyaks, Kukis, Lothas (Lhotus), Maos, Mikirs (Mikhirs), Phoms, Rengmas, Sangtams, Somas, Thankuls, Yimchungars and Zelliang.

English is the official language of the state for administration and education. However, the common language used by the tribal population is Nagamese and English. About 49 per cent of the total population is literate and only 15.5 per cent lives in urban areas.

Geological Features

The entire Nagaland has almost identical geological formations. In fact, Naga Hills is a continuation of the Himalayan folded mountains. The formations belong to the Tertiary period.

The southern Nagaland has the Barail and Disang formations. The Disang conforming to the oldest rocks are dominant towards the east between Japfu and Seramati at an altitude of 3,000 feet to 4,000 feet, but the Barail series are more conspicuous towards the west. Disang series exhibits thin splintery grey shales interbedded with hard hands of fine-grained flaggy sand stones. In addition ferruginous varieties are not uncommon, which concretion are detected in the shales extending to Mokokchung. Iron pyrites are found in the shales admixed with carbonaceous matter.

But sandstones even appear to be little more than massive impure varieties of shale. Where Disangs show increasing metamorphism, the argillaceous beds become more slaty with variations of blue slates weathering to pale grey green. Phyllites, talcose and chloritic, green in colour and soapy to touch are admixed. Slate of superior quality is abundant in Tizu valley, which is used by the Nagas for their house building and for commercial purpose. Slate in a more metamorphosal zone is combined with quartz. Serpentine intrusions are noted in a thick band of conglomerate near the Seramati Peak. Disang beds generally dip at steep angles.

The structure is soft their splintery character has helped to cause frequent landslides around Kohima. Pyrites and carbonaceous matters are also admixed. Deposits of chrysotile asbestos are found towards the south bordering on Nurma between Puchimi and Keromi in Tizu Valley.

The Brail contains fine-grained sandstones, hard, bluish, grey, thin-bedded and flaggy in nature. Apart from carbonaceous elements which when traversing northwardly from Chumukedima terminate in the Doyang Coal field. Towards the southwest, the Brail exhibits the formation of massive sandstone but the shale is absent.

The general elevation of the state ranges from 914 metres to 3,840 metres above the sea level. The Brail range locally known as Radliura, enters the state from north Kachhar and after passing through Kohima runs in the direction of Wokha. Japava which lies to the south of Kohima is the highest peak of Barail (Radhura) Range and attains a height of 3,804 metres above the sea level. At this place the range is met by the meridinal axis of axis prolonged from the Arakanyoma (the major mountain system of Burma), and from this point the main range runs in a north and northeasterly direction. Owing to a sudden rise of the Barail Rang on its northern face, about 12 km wide miniature type of Dun (valley) is formed in between the barail Range and Samaguling Hills. Kohima and Naga Hills are located further east. The Patkai range forms a watershed which constitutes the International boundary between India and Burma. Saraniati situated in Thensang district is the highest peak of Nagaland which is 3,877 metres above the sea level.

There are two other small ranges that connect Barail and Patkai Ranges. One of these ranges connects Barail with Patkai Range in the vicinity of Kohima and Ukhrul. Up to Mao it has a direction from southeast to northwest. From Mao the range takes an eastward turn and continues in this direction for above 24 kilometres and then follows a southward direction. The other linking range also follows a zigzag course. It joins the first range at Mao and crosses the Patkai Range slightly east of Tuensang. Similar to the main hills of Nagaland these ranges also send out many ridges, spurs and small offshoots of hills. The ramification of numerous mountain ranges, ridges and spurs have made the topography and geomorphic features of Nagaland most complex. Relif and topographic features have however, closely influenced the spatial distribution of tribes, their settlements and culture. The important peaks of Nagaland are Saramati (12,553 ft), Japfu (9,890 ft), Ezupu (9,320 ft) Paona (8,157 ft), Angola (6,764 ft), Laishing (6,755 ft).

Parts of the Japfu mountain summit owing to its high altitude are snow-bound during the cold weather (December, January), summits of the lofty peaks are thickly wooded, clad with an evergreen vegetation.

Owing to the scanty undergrowth, the loose and less compact soil texture and structure, absence of hard rocks and widespread soft clay across the precipitous slopes, landslides are frequent which cause serious impediments in the maintenance of communications. Such soils which usually retains bare and weak vegetation often shrinks easily after the showers, the soft clay (subsoil) tumbling down the hillside causing at places a gigantic formation of slough. The lower hills have for the greater parts become deforested owing to the practice of Jhuming (shifting cultivation).

Despite landslides and Jhuming the state commands a majestic landscape. Rolling hills skirting over the horizon with terraced and undulating fields, the narrow glens at their base, the profuse vegetation which clothes the mountain summits on a higher altitude, the diverse flora which lay scattered on the hills blooming in their verdant colour are panoramic view. The invigorating breeze and the temperate weather make life pleasant and lay incentives for manual works and physical exertion; and how magnificent are those beauty spots which set a thrill to a watchful spectator.

All over the state the oblong and sturdy ridges, their precipitous slopes — the elongated chains which merge themselves into the imposing plateaux, at places intersected by tribal traditional tracks and newly constructed roads widening up and down the cliffs, at times touching the villages with their age-long existence on the spurs. Glen at places open out into the diminutive valleys.

Location

Nagaland location shows the geographical and the strategic position of the state in the country. Home to a number of tribes, the state of Nagaland is located in the Northeastern Region of India. The capital of the state is Kohima which is located at an elevated altitude of 1,444.12 metres above sea level. Some of the major facts about the geography of Nagaland are given below.

The state of Nagaland encompasses the geographical coordinates of 25°6' N to 27°4' N latitude and 93°20' E to 95°15' E longitude. On the eastern boundary of Nagaland lies the international border that India shares with Myanmar. The southern end of the state is bordered by the state of Manipur. The state of Assam borders in the western and the north western sides. The state of Arunachal Pradesh borders on the north. Sixteen different tribes inhabit the state. The tradition of the tribal inhabitants is revealed through the different customs, dialect, attires and habits.

The location of Nagaland reveals the political and geographical significance of the state which is marked by the international border on one side. The border regions are patrolled by military and the border security force who prevent the encroachment of the infiltrators.

Land

Bordering Assam, Myanmar (Burma), Arunachal Pradesh and Manipur Nagaland takes the form of a narrow strip of mountainous land from the plains in the south the land changes through tea plantations into heavily forested mountain regions. There are green valleys, high mountains and deep gorges, which sustain a huge variety of fauna and flora.

Mountains and Hills

Nagaland is a small state in the northeastern part of India. This tribal state is blessed with great valleys, meandering streams, high mountains, deep gorges and a rich variety of flora and fauna.

The entire state is covered with ranges of hills that are the northward extension of the Arakan Mountain system. Nagaland's capital is Kohima, a charming hill station perched at an altitude of 1,495 m above sea level.

Naga Hills

Naga hills, reaching a height of around 3,825 metres, lie on the border of India and Myanmar. These hills are part of a complex mountain system, and the parts of the mountain ranges inside the Indian state of Nagaland are called Naga hills.

In Undivided India, Naga Hills was also the name of an administrative district of the British Raj.

The hills, due to their complexity and position form a barrier between India and the former Burma. Extending northerly this rock formation and frontier known as 'Arakan Yoma' reaches 12,552 feet.

Naga, derives from the ancient Assamian God of Rainfall (Colitawobiao Naggsi). The ancient Myanmarian people decorated their livestock, such as pigs, with colourful tassels and skirt-like decorations. At such times, village elders would spin on one leg and chant for rain.

In 1963, the area became known as Nagaland in-line with its position within India.

Khasi Hills

The Khasi Hills are part of the Garo-Khasi range in Meghalaya, India, and is part of the Patkai range and of the Meghalaya subtropical forests ecoregion.

The region is inhabited mainly by tribal Khasi dwellers, which are traditionally in various chieftainships, petty states known as the Khasi Hill States. One of its capitals, Cherrapunjee, is considered the wettest place in the world.

Garo Hills

The Garo Hills are part of the Garo-Khasi range in Meghalaya, India. They are inhabited mainly by tribal dwellers. Shillong, the capital of Meghalaya, is located in this range. It is one of the wettest places in the world. The range is part of the Meghalaya subtropical forests ecoregion.

Garo Hills comprises 3 districts. Tura is the largest town with a population of about 70,000 located at the foothills of often cloud covered Tura peak. The town is centrally located to other popular game/wildlife sanctuaries in the district such as Balpakram and Nokrek, natural caves (the Siju cave being one of the longest in Asia). These places are rich reserves of natural flora and fauna.

Japfu Peak

The Japfu Peak is set amidst the verdant locales in the North-East Indian state of Nagaland. At an elevation of 3048 metres from the mean sea level, the hill retreat is overshadowed by thick bamboo bushes that have an appearance of a lawn. A trek up the Japfu peak can be tough and trying, but the verdant and beatific landscape from the top gives a captivating sight that is certain to enrapture tourists. The peak is the second highest peak of Kohima and is just 15 km from this capital city of Nagaland. The hill top portrays a bird eye view of the entire city of Kohima.

The Japfu Peak ranks high among the Nagaland attractions and the mystical sun rise view from the peak is a cherished memory. The dry months from November to March are best for a trip to Japfu Peak. After the rain drenched monsoon, the air becomes fresh along with the clear skies and the surrounding appears all the more green in Japfu.

The Northern Montane Wet Temperate Forests predominate the landscape of Japfu with evergreen covers of Michelia, Magnolia, Quercus, Prunus, Alnus, Schima and Betula. Rhododendrons run a riot of colours as the summer sets in the Japfu Peak of Nagaland. Incidentally, the world's tallest Rhododendron tree has been identified in Japfu peak that towers up to 130 feet and the base has a circumference of around 11 feet. The name of the tree has been enlisted in the Guinness Book of World Records for its rapid spread.

Saramati Peak

In Nagaland Saramati hill range is the biggest in the mountain range of Nagaland and is situated on the extreme south east of the state. At 3,841 m, Saramati Peak is highest in Nagaland and it remains snow covered during winter. The mountain range is covered with rich, natural and diverse forests, visible at various altitudes, ranging from subtropical ever green and semi ever green to temperate broad leaved and Alpine vegetation. It also has good biodiversity with natural flora and fauna and various kinds of orchids.

Mount Tiyi

Mount Tiyi is situated at an altitude of 1,969.61 m from sea-level. It is a hill which has supernatural legends associated with it. Most Nagas believe that this mountain is the abode of departed souls. According to local Wokhan folklore the mountain had an orchard that could only be found by the 'lucky ones.' Rhododendrons are found commonly on Mount Tiyi.

Rivers and Water System

The state of Nagaland is drained by numerous streams and rivers. Some of the important rivers are Dzulu, Dhansiri, Dikhu, Milak, Zungki, Tizu. Most of these rivers originate from the central mountain ranges. From the centre the rivers move north and southward.

The hills in Nagaland are serrated ridges that are separated from each other by deep gorge-like valleys through which rivulets streams and rivers make their ways to the Brahmaputra Plains in the north and to the drainage system in the south. The Doyang river which originates from the vicinity of Mao Village of the Angami territory of the Kohima District is the largest stream of the Nagaland State. It flows northward and is navigable for a short distance before it enters the Valley of Brahmaputra.

Dhansiri (Temaki) rises in the southwest of the Kohima District. It first flows westwardly and then takes a northwardly course and forms a natural boundary with North Cachar Hills. Having debouched North Cachar, it bends eastwardly and flows past the Rangpahar-Dimapur Plains in Kohima District and again leaving the district, it flows on northwardly until it falls into the Brahmaputra at Dhansirimukh: It receives all the western and northern drainage of southern Nagaland. It is in Sibsagar that its real size is noticed before it confluences with Brahmaputra and becomes one of the latter's largest tributaries having carried out all the hill drainage. It is navigable only during the monsoons near Golaghat with country boats and small steamers plying up and down stream.

Diphu (Duidiki) originates from near Paona Peak. Flowing northwardly till it leaves the hills, where near the point of debauching for the plains, it receives an addition of

Khukhi river which has drained a northwestern portion of the district. Its confluences with Dhansiri is near Dimapur. Tizu is another important river which flows towards south. The Tizu and several other small rivulet flow in a southern direction and drain the Tuensang and Phak Districts and discharge their water into Chindwin river of Burma. Tasangki river originates from the west of Peren which flows southwardly till it confluences with Barak (Mbeiki). Tuilang is another river on the southern extremity: Duknaki, Manglu, Langlong, Tahaki or Khova, Disagfojan and Teipuiki are the other small rivers of the southern parts of Nagaland. Those rivers whose exits lie in the southwestern extremity such as Tasangki are emptied in Barak at Tullong (Mbeiki), a torrential river which rises in the Kapamezu range, and flows southwardly into Manipur but later on bends westwardly to Silchar Plains. Its course is through the very difficult mountain terrain.

All the rivers of Nagaland discharge little quantities of water during winter seasons but in the rainy season they suddenly assume threatening posture. The inundated streams and rivers cause heavy soil erosion and become difficult to ford during the summer monsoon season. Most of the rivers are not navigable owing to mountainous topography, swift speed over cascades and rapids. There is a famous Lacham, a natural lake in eastern Chakhesang, east of Meluri. It lies in a glen amidst the grotesque heights of the overstretching ranges. There is another small lake called *Achie* in pfutsero. At Dimapur, tanks surviving as historical relics of the old Kachari Kings are still to be seen in Puranabazar, but many yet (totalling more than fifty in number), have become mere pits and hollows as they are all dried up. The most important tanks are: (i) Bongola Pukhuri, (ii) Padum Pukhuri, (iii) Jor Pukhuri (iv) Bamon Pukhuri, (v) Dipo Pukhuri, (vi) Thara Pukhuri, (vii) Podo Pukhuri, and (viii) Garani Pukhuri.

Plants and Animals

The state of Nagaland is well endowed with forests. The prevailing high temperatures and fairly high precipitation throughout the year are conducive for the luxurious growth of numerous types of trees and plants.

The natural vegetation of Nagaland has great diversity, ranging from the alpine and bamboo forests to scrub forests of the foothills to the deciduous forests, at the lower altitudes and gentle slopes. Thus the vegetation of Nagaland is rich in the tropical, subtropical and also the temperate species. The natural vegetation of Nagaland is mainly classified into:

- Wet evergreen,
- Sub-tropical wet hill,
- Wet temperate, and
- Pine forests.

The plain area around Dimapur and the tracts adjacent to the Assam valley abound in wet evergreen vegetation resembling to some of the species of the equatorial climate. The main species of this region comprise Nahor, Sam, Poma, Khokan, Jhar, Makai, Gonseroi, Amari, Hingari, Hollong, Lali, Rata; Titasopa, and Nagaser. This zone constitutes a tropical broad-leaf vegetation, some trees reaching the top canopy in gigantic height.

The sub-tropical wet hill vegetation thrives at an altitude, ranging from 300 metres to 1,200 metres above the sea level. This zone is characterised with chestnut, Michelia, Champaca, Schima Wallichii, Gmelina arborea, Albizzia spp and members of meliaceae. Rengma foothills adjoining sibsagar plains abound in deciduous riverain canes and sometimes impenetrable bamboo groves.

In between 1,000 metres to 1,300 metres is the home of pine-trees. Oak is also found in this zone. Beyond 1,300 metres to 2,000 metres are the wet-temperate forests. The main species are Betula, Rhododen-drop, Magnolia, Juglans regia and Runus.

Owing to Jhuming, the lower hills have largely been reduced of vegetation because of a large scale deforestation. The central and eastern parts of the state are still covered with thick forests, sheltering a host of birds, animals and fowls, where Burmese fauna is said to have traversed through those dense jungles to India's eastern fringes. Jhun fields after the completion of Jhun-cycle generally gets converted to grassland but there is no denying the fact, owing to this practice, there is much degradation of ecosystems.

The forests have great economic importance for the people of the state. Posts, pillars, planks, troughs, mortars, etc. are scooped of wood. Sappers, creepers, barks, wild vines, tubers, bamboo and cane have a multifarious use connected with the manufacture of rain-proof coats, rain hats, utensils, and furniture. Bridges and house building and other domestic items are also prepared from the materials obtained from forests. Nagas make robes out of strong creepers and strings out of bamboo skins. Orchids are much loved as decorations. Wild vegetables, roots, fruits and others are much loved as decorations. Wild vegetables, roots, fruits and tubers are eaten raw or prepared into food. Plantain leaves which grow wild are used as packages of food stuffs such as meal, fish, salt, meat, pan, and for wrapping the rice preparation during the process of fermentation. Straw is used for house thatching.

According to the statistics published by the Forest Department of Nagaland, the forests cover an area of about 287,556 hectares (1986). Out of which 28,560 hectares or 9.93 per Cent are clothed with reserved forests, 51,799 (18 per cent) by protected forests and 207,198 hectares (72 per cent) by private forests. The Forest Department of the State Government of Nagaland has launched a programme to arrest the forest wealth depletion and to afforest the depleted tracts.

Fauna

The state of Nagaland has great diversity in physiography, climate and vegetation. This diversity in geo-ecological conditions provides the required habitats to varied animal kingdom. The fauna of the state, consequently differs from latitude to latitude and altitude to altitude. Moreover, Nagaland constitutes a meeting ground of the sub-Himalayan, Indian, Chinese, and Burmese type of fauna and therefore it is quite varied and rich. A great deal of game has, however, become extinct owing to the indiscriminate hunting and burning of forests by shifting cultivators.

The game among the Nagas is valued not only for its meat but hide and skin, skull, tusks, and feathers which the people have great liking as part of their ornamentation and decoration. Wild animals are found in the foothills and are fascinating game to the Nagas who hunt them for their meat and tusks but elephants are not domesticated for any purpose of transport. Tiger has its caves in the dense jungle. The dear family comprises the barking deer, sambar and serow.

The barking deer have their home in altitudes varying from the plains to 1500 metres and are a prey to tigers and leopards. The monkeys and jackals are also widely distributed in Nagaland. Other species comprise wild buffaloes, wild pigs, wild bears, wild dogs, antlers but the games vary to squirrels, bats, others and musk-rat, etc. Snakes comprise vipers, kraits, grass snakes, cobra, lizards, toads, monotors and pythons.

Numerous species of birds are found in higher altitudes. The main birds of Nagaland are partridge, nightjar, warbler, rokin, quail, woodpecker, hornbill, pheasant, porcupine, swift, hawk, crow, spine and other wagtails. In the lower hills cuckoo, sparrow, sun-bird, parrot, parakeet and other colour wrens are important.

Minerals: The development of industries and tertiary sector largely depends on the availability of minerals in a region. Nagaland is however not very rich in minerals. Till recently only coal had been known as a mineral of some economic significance. The Nazira coal field and its southwesternly extension is the major coal-producing centre of Nagaland. In this field coal has been mined at Barjan in the Saffrai area. The coal of these mines contains moisture (4.35%), volatile matter (48%), fixed carbon (47.7%) and ash (1.95%). The coal obtained from this area is consumed in the tea gardens and brick kilns in the neighbouring areas of Assam and also by the railways. Still most of the labour working in the coal mines of Nagaland comes from outside the state.

Coal is also found at Janji and the Disai valley, about 13 and 32 kilometres southwest of Nazira fields. In Disai valley the coal seams are located around the settlements of Lirmen, Aonokpu, Merinokpu and Lakhuni. All these settlements are located with 16 to 19 kilometres of Marapani railway station. A coal horizon has also been reported about 9 kilometre away from Tuensang town. Promising coal seams to have also been located in Tiru valley area of Mon District. Exploratory drilling for coal in Borjan area and follow-up action for reopening the Borjan coalmine have also been taken up. Some coal seams found in Jhanji-Desoi valley (Mokokchung District) are also being worked out. Detailed geological investigations are being carried out in Tuensang coalfield.

Oil seepages are known in the Dikhu valley. The people of adjacent settlements collect the crude for local use. Marapani tract in Wokha district also shows some prospects for oil reserves. It is of interest to note that the Whitehall Petroleum Corporation Limited had carried out prospecting work in Northern Cachar Hills, Southern Mikir Hills and Southwestern Naga Hills and drilled three wells without discovering any ail. According to Brown and Dey, the anti-clinical structures tested were cut off at depth by thrust faulting and in the comparatively small thickness of beds above the fault no productive sand were found.

Marble has been found near Burma border in Tuensang district. Detailed geological investigations for limestone, nickle-cobalt, chromium-bearing magnetite, and clay deposits were intensively carried out. Limestone deposits around Nimi (Tuensong District) and Wazeho (Phak District) have been located. Magnetite deposits have been reported in Pokphur tract (Tuensang District and Phek District). Investigations in detail are in progress. Tuffacceous material occurs along some of the streams as encrustations on the exposed rocks and boulders. Though the deposits are small yet the villages of Kezoma, Thenizuma, and Kekrima are important from this angle. These deposits have, however, been worked in the past for making building lime in small kilns in above villages. The kilns are still in good conditions and small-scale lime burning can be taken up again.

The Acro-magnetic surveys were carried out in the ophiolite complex of Nagaland occupying the eastern parts of Phek and Tuensang districts.

Where earlier very promising multi-metal deposits of nickle cobalt chromium were located. Indications with regard to the existence of other base metals were also received. The geological data and samples collected from the field are being processed and analysed in the petrological and chemical laboratories. Occurrence of pyritiferous shale near Wokha and asbestos in ultra-basic rocks in the neighbourhood of Yisi, Purr, and Lasori have also been reported. The asbestos probably belongs to the Chyrysotile variety. Silver are in also reported to occur in Tuensang area.

Sandstones, slates, stream-gravel and boulders are other building materials found in Nagaland. Sandstone is found and mined near Kohima, Mokokchung and Wokha. Good quality slate is mined in Tuesang district where it is used for roofing purpose. Strearri gravels and boulders are found in large quantities along river courses in the foothills regions.

Salt is produced from the brine water in some of the wells located in the settlements of Akhegwo, Yisi; Purr, Molen, Ozeho (Kohima Division) and Longzang near Lungwa outpost in Mon subdivision. The walls are dug to the depth of about 4 metres to strike the brine-bearing strata. The upper walls of the well are lined with timber to prevent dilution of the brine by the percolation of water coming from surface layers. Brine is taken out in the bamboo pipes and heated to be dried. The salt obtained in the village of Yisi and Longzang in white while other areas produce blackish salt. Brine is always heated for evaporation. Now when Nagaland is comfortably placed on the road and communication map of the country, the practice of preparing salt from brine water is fast dying out as cheaper salt is now available everywhere in Nagaland.

Environment

In general, the climate of Nagaland is modified tropical monsoon type. In the scheme of Koppon's classification of climate, Nagaland has a Tropical Rainforest climate (Monsoon type). In this climate, temperatures at low altitudes remain high throughout the year, excepting the months of December and January. The summer monsoon is strong which generally lasts from mid-June to mid-October in Nagaland. The monsoon climate is characterised by a rhythm of seasons which is caused by the southwest and northeast monsoons. The reversal of pressure takes place regularly twice in the course of a year. At the time of northeast monsoon winds are of continental origin and blow generally in the state from west to east, while during the southwest monsoon they are oceanic in origin and blow mostly in Nagaland from southwest to northeast. Almost all the rainfall recording stations of Nagaland record over 75 per cent of their total rainfall during the rainy season (mid-June to mid October).

Winter season in the state commences in November and lasts till the end of February. During this period a high pressure belt extends over the North-East India. The prevailing direction of winds is from west, northwest to east, owing to the pressure distribution and the influence exerted by the Himalayas.

The mean minimum temperature in the month of November at the station of Kohima is 10°C, while the mean maximum temperature in this month reads up to 17°C. The month of December records further decrease in day and night temperatures with the minimum temperature occasionally less than 5°C. The mean maximum temperature of December at Kohima is around 14°C.

January is the coldest month of the year. Occurrence of fog and mist are the common phenomena in this month. The fog and mist often reduce the visibility substantially. In January the mean maximum and mean minimum temperatures at Kohima is about 12°C and 4°C respectively.

In February the meteorological station of Kohima records 7°C and 15°C as the mean minimum and the mean maximum temperatures respectively. The relative humidity in December and January varies between 40 to 60 per cent. Areas situated above 2,000 metres record very low temperatures during winter. Consequently on certain occasions slight to light snowfall has been observed on Saramati (3,877 metres) and other loftier peaks, yet in the inhabited areas snowfall has never been recorded. On the whole winter can be severely cold and uncomfortable especially at the occurrence of rains and hailstorms.

March to mid-June is the period of warm summer. During thin period skies are generally clear and at the low altitudes day temperature becomes unbearable. In summer season, depending on altitude, the temperature ranges between 15°C to 38°C The month of March records a sharp upward trend both in the day and the night temperatures. In this month the mean minimum monthly temperature at Kohima is 10°C while the mean maximum reads up to 22°C. The increase in temperature continues in the month of April and May. The mean maximum temperature of April and May at Kohima being 27°C and 31°C. However, the mean diurnal temperature is almost identical in March, April and May. The relative humidity in summer months at Kohima ranges between 60 per cent to 78 per cent. Peculiar phenomenon of the summer season is that two or three days of intense heat are followed by cloud and wet weather which reduces the intensity of heat and make the weather pleasant and invagarating.

The pre-monsoon showers occur it the latter part of April which continue with intermittent gaps till the outset of summer monsoon. The pre-monsoon showers are highly beneficial to agriculture as they help in the sowing of cereal and vegetable crops.

June to October is the period of summer monsoon rains, and also known as the season of general rains. During this period the skies are generally overcast. Under the overcast conditions both the mean maximum and mean minimum temperatures show downward trend. In the rainy season rainfall alternates with short rainless gaps of two to three days. July and August are the rainiest months of the year as they receive more than 70 per cent of the total annual rainfall. July is the wettest month, recording 55 cm of rainfall at Kohima followed by Jun. (48 cm) and August with 45 cm. November and December are the dry months of the year and they record insignificant quantity of rainfall. Rainfall normally, slackens in October and the rainless intervals become longer The mean maximum and the mean minimum temperatures in Kohima are around 23°C and 13°C respectively. On an average Kohima receives about 25 cm of rainfall annually. October to May are considered as the most enjoyable months of the year.

So far as the movement of winds in Nagaland is concerned in most seasons of the year, they blow from valley to slopes in day time and from mountains to valley in the night time. The winds debouch with great violence in the valleys during nights, especially during winter. In the interior mountainous areas they are more moderate, and at great elevations the nights are almost calm. The direction of winds is however subject to local variation as the orographic features change their directions.

In brief owing to elevation, Nagaland has a salubrious climate of temperate type in which winters are cold but the summers are warm, the spring season is warm and humid, but the breeze though invigorating is interrupted at times by the gales. The heat decreases during the autumn, November and December being the finest parts of the year. Dimapur and the areas in the vicinity of Assam valley have sub-tropical weather. Dimapur and the areas along the road up to Ghaspani (Medziphema) is hot and damp, characterised with mosquitoes and Malaria.

5

Society

Before examining the various facets of population and people of Nagaland, it is imperative to discuss origin of Nagas, and their arrival in the Naga territory. The arrival of Naga tribes in Nagaland, their pre-history and migration pattern are shrouded in obscurity. The cultural anthropologists, archaeologists and ethnologists hold different opinions about the place of their origin and the time of their arrival in their present abode. Till few decades age, many of the Nagas were also quite ignorant of any distinctive tribal name ascribed to them. Even as late as 1954, Verrier Elwin found the people of Tuensang district (Konyak, Change, Phoms) seldom speaking of themselves as Nagas.

Though applied to the ethnic groups and tribes living in Nagaland, the origin of Naga word is not known and has been a matter of opinion among the social scientists. There had been endless controversy and speculation on the intriguing word (Naga) and how it came to be. A brief discussion on the various opinions about the 'Naga' word may not be out of place which have been given in the following paras.

J. H. Hutton, the leading authority on the tribes of North east India is of the opinion that the 'Naga' means 'mountaineers', Hutton originally thought that 'Naga' was a corruption of the Assamese Naga, probably meaning a 'mountaineer' from the Sanskrit Naga, mountain or relatively inaccessible areas. Later, he recorded this opinion in view of the fact that Ptolemy and Shyaph-al-Drn Talish (16th century AD) both speak of the Nagas as 'Nanga' or naked. This theory has little credibility as it is based on assumption.

If the term Naga means mountaineers, then why the other neighbouring hill tribes are not called Nagas. Another theory which is also based on reasonable conjecture traces the origin of Naga word back to Nangta, i.e. 'Naked Savages' applied to hill tribes; 'Naga-Manuh' means 'naked man'. In the opinion of Hutton "all along the foot of the hills an Assame may still be heard daily addressing to the scantily dressed man with "Oh Nanga".

He says the change of the long 'a' to a short 'a' (pronounced to) is typical to the Assame dialect in which the Bengali Toka (Rupee) becomes Taka and Raja as Roja. Hence, Nanga (the second 'n' is nasal) becomes Naga.

Social System

The diverse Naga tribes has never been united under one head. In fact, each major and minor ethnic group has its own head. The head of a tribe commands great respect from its people. Even the village headman is considered as the most reverend person who is to be treated with great respect. In the past there used to be inter-tribal, intra-tribal, inter-village and inter-Khel disputes, battles and declared wars. They fought merrily and head-hunting was quite prevalent. Despite the atmosphere of perpetual enmity, a tribal and ethnic group feeling was existing and a very sharp distinction was drawn between the Angamis, Aos, Lothas, Rengnias, Konyaks and Semas. Each tribe used to consider the people of other groups as inferior and unfortunate for being born in some other tribe. Even in the old head-hunting days loosely knit leagues gave the tribe a certain amount of administrative and political cohesion.

The real administrative and political unit of all Naga tribes is the village. The 'Khels' are run with separate organisations, but a village usually united for Jhuming operations, war and peace treaties, and keeps at least the more important Ainungs in common. The festivals, fairs, communal dances, games and other cultural functions are also organised at the village level. For example, the Mongsen 'Khel' and 'Cliouxh' Khel of Aos of the Mokokchung has each its council, but the people of this settlement always united against a common enemy, and all the chief Arnungs are observed by the whole village on the same day. For most purposes, however, the social unit is the 'Khel'.

The traditional administration of Naga village is based on two basic principles. First the whole village is divided into age-groups to which the various communal duties are assigned. Secondly, the control of affairs lies with a council, whose method of election and tenure of office vary in the different tribes and language groups. There is nothing corresponding to a hereditary chieftainship. The system is in brief as follows.

Every three years a new group of boys born within the same three years enter the 'Morurtg.' A boy or a girls remains in his original age-group till he or she dies, each group taking its name from some eminent member. The prominence of a member is decided on the basis of his performance in various socio-economic and cultural activities. Girls also have their age groups, but the system does not play a very prominent part in female life. Boys on first entering the 'Morung' have certain menial duties to perform, till in three years time, a new-age group takes their place and the fags of yesterday blossom into bloods for the next three years of 'Morung' life. After his time in the 'Morung' is over, a man settles down and marries, and probably in tune becomes a councillor. His term of office over, he very likely becomes a priest till he dies. But all through his life he remains a member of his original age-group. For instance, when pigs are being ringed each group is assigned a particular portion of the fence to make, or when village paths are being cleared each group is given a stretch. From the cradle to the grave a man is a part of a machine. Only on these lines could a village of perhaps two husband souls, without King or chief, be run.

The age-group system of Naga tribes may be understood clearly by citing an example from the Changki group of Aos of the Mokokchung District. Every three years a new group of boys, of age ranging from about twelve to fourteen, enter the Morung. NoZalurlhori The boys are called (unripe gang). These boys must sleep in the Morung and work like servants of slaves for elder boys. In three years a new group takes their place and they become servants of slaves for elder boys.

In three years a new group takes their place and they become Tukapbahori (ripening gang). They now make the newcomers work for them just as hard as they worked. They need not sleep in the Morung, if they do not want to, and may marry towards the end of their times. Their duty is to carry messages. Under this system a message can be sent from end to end of a tribe's territory by day or night, the man or boy on duty for the time being carrying on the letter to the next village.

The same system is also followed in the tribes of Fiji. These boys also work in general for the village. After three years of this they become Chuchenbahori (Morung leaders gang). The Morung is under their control, and the old days youths first went on raids when they reached this stage. Then after another three-years they become Okchangshanucharihori (Pig's leg eaters). The name indicates that they get the legs of pigs killed at Morung feasts. Their duties are much the same as for the previous three years. For the next three years they are Kidong Mabang (clan leaders). On entering this period they have no more to do with the Morung, they have left their youth behind them and they are villagers of standing.

After this they become Khonn (load carriers) for three years. They supply men to carry loads containing sacrificial pigs, fowls, and so on the ceremonies, and receive small shares of the councillor meat. At the end of this period they become Tataris (councillors) for three years, and with the advice yet older groups, run the village. After this short term of office, during which they get the biggest shares of meat, they become Maozanrlu Tclakba (Assistant Councillors). They still obtain shares of meat, but only very small ones.

Finally after three years a assistant councillors, they become Maozarnba Tonrarrrba (Councillor Dross). A few of his last groups pass on to be Pafir (priests), but for most men this is the last stage. They represent the age and experience of the village and the Tatari are expected to ask their advice on any matter of importance. The old-age people with poor physique who are not of any economic importance become liability on the family and the society, for which they pray for peaceful end to get rid of the miseries. In the past the condition of elderly was even more pathetic and miserable. In olden days, such people were ignored and in some of the more backward and poor tribes became the victims of cannibals. They used to be killed while sleeping in night and cannibals had feast with their relatives and friends. Such feasts were given the name of flood revival ceremony.

In most of the Naga tribal groups immovable and landed property is classified under four categories, i.e. (i) Private land, (ii) Morung land, and (iii) clan land, (iv) Common village land. All but a very small portion of the land is private property. But they say it was not always so. According to them when a village was founded each clan took a portion of the land and held it as common clan land. The tendency has been for this to become private property; men cultivating a particular piece would acquire a rescriptive right in it; or a clan would transfer to the aggrieved party a piece of land as a fine inflicted on one of their members for according to custom if a man cannot pay a fine himself his clan must pay it for him; or a clan would become reduced in numbers and the survivors would sell off their surplus land to individuals of other clans.

The result is that there is no cultivable land which is permanently clan land. Should a man die leaving no hairs his land becomes clan land, but probably only for a month or two, till the oldest man of the clan divides it up and it becomes private property again. Morung land is invariably land near the village on which are timber and bamboos used for repairing the building. A Morung never owns rice fields. The common village land usually consists of Jungle unsuitable for cultivation. Excepting the terraced fields of Anganis around Kohima, rice land is rare, and where it exists, it is due to special circumstances.

The law of inheritance provides that immovable property is to be inherited in the male line. Sons, brothers, brothers' sons and so on inherit in that order. Though a woman can possess a property she cannot inherit it. For example, a widow receives sufficient property for her support. If a man with only a daughter and no sons were to give land and money to his daughter during his lifetime those gifts would remain valid after his death, provided the girl had made her father even a nominal payment for the land. But all property remaining undistributed at his death would go to his next male heirs, whatever his known wishes might be. They would give the daughter a share if they liked, but need not to do so. A man cannot will his property away contrary. If the daughter in the care mentioned above made for father a payment for the land, it becomes her private property. She can sell it or give it away if she likes, but if she does not transfer during her life it goes on her father's male heirs.

But if she makes no payment she can only have the use of the land for life and may not dispose of it, and after her death it goes back to her father's heirs. All sons inherit equally. A widow receives a portion of the rice and the use of the house, and as such as she requires of her husband's land till death or remarriage, or till she becomes so infirm that her sons have to support her. Very often a women lends out and thereby increases the rice she received at her husband's death. Anything she buys with this rice becomes her absolute property.

If a widow has to support a young son or daughter the land assigned for her use is increased accordingly. Land bought by a woman - perhaps with money given her by her father - goes to her son if she has one or, failing him to her brother or other male heir of his father. It cannot go to husband. Of her rice, on the other hand, the greater parts goes to her son or to her father's heirs, but her husband is entitled to a small share. If she has a daughter, and no son, the daughter gets a small share and her husband's heirs the rest.

Pronounced Noga

There is another school of thought of the ethnologists and social anthropologists who are of the opinion that the word 'Naga' simply means people. This theory holds that the term occurs in Buranjis and that its correct form should be 'Noga' and 'Naga' which is derived from the generic word 'Nong' or 'Nok'; both words meaning 'people' in the language of Yimchunger Khemungan tribes.

In the opinion of Cait also the word Naga has been derived from 'Lo' or 'Log' or 'Nok' which means 'folk' or 'people' in Hindi and some tribal dialects. Whatsoever, the source of Naga word may be the Nagas knew each other by the name of the respective tribe to which they belong. Even the present tribal names like Anganis, Aos, Lothas, Seme, etc. seem to have been coined by the people of plains and outsiders, most probably by the Britos.

There are various stories which attempt to throw some light on the origin of the word 'Naga' and are still current among the Nagas. Some of the Naga tribes believe that the Nagas immigrated from Philippines where there is still a place called Naga. Among the Burmese the word 'Naka' means people with pierced ears. The word 'Naka' is said to be another form of 'Naka' as the Nagas — both men and women — pierce their ears. Horam, who conducted several field studies in Naga tribes opines that the meaning of this word has its origin in the word 'people' or 'folk'.

About the origin of Naga tribes the Vedic Hindu literature speaks of the presence of an Indo-Mongoloid race (Kirata) as far back as 1000 BC. More than ten centuries later, Ptolemy wrote about the Nagalog. The various conjectures reveal that Nagas belong to the 'Indo-Mongoloid' race. It is speculated that most probably they moved south and east from Sikiang (China). Some of them trekked along the Brahmaputra and into present-day Arunachal Pradesh, some pushed southward into Indonesia and Burma, and evidence of strong cultural parallels remain. There can be little doubt that at one time the Nagas might have wandered about before they found their present permanent abode from their myths and legend as one gathers that there is some relationship with natives of Borneo in that the two have a common traditional way of head-hunting, with the Taiwan (Formosa) through the common system of terraced cultivation, and with the Indonesia as both use the lion-loom for weaving cloth. The embroidery on the Naga clothes especially shawls resemble the kind done on Indonesian clothes.

The Nagas show a high degree of amalgamation of food. Each tribe has combined elements due to immigration from, at any rate, three directions, i.e. the northeast, the northwest, and the south. It may be speculated at certain stage, a Negrito race, later an Astric race of Mon-Khmer type was in occupation, leaving traces in implements and perhaps folktales now found.

Then came Bodo immigration from the northwest. There is beyond dispute, a mixture of Thai blood from the east also. The immigration wave from the south is obvious enough, and possibly brought up elements of population from southern Burma wedged in among migrating tribes. They perhaps also contain some Aryan elements from the other side of India caught up among migrating tribes. There are several marked points of similarity between the Ao-Nagas on the one hand and the Dyaks of Borneo and the Igorot of the Philippines on the other. They have had more or less same practices of head-hunting, platform-burial, tattooing, Moryng (bachelor's house) and terrace cultivation.

While in-migrating from the different directions in Naga Hills, some of the Naga tribes moved together bound up a compact to cling together in their wanderings and to live as one in their new homeland. The Augamis, the Rangmas, the Lothas, the Semasall separate tribes, though, one tradition holds that they have had descended from four parallel ancestors who were brothers — moved together until they reached the foot of mount Japfu in the southern part of Nagaland. Here they split up says another tradition, to choose the routes of migration to the tracts they had marked out for their own.

Meikhel, a place in the southern part of Nagaland is considered by most of the Naga tribes as the places where from they dispersed into different directions. Meikhel is a village between Mao and Maram areas, about ten miles to the southeast of the present town of Kohima. Near Meikhel is the second highest peak of Naga Hills Known as Japfu (Japvo). The Angami, Lotha, and Tangkhuls tribes declare Meikhel as the place their origin, while the Aos and Phomes trace their origin to the Lungterok (six Stones) on the Chong Liemdi Hills.

Whatsoever the place of their origin may be, the Nagas entered the Naga Hills through the succession of waves. It is most probable that the tribes which are occupying the more interior, less accessible parts and remote tracts of central Nagaland were the first to enter Naga Hills. Their point of entrance was from the south. The Sangtam-Chang; Aos and Lothas were most probably first to reach Nagaland. Under the pressure of successive waves of migration they were pushed in the north from the south. The Angamis, Zelhangs (Kukis), Kazamas, and Tengima are the tribes who reached in the last phase of immigration and occupied the southern parts of Naga-territory.

Another common tradition in southern Nagaland associates the Aos with this historic migration which preceded by the Aos who uphold that their origin lay in Chungliyimti (in modern Tuensang District) before they migrated to Ungma (Mokokchung District) and got diffused to other places. A tradition further refers to a great havoc which occurred in their ancient homeland causing this migration simultaneously.

The movement of the Naga tribes, however, had been sluggish and they did not follow a definite direction to reach the known destination of their permanent settlements.

Irrespective of time and direction of arrival of Naga tribes in their present homeland, they may be divided into the following four major groups. These groups show strong cultural affinities.

Major Naga Groups

	Group Territory	Tribes
I	The Southern Groups	Kachasw, Zemis, Lyengmis, Marong, Mais, Kabuis.
II	The Western Nagas	Angamis, Memis, Semas, Rengmas, Lothas.
III	The Central Nagas	Aos, Tangkhuls, Sang tams, Yachumis, Chaings, Phoms.
IV	The Eastern Nagas	Konyaks.

The common characteristics identified by Smith in the twenties of the last century are: (1) Dwelling houses built on posts or piles; (2) Disposal of the dead on raised platforms; (3) A sort of trial marriage; (4) Betel chewing; (5) Morung (common sleeping houses); (6) Betal chewing; (7) Tattooing; (8) Absence of any strong political organisation; (9) A Double cylinder vertical forge; (10) Simple loom of weaving cloth: (11) A large quadrangular or hexagonal shield; (12) Residence in Hilly areas; (13) Jhuming or shifting cultivation; (14) Head hunting (the practice of head-hunting no longer exists in Nagaland.

These characteristics do not appear uniformally in the various Naga tribes for, though there is little doubt that they originally belong to the some stock, they have since their separation from their 'primeval cradle land' came under different local influences. While some of them remained isolated till a couple of decades ago, others came into close contact with the relatively more advanced people and adopted new customs. As an example of change suffered by some, Smith cited the disappearance of the bachelors or young 'mens's houses (Dekha Chang) among the Sema Nagas.

Looking at the tremendous amalgamation of blood, there is hardly any pure ethnic group in the world. Considering this fact, it should not be surprising that the Nagas are basically one people in spite of various mixtures. Thus it can be said that the various tribes grouped under the general name 'Naga' are essentially one.

It is difficult to delineate the territorial boundaries of the various Naga tribes as there are transitional zones in which two or more than two tribes live together. In general, the south west Nagaland is occupied by Zelliangs (Kukis), Angamis, Rangmas and Chekhesang. The people of these tribes have long exposure and interaction with the sedentary population of Brahmaputra Valley through the Corridor of Dimapur. Owing to thin interaction with the people of the plain they are more progressive and wherever possible have developed terraced fields in which provisions of irrigation have been made. On the slopes of hills they practice shifting cultivation (Jhuming). Consequently, depleted slopes, devoid of vegetation may be seen on the way while going from Dimapur to Nagaland.

The central and Western parts covering the districts of Wokha, Mokokchung, and Zunheboto are the areas dominated by Lothas, Aos and Semas. Aos are well known for their progressive outlook which may be owning to their high literacy rate. Lothas are confined to the areas of low altitudes, their major concentration being in the Wokha District. Lothas are economically poor, socially more conservative and possess relatively poor physique.

The Konyaks, Changs, Sangtams, Phoms and Yimchungers live in the Mon and Tuensang Districts. The poor physique of these tribes indicates of their poor diet and malnutrition. The District of Phek is populated by Pochury (Sangtam) and Chekhsang tribes. Being located in the far-flung areas, these tribes have very little interaction with the rest of the people of the country. They are quite conservative in their outlook. According to the census of 1981, Konyak (72,338), Ao (65,275), Sema (65,227), and Angami (43,569) are largest tribes in Nagaland.

Population Growth

The population of Nagaland like all the other tribal populations of the country is growing at a faster rate. According to the census of 1971 the total population of the state was 516, 449 which rose to 774,930 in 1981. The population growth in Nagaland is among the highest in India. The birth rate average more than 35 per thousand and the death rate hovers near 15 per thousand. In some of the tribes like Konyaks, Sangtams, the birth rate exceeds 40 per thousand and the death rate is less than 20 per thousand.

The resulting population growth rate exceeds 25 over thousand or 2.5 per cent per annum, creating a population doubling time apparently twenty-five years. General health and living standard of Naga Tribes is low. Literacy rate is below 50 per cent (1981), the incidence of preventable disease is high and infant mortality rates are more than 120 per thousand during the first year of life. Medical care is available to only a small proportion of the total population. Moreover, vast majority is subject to malnutrition, undernutrition and deficiency disease.

Drinking water and sewage disposal systems are missing. The people are dissatisfied about their living conditions.

Over 92 per cent of the total population of Nagaland is tribal in character which is living in the tradition-bound society. The Christian Missionaries are rendering valuable services in respect of education and medicines. They are however, making them more orthodox and conservative at least in the affairs of family welfare. These Missionaries have not only converted the animistic Nagas to Christianity, they are interested in seeing the Christian population in India increasing at a steady growth rate. Consequently, the Family Planning drive could never have its roots in Nagaland. The high birth rate and low death rate are leading to tremendous growth in population.

It is shown here that nearly one-third (32.27%) of the total population of Nagaland lives in Kohima District. The Western part of Kohima especially the environs of Dimapur are levelled plains which are highly productive and capable to support large population. Tuensang and Mokokchung have about 20 per cent and 13.45 per cent of the total population of the state respectively. Mon and Phek Districts have over 10 and 9 per cent of the population of Nagaland respectively. Wokha and Zunheboto are relatively small in area and consequently sustain around 7 and 8 per cent of the population respectively

There had been oscillations in the growth pattern of population of Nagaland. Reliable data on the population of Nagaland is available since 1901.

Between 1901 and 1911 the population of Nagaland rose from 101,550 persons to 149,038, recording an increase of 46.76 per cent. Between 1911 and 1921 the population grew only 6.55 per cent. This slow growth of population during this decade was owing to the occurrence of Malaria and cholera. The population grew at a steady rate of 12 per cent but during the subsequent two decades again the growth rate was less conspicuous. Between 1961 to 1981 the population recorded tremendous increase recording about 40 and 50 per cent in population in the respective decades.

Density of Population

The density of population is determined by dividing the total population of a given region by its total area, in other words density of population means land-men ratio. As per the 1981 census in respect of density of population, Nagaland occupies the 20th position among the states. The density of population in 1981 was 47 persons per sq km as against 247 for the country as a whole.

The population of Nagaland is highly unevenly distributed. Surprisingly, contrary to other areas the population at the foothills in this hilly and mountainous state is sparse. Comparatively thick density of population is found at and around hill tops. Traditionally, because of strategic reasons the Nagas build their villages on hilltops at an altitude ranging between 914 to 1250 metres above the mean sea level. The harsh and inclement weather above 1250 metres do not permit human habitation. Thus as one climbs higher, elevations towards the Indo-Burma border on Barrail range the population thins out. The River valleys because of uninvigorating climate, otherwise also do not attract Naga people.

According to the census of 1981 the average density of population of Nagaland was 47 persons per sq km, as against 170 persons per sq km for the country as a whole.

According to the Census of 1981 the average density of population of Nagaland was 47 persons per sq km, as against 170 persons per sq km for the country as a whole. The density of population is higher in District Mokokchung, being 65 persons per sq km. It is followed by Kohima District in which 62 persons reside per sq km. Zunheboto and Mon district rank third and fourth with an average density of 49 and 44 persons per sq km. The density of population is 36 persons per sq km in Tuensang district, while Phek and Wokha districts have only 35 persons in one sq km crude arithmetic density in a rugged and mountainous state like Nagaland hardly makes any sense and has no meaning. The physiological density in settled parts exceeds to 1,100 persons per sq km in Nagaland. It shows a very high human pressure on the limited arable resource base of the state.

In Nagaland only 10 per cent of the total population lives in urban areas and 90 per cent in village. In fact's in the Naga society village is the main pivot on which the activities of each individual revolves, according to social norms and traditions of the village.

Up to 1951 census, Kohima was the only town which was also a class VI town. After 1961 census two more towns — Dimapur and Mokokchung were added and Kohima town became a class V town. In the 1971 census, Kohima became a class III town and Dimapur and Mokokchung entered class IV. In 1981 census there were twelve urban places in Nagaland. Between 1961 and 1971, the urban population of India rose by two per cent from 17.97 in 1961 to 19.91 in 1971. In Nagaland the rise was by 4.76 per cent which is double to that of India. Between 1971 and 1981 the urban population of Nagaland rose to per cent of the total population.

A Naga village is usually well-defined and demarcated by natural features based on customs and traditions. A village boundary with its neighbouring villages is marked either by natural ridges or rivers. The village would contain village reserved land, wood land and sufficient Jhum land as the villagers practice shifting cultivation. Establishment of new village is to be done now through permission of some of the old villages so that the new village shall be able to acquire rights over the land surrounding the new villages. Naga villages are not clearly surveyed but every village has a traditionally-recognised boundary.

According to the census of 1981 there are 1112 inhabited villages in Nagaland as against 960 in 1971 and 814 in 1961. Owing to the growth of population in the old villages, the Jhum land at the disposal of the people could not accommodate the excess population and therefore, the surplus population moves to a new place after having obtained the approval and permission of the mother villages to establish new villages where Jhum land was available.

The District of Kohima has the largest number of villages, being 341 or 30.67 per cent of the total villages of the state. The large number of villages is partly to its size and partly to easy access and plain areas around Dimapur. Tuensang has 236 villages accounting for 21.23 per cent of the total villages. Zunheboto and Mokokchung have 155 and 109 villages respectively. The mountainous and rugged districts of Phek Wokha and Mon have only 96, 95 and 80 villages respectively.

In Nagaland the average population of a village is about 484 persons. There are quite a large number of small villages (69 per cent) with a population of less than 500. There are 174 villages, each having a population of more than five hundred but less than 999. There are 114 villages each having a population within the range of 1000 and 1999. There are 17 villages having a population in the range of 2000 to 4999.

Sex-Composition

Sex ratio in the Indian census represents the number of females per 1000 males. When we refer to the sex-ratio being high, it will mean an excess of females over males in a population, a low sex ratio will denote a deficit of female population and masculine dominance.

Against the all India sex-ratio of 930 the sex-ratio of Nagaland was only 863 in 1981. The sex-ratio of Zunheboto, Wokha and Mokokchung was 964, 918 and 906 respectively. In Phek, Tuensang and Mon Districts the sex ratio was 873, 892 and 869 respectively. The sex-ratio was lowest in Kohima district being 790 females per thousand of males. In Kohima town and Dimapur there are substantial businessmen, defence personnel and labour who stay there without their families. Consequently the sex-ratio is very low.

The sex-ratio of three big urban centres, i.e. Kohima, Dimapur and Mokokhung was only 472 which is one of the lowest in North East India. The fall in the sex-ratio of these towns is due to the influx of males to the towns for the sake of education, employment and business. Contrary to this the sex ratio in the rural areas being 900 is almost at par to the national level.

The age structure of the population also varies from place to place. The population of a state may be divided into (i) children below 15 years of age, (ii) workers between 15 to 59, and (iii) elderly persons of 60 years and above. The working group of population in Nagaland is 55.4 per cent against our country's workforce of 52 per cent. The higher workforce indicates a high female participation in the economic activities. The dependency ratio is 45 per cent, out of which 38 per cent are of youth age group and 7 per cent of senile age group.

People

Most of the people of Nagaland are part of the various tribal groups that inhabit the rural corners of the state. Apart from tribes the state also has many subtribes. The prominent tribes include Chakhesang, Angami, Zeliang, Ao, Sangtam, Yimchunger, Chang, Sema, Lotha, Khemungan, Rengma, Konyak, Pochury and Phom.

The people of the state are known to have significant contribution towards the Nagaland society and culture. The prime religion followed by majority of people is Christianity. Those people who live in the plain areas call the inhabitants of the upper regions of the state as Nagas. The Naga people belong to the Mongoloid group. Majority of the Naga population is engaged in farming and weaving activities. Naga people are known for their simple and hospitable nature. The fairs and festivals of the different Naga tribes showcase the inherent local beliefs of the people of the state.

Since there are different tribes with subsections hence each of the Nagaland community celebrate its own array of festivals with devotion and enthusiasm. Also, the peaceful cohabitation of various tribes show the harmonious attitude of the people towards each other. Nagamese is the language which is spoken by almost all the people. However, each and every tribe has its own chain of linguistics. While the urban people of the state live in comparatively developed areas, the tribal communities make their houses in the remote zones.

Having their own set of customs, languages and beliefs the Nagaland people symbolise a bright picture of unified diversity of the state.

Ethnicity

Ethnicity in Nagaland includes a number of tribal communities which are again divided into several subtribal sections. The various Naga tribes that form the core of ethnicity are known to have derived their origin from the Indo-Mongoloid family. The unique trait of the different ethnic groups is that they prefer to live in the rural zones of the state instead of the prominent and posh areas.

The ethnic communities of the state enrich the society and culture by providing a vibrant platform of dynamism. The festivals and rituals of the various ethnic groups differ considerably. Also, the spoken language of one ethnic group is different from another. This shows the diverse nature of the various ethnic groups present in the state. The tribes under the ethnicity follow a common faith. Most of the tribes are Christian. Nagamese is the common language spoken by majority of the people. As per the political records the ethnicity has played a major role in developing the social format of this state.

Since ethnicity is a key indicator of the social progress hence the ethnic groups of Nagaland are expected to perform on the same level. Although initially the various ethnic communities were not on the same platform, later through Christianity they have been provided with the same. Today, ethnicity has become a vital factor which bears sufficient possibilities of bringing in a rapid and progressive change in this Northeastern State of India.

Status of Women

The females have a fairly high status in Naga society. They are not treated like slaves or servants. Generally, a Naga lady always has her clan behind her, and were a bad tempered husband to bully his wife he would soon have a swarm of angry in laws buzzing round his ears, and his wife may promptly leave him. All her life 'a woman enjoys considerable freedom. In and around the house there is division of work. The husband generally does the heavy work, while his wife cooks and makes the clothes. She can have rice trade independently of her husband. Both work in the fields. At feasts of merit, which are perhaps the greatest of all the occasions in a man's life, his wife plays a prominent and honourable part. On days of lesser festivity she acts as hostess and freely with the guests.

Character: As stated at the outset, Nagas are generally well built, industrious and honest and people of integrity. They are brave enough when things go well, but subject to panic when plans go awry. The Changs and Semas are reputed as the most war-like tribes. This is perhaps a matter of crowd psychology. They are however, not the people who can fight and finish to the last under adverse conditions. Throughout the Naga chronicles one finds that their normal methods of carrying on war was characterised with guerrilla attacks rather than big open fights. They generally attack the enemy from behind.

In the guerrilla warfare the Naga warriors manoeuvre like a cat, enter a forbidden territory like a poacher, come out from behind the bush like a panther, pounce on the enemy with the paws of a tiger and after hurriedly going through the raid melt into the thin air. They conduct their operations with such swiftness and accuracy that there is no time left for the defender to recover or reorganise. The defender would not know the direction in which the warriors withdrew. Even if they know, they found obstacles in the way and thus to keep contact with them would be a wild goose chase.

Every Naga considers himself as a fine fellow and resents an insult. With regard to their sex moral Nagas have an uninhabited attitude. They are exogamous and do not have intra-clan marriages. Among exceptions a Konyak chief, must have principal wife within the clan as he is considered sacrosanct and awfully reverenced Marriage price is a lure with many parents. Though most of the Naga communities are permissive but their affairs are carried secretly. The Khemungan Naga still follow the custom of abduction.

Nagas are superstitious and care too much for good omens and ill omens. On occasions they become very brutal to human beings and animals. Mithuns are tortured before they are sacrificed, and plucking the fowl alive formed part of many ceremonies. They do not hesitate to pluck dogs and goats alive for the sake of getting hair. Theft and crimes of violence are uncommon and most of them have a great sense of humour.

Marriage

In any society relationship between man and woman whether restricted or loose is bound to exist in many forms because of flexibility in human nature — thoughts, actions, sentiments and emotions. Though satisfaction of sex appetite is the primary force, social obligations and restrictions which are dependent on the standards of cultural development greatly influences such relations. Marriage is one of the oldest institutions of human society. It is a dynamic concept which has passed through several stages of change. Marriage, perhaps was a casual affair for the Palaeolithic (old stone age) men.

It is highly debatable to know how monogamy came into existence. A general study of Naga marriages can throw some light on the evolution of the institution of marriage in the various ethnic and social groups. The institution of marriage in the Naga tribes has been closely influenced by the harsh physical environment and the prevailing social milieu of the tribe. The marriage institution in the tradition-bound Naga tribes depends on the institution of Morung (Bachelors sleeping dormitory). It is therefore to discuss in brief the institution of Morung of the Naga tribes.

Occupational Structure

According to the 1981 census about 49 per cent of the population of Nagaland forms the workforce. This participation ratio is appreciably higher to that of the average for India (32.9%). Nonetheless, this rate is also higher than the total Indian tribal workforce (38.5%). The participation rate in Nagaland in 1971 was 50.78 per cent. The decrease in the participation rate has been the result of changed definition of worker adopted in 1971.

The poor economic base compelling every hand to take up some job and there being no prejudice against women participation in different economic activities are largely responsible for higher participation rate. This phenomenon is, however, consistent with a high level of underemployment as well as much idleness. Thus participation rate among the tribals is affected both by social and economic factors.

In the working force, about 77.48 per cent of the workers are engaged as cultivators while only 1.52 per cent of them work as agricultural labourers. On the whole, about 80 per cent of the total population is directly or indirectly dependent on agriculture. Barring other services which employ about 15.27 per cent of the Nagaland workers, no other occupation has so far attracted any significant number of workers. Forestry, livestocking and fishing, etc. have attracted only 0.38 per cent of Nagaland's workers. Household industry offer employment to only 0.38 per cent and 0.76 per cent of workers in the state. Construction, trade, commerce and transport-storage, engage only 1.15 per cent, 1.90 per cent and 1.15 per cent respectively of the state's workforce. Thus the occupational structure of Nagaland is overwhelmingly dominated by primary economic activities.

The non-agricultural activities are limited to construction of houses, manufacturing of utensils, baskets, clothing, hunting equipments, tools, etc. Cloth is woven by Naga women on lain looms. Metal work is confined to the manufacture of Dao and ornaments. It may be made clear that spatial segregation and cultural isolation of the Nagas is largely responsible for the lack of inventiveness related to secondary and tertiary economic activities. The absence of secondary and tertiary workers in the work-force of the state indicates the state of underdevelopment and over dependence on the primary sector of the population.

Linguistic Composition

The linguistic composition of Nagaland is somewhat peculiar. Only about 7 per cent of the total population of the state speak language listed in the Schedule VIII and 93 per cent speak local language.

According to the census of 1981, there are 16 dominant tribes in Nagaland and each tribe is having its own dialect. None of these is used as state language. There is a speech form known as 'Nagamese', composed mainly of broken Assamese, Bengali, Hindi and Nepali. This peculiar speech is used as a common language next to English. Naga tribes use Roman script. The Angami and the Ao (Chongli) languages have now been developed to an extent that students appearing for the High School Certificate Examination can also offer these two languages as vernacular subjects.

In Kohima district Angami is the principal language. Its speakers comprise 39 per cent of the population of the district. In Mokokchung district, the (Chongli-Ao) speaking population form 41 per cent. Sema speakers Form 28 per cent followed by Lothas with 21 per cent. In Tuensang district the Konyak speakers with a total of 42 per cent occupy the first position followed by Sangtam and Phom with 12 and 10 per cent respectively.

In the urban English and Hindi are the dominant languages. Hindi speakers constitute 22 per cent of the urban population followed by speakers of English, Chongli-Ao and Angami languages. The remaining urban population speaks, Nepali, Gorkhali, Bengali, Assamese, Sema, Santali and Lotha in a descending order. Only about 35 per cent of the local tribals form the urban population of the state.

Literacy Rate

Nagaland has a literacy rate of 72.5 per cent which is far higher than the overall tribal literacy of only 11.30 per cent in India. The literacy in Nagaland is also very high when compared to the Scheduled caste population literacy (14.67%) in India. The male literacy (35.02%) and female literacy (18.65%) in Nagaland are also quite close to the male (39.45%) and female literacy (18.72%) of the country as a whole. Some amount of literacy is no doubt the result of immigrating floating population, yet the higher incidence of literacy in Nagaland cannot be totally because of this factor. The only plausible factor for such a high degree of literary is the spread of Christianity. The Christians who have relatively progressive and advanced outlook lay a greater emphasis on education. Thus we find higher literacy rates in Christian-dominated parts of India. Christian missionaries of course, with vested interests entered long back. Along with other facilities Christians missionaries made it a point to open school in Naga villages. Today there is a school in almost every Naga village. In 1985, the state had 1,045 Primary Schools, 312 Middle Schools, 109 High Schools, 12 Colleges, 425 Adult Literacy Centres, one Industrial Training Institute, one Polytechnic, one Training College and four junior Teachers Training Institute. Obviously a higher literacy rate of literacy is expected in such an environment.

Faith and Religion

Naga religion is described by sociologists to be animistic which lay emphasis on the existence of the defied manifestations of nature and propitiation of spirits both benevolent and malevolent. The cause of troubles and torments which befall the family and the inhabitation are attributed to the action of the evil spirits. They hold that commitments, omissions and occasional failures to appease them are the reasons for incurring the spirits' displeasure. By divination they trace such sufferings, ailments and ill-luck to the influence of the evil spirits, and the spirits having been traced, appeasement to them follows.

But Nagas also follow theistic principles, although on the nature, attributes and functions of the Supreme being whom they call *Ukepenuopfu*, the Angamis cannot explain. Him they attribute to the author of the creation but at times lie is personified with a progenitor of the race and of all the living beings. Curiously this deity has both male and female attributes. About his relations with the other deified spirits, his retribution of the human beings and his position in the circle of the pantheon, they could not answer definitely. All the Naga tribes believe that there is an unseen divine power behind the creation, behind the course of events and behind the destiny of mankind.

Naga tribal religion being a mixture of theism, animism, supernaturalism and superstition is connected with the practice of sorcery, exorcism and magic. Naga priests receive special training for wording off evil spirits and for the conduct of ceremonies. Several practices are held to avert epidemics, believed to be a representation of an evil spirit's shadow, which in cases of failures of being appeased, has come to ravage the village. A sacrificial offering in such situations consists of eggs laid in the path wrapped in a leaf, while the village paths are strewn with pieces of ornamental decorations and clothings. Invocations to such a spirit are made to ward him off. But the system of invocation and appeasement of spirits varies from tribe to tribe, from village to village and from one household to another. Sacrifices are also offered with a cooked liver, entrails and slices of meat in addition to eggs.

During the last one hundred years the Christian Missionaries have done a highly commendable job and they converted a large number of the followers of the tribal religion into the followers of Christianity. Nagas have no idols and they do not believe in image worship. The Aos, Konyaks and Lothas attach some importance to certain stones but they do it without the idea of worshipping them. At present, most of the Nagas are Christians by faith. In their daily life they practice a modified Christianity which is not a moral code.

The tribal religion is a system of ceremonies. Since habits die hard, the Naga Christians who believe in the Cod and the Jesus Christ as his messenger are still practising many rituals of their tribal religion.

The Nagas believe that they will not prosper if they omit the sacrifices due to the deities around them, who unappeased are never ready to blight his crops and bring illness upon them and their families. This does not mean that a Naga is a devil-ridden, terrified wretch, unable to distinguish right from wrong. He cheerfully performs the necessary sacrifices and hopes for the best. When the inevitable day comes at last on which offerings for sickness are no longer of any avail he meets his end with resignation and unafraid goes to join his ancestors and forefathers.

There are several deities which are worshipped by the Nagas to bring prosperity to the family. The sacrifices prayers begin with an invocation on the Sun and the Moon. It is Tsungrarn (spirits) who play an important part in human life. On their good will 'largely depends x man's health and happiness. These spirits are everywhere in the village. They are present in the fields, in the jungles, by streams, in trees, and in the huge boulders. They are regarded as resembling in some way the people of the locality they live.

By the tradition-bound Nagas, the large-sized boulders are also worshipped. There is hardly any conspicuous boulder which escapes attention. Offerings are made to stones to bring fine weather. An offering of a small pig and two cocks assures safe fishing and good crops for the year.

An annual ceremony is performed in every village in honour of all Tsungram (spirits) in general. This ceremony takes place in the month of July or August. On the first day a pig is sacrificed outside the house of the village Head-man, and a piece of meat is given to the houses at each end of the main village street. Distributed in this way he is bound to find it ready for him whichever direction the Tsungram (spirit) enters the village. The rest of the pig is eaten by the elders. On the evening of this day every family makes a small offering at the hearth. The next day is a very strict Amung (period of chastity). On this day no one is allowed to leave the village and even rice may not be husked, women and girls play games with sword-bean seeds and boys spin tops.

It is a common belief among the Nagas that Lachiba (Brahma) created the world in summer. Lachiba is worshipped in the month of June. This spirits prevents landslides, and other natural calamities. On this occasion a pig is sacrificed outside the village fence and eaten by the village councillors. On this day no one can husk rice or fetch firewood from the stacks outside the village settlement. Next day everyone offers an egg in front his field house.

Among the minor spirits the most important is the house spirit. This spirit is made offering only when a house is being built, but at least every three years a sacrifice is offered, if necessary. A three-year pig is killed in the house at the foot of the centre post of the back-wall. The head liver and heart are eaten by the householder and his wife, and the right half of the body is laid at the foot of the post. Later in the day the pork is distributed between the members of the household and near relations.

The Naga belief about the soul is curious one. He believes that every man has a fate which lives in the sky. This is in no sense a soul. The Tiya (soul) of a man is male and that of a woman is female. Every Tiya has a name but only medicine man can find out what it is? One of the main reasons given for divorce is that the Tiya of man and that of woman do not agree. Some hold that the soul which always occupy a main lives in his head. This theory is clearly on the basis of head-hunting. The soul of dead men are wanted to fertilize all plant and animal life, and to the general stock of vital essence in the village.

Since the soul is located in the head above all other parts and therefore the dead at any rate is carried back (with the soul in it) to add to sum of vital essence in the head takers village. Head-hunting is really life hunting and implies the capture of the soul and its utilisation to increase the stock of life essence already possessed by the village and its utilisation and so promote the welfare of the crops, of the livestock and of the human inhabitants. The past practice of head-hunting has been discussed separately in the sub-topic of social life of Naga tribes.

Illness is most commonly believed to be due to the capture of the patients, soul by Tsungram. These spirits lie in wait for man's soul and pounce upon them and devour after holding them ransom for sometime. It is the soul always accompanies a man that is held prisoner in this way. Its owner at once falls ill, and if his soul is not restored to him he will die. A 'medicine man' is called without delay to remove the ill-effect of Tsungram. The medicine man, having taken the omens by gazing into a leaf cup of Madhu announces that the sick man's soul has been caught by Tsungram at such and such spot. Further omens are taken if necessary to find out how much the Tsungram will accept for the soul. Then certain offerings are made to appease the Tsungram.

In addition to the said spirits which are more or less heavenly in their nature, there is another category, namely the ghost spirit of those human beings, who die an unnatural death or those who after death are not treated as per the rites of that tribe. It is believed that by not performing the traditional ceremonies on the dead body of a person, the spirit that left it for its own home does not rest in peace and it remains disturbed and annoyed with the relatives for their indifference and negligence. This spirit can literally play up hall with the members of the family.

Such spirits roam about to take revenge from the wrong-doers by cursing their crops, bringing sickness, setting fire and even resorting to killing. To avoid unnatural death, fire accidents, epidemics among the crops and cattle, the spirits have to be appeased. An unnatural death is a curse to the family whereas natural death is accepted without any reservations or ill feelings. When a man's days are completed, he has to leave for the world of the dead. The dead body must be paid reverence and given all assistance so that the dead may enjoy the same status in the abode of the dead which he enjoyed before death in his community and society.

In case of unnatural death, the observance of customs can throw the family of the dead in real frenzy. Since the death is the result of anger of a hostile spirit, the family is made to leave the village home and asked to stay in the forest for a certain period. To further the act of purification, the house can be destroyed and all other property set aside. The granary is also destroyed and the relatives of the bereaved family are expected to go to jungle and give food but without taking to the outcasts. The family however, comes back after the expiry of the due period of penance. This practice is still strictly followed in Naga villages for any death caused by lightning, snake bite, attack by wild beasts, drowning, burning, landslide, fall from a tree and childbirth. In the urban areas, especially among the educated families this concept is losing significance and been considered as superstition and outdated conservation.

The ways in which a man can be brought by spiritual forces to sickness or even to death are numerous. Only a 'medicine man' can diagnose a case correctly and select the proper ceremony to be performed. 'A man's soul may be retained by a Tsungram (spirit); or his celestial mithun-soul may be sacrificed; or his dead relations may draw his soul away; or a kitsung may harm him; or careless words spoken by some one in all innocence may cause him to sicken; or the soul of game he has killed may take vengeance on him. With his formidable catalogue of ghostly perils before one, one marvels that a Naga is ever healthy.

But he generally is. Once he is ill, however, sacrifice after sacrifice is offered. This is not usually an expensive business, though an unsuccessful sacrifice often means a more costly effort to follow. The limit is however, always reached before a man is reduced himself to poverty, for even if a man desperately ill should- wish to offer all he has, he cannot do so; his expectant heirs put the brake on without delay. Probably at one time the supreme sacrifice was that of a human being. A relic of this practice lasted till the early parts of the present century, when in case of desperate illness, a formally offering a slave to the Tsungrarn, but instead of killing him, cutting off one of his fingers and letting him go.

Religious Composition

Religion plays a very important role in the life of a country because it influences its citizens in several ways. Till 1941 census data like age, sex and literacy were presented separately for persons professing various religions. Since 1951 census data merely show the total population under each religion.

The census of 1981 listed six principal religions, namely, Hinduism, Islam, Christianity, Buddhism, Sikhism and Jainism. Religions other than these six came under the head 'other religions'. During the census of 1981 some of the persons of Nagaland said that they had no religion, therefore, they were enumerated under the head' religions not stated'.

Prior to 1872, Nagaland was a land of Animis (Tribal religion). Even now a number of Nagas is following this religion. The followers of Animism perform sacrifices by killing animals like the pigs, fowls, and dogs to propitiate spirits, offer their prayers to the Moon and the Sun and the good and bad spirits of the village. Their aim is to receive blessing from deities and spirits for a bumper harvest, for health and happiness in this world and beyond.

Nagaland is the only state in the country where the Christian population was more than the percentage of the total population. The other states and Union Territories in which 20 per cent or more of the population is Christian are Meghalaya (46.98%), Goa Daman and Diu (31.77%), Andaman and Nicobar Islands (26.35%), Manipur (26.03%) and Kerala (21.05%). During the decades of 1961-71 and 1971-81, the Christian population registered the highest growth all over the country.

Hindus form 11.50 per cent of the total population of the state. During the decade of 1971-81 their population rose by about 70 per cent. The increase of the Hindu population in the state may be attributed to the influx of outside population for employment and business purposes. About 50 per cent of the total Hindu population lives in rural areas and the remaining 50 per cent in the urban places.

The followers of other religions such as Islam, Buddhism, Jainism and Sikhism do not occupy a significant proportion to the total population of the state. The majority of the population of these religious communities live in urban areas.

The notable feature of the population of Nagaland in the other religions (Tribal Religion, etc.) come next to the Christians, constituting 20.62 per cent of the total population.

The maximum concentration of Christian population is Mokokchung and Wokha Districts, followed by Zenhaboto. In Mokochung, 89 per cent of the total population is Christian. The Christian population in Kohima district is about 55 per cent. Kohima district has got the maximum number of Hindus as the State Capital and Dimapur town being located in this district. Muslims, Sikhs, Buddhists and Jains also occupy fairly high proportion in Kohima compared to other districts of the state. Tribal faith accounts for about 22 per cent of the total population of the district.

Christians constitute about 57 per cent of Tuensang districts population. This district has the largest number of 'other religions', i.e. Tribal Religion (38 per cent of its population, Followers of Hinduism, Islam, Sikhism and Buddhism are comparatively fewer. There is not a single follower of Jainism in this district.

In other States Christianity has been taken as an 'Urban' religion, but in Nagaland the reverse is the case. 'Hinduism' can be taken as an 'urban' religion because 52 per cent, 94 per cent and 46 per cent constitute the Hindu population at Kohima, Dimapur and Mokokchung towns respectively. The Christian population at Dimapur is only 11 per cent. At Mokokchung and Kohima it accounts to 50 per cent and 43 per cent respectively. The followers of Tribal Religion are declining at a faster rate in the three major towns (Dimapur, Kohima, Mokokchung). The Muslim population at Dimapur is 9 per cent, 1.4 per cent at Kohima and 2.40 per cent at Mokokchung. Jains form about 5 per cent of the population of Dimapur town.

Religious Officials

The Nag as one know nothing of any priestly caste, or priesthood upon which special powers have been conferred by consecration. For the simple ceremonies of the home and field a man acts as his own priest. For ceremonies such as the Mithun sacrifice, where the clan as a whole is concerned, one of the clan priest is called in. There are old men who have been councillors and their qualifications are age, experience and free from any serious deformity.

Each clan in a village may have from one to four priests, the number varying from village to village. Public opinion dictates who among the old men are fitted to be priests. Attached to each priest is another old man who acts as his assistant. On the death of a priest his assistant takes his place, and a new assistant is chosen. A simple ceremony is performed by a new priest to celebrate his entry into office. He kills a cock in front of his house and announces that he is following the customs of his ancestors. For most village ceremonies the priests take it in turn to act, but at the bigger festivals they are all expected to be present.

Life after Death

There is no word for that part of the man which passes after death into the next world. The man is regarded as going himself. For instance, a Naga would say: "Asam-Chibas some has gone to the land of dead"; he would not say: "Asam-Chiba's soul has gone to the land of the Dead." One of his souls may have caused his death by going on there ahead, but Asam-Chiba himself followed later. Certainly one of the souls reappears as a hawk, or according to some, as a butterfly or cricket, after Asam-Chiba has departed, and one is believed to linger near the body for some time.

The soul according to Ao ideas, is not an ethereal personality, cumbered on earth with a body from which it is only freed at death. Rather the Ao souls are very troublesome appendages of real ego. These appendages require a great deal of looking after, for though the temporary absence of one, perhaps captured by a Tsungrem, only cause illness, its permanent loss involves its owner's death.

As the Naga knows he must go to the Land of the Dead some time, whether he likes it or not, he does not worry his head much as to where it is. Consequently opinions differ as to its locality. Some regard it as in the sky. Others say that it is under Wokha Hills, and that some at death approach it via the plains and others by Lungkam, each taking the path his ancestors took before him, though no one can say why any family originally took its particular route.

The Aos place the entrance to the world of the Dead which lies under the earth at the same spot at Wokha Hill as do the Lothas, and call the line of white rock leading up to it — Lyasuphu (girls cloth drying), regarding it as a collection of dead men's cloths laid out to dry by their dead girl friends. Whenever this land may be — whether in the sky or under the earth — certain beliefs concerning it are fairly clearly held. On their way to it the dead must cross a stream called Lungritsu, the boundary between the dead and the living. If a man reaches this stream, but does not cross it, he can return to the land of living.

But should he so much as wash his hands and feet in it he can rarely return, and for a man to dream that he washed presages his death within the year, for his soul has bathed in the fatal waters of the Naga Style. Occasionally, however, a man crosses the stream and is turned back by Moyotsung — the King of the Dead, with the good news that he is not yet fated to die. Such a man will recover from his illness, but all the skin peels off his hands and feel where the water of the Lungritsu has touched them.

For most of the journey to the gates of the village of the Dead (asuyint) is easy, but not for all. Unwanted babies, killed because they are bastards, or infants dying before they have been acknowledged by their fathers and named, turn into wild animals on the way and never reach it at all. It is the duty of all to marry and increase the strength of their village, and elderly bachelors and spinsters who die unwedded find the road to the Land of the Dead blocked with prickly creepers, which scratch them badly. For ordinary men and women the way is not so arduous. A man carries his load of clothes, food, etc. and walks with his spear in his hand. Having crossed the Lungritsu he first comes to Moyottsung's house, outside of which there is a tree. At this he must throw his spear, calling out his own name as he does so. If he has lived a honest life he will hit the tree, but if he has been a thief he will miss. Moreover, in the later case his load will' give him trouble.

For every thing he has ever-stolen will be in it, and, try as he will back them at the bottom, these proofs of his guilt keep working up to the top of his load, where 'no one can fail to see them. Meanwhile Moyotsung watches and judges. Honest men he calls into his house and sends straight through it into the village of the dead. Thieves have to go 'by a side path, though all seem to reach the same goal. A rich man leads along the road to the next world the Mithwi he has sacrificed in this. Their actual heads are still in his heirs house on earth, but wooden models were placed in front of his corpse-platform and it is the ghostly animals enshrined in these models that he takes with him.

With the trophies of war the case is different. Heads were not left to heirs but were put in front of the corpse-platform. Models are only used now because the sacrilegious hand of the British Government has destroyed the originals. On the road the warrior meets the men he has slain. They have been earthbound till now, poor wretches, for they could not go to the world of the Dead without their heads, which were in their conqueror's keeping. The latter now gives one of them his load to carry. The victim protests and says it is not his business to carry a load. For this he gets a good thrashing with a cane especially placed in front of a warrior's corpse-platform for his purpose. Grumbling, the victim picks up the load and on they go till they reach Moyotsung's house. Here the quarrel breaks out afresh and Moyotsung is called in to arbitrate. The warrior triumphantly points to the rice flour on his victim's forehead, placed there when ceremonies were done with the head, and the vanquished foe is non-suited at once.

A woman has a more adventurous journey. At a certain point on the road she meets a fiend with long hair called *Aonglamla*. The fiend will chase her and demand a present. Now a swordbean seed was carefully placed with the other things in the carrying basket hung up on her corpse-platform. This is where it comes in useful. She takes it out of the load and rolls it along the ground. The fiend scampers after it, thinking it is something valuable, and the woman slips by. Arrived in front of Moyotsung's house she must prove her honesty by throwing her weaving-sword at the tree. If it hits she has passed the test and goes through Moyotsung's house to join her dead forbearers. If she misses, she is proved to have lived a life of dishonesty and, disgraced, must go round by a side path.

All the dead are the servants of Moyotsung, and when he is about to rebuild his house many men on earth die, in order that he may be supplied with workmen. The Mithun he sacrifices are the souls of the men, and every animal slaughtered means a death on earth. It may seem strange at first sight that an Ao, who lives under a talkative and accommodating village council in this world, should believe that he becomes the subject of an autocrat in the next. But, as a conservative politician once pointed, in no religion are the arrangements of Heaven democratic. Dr. Clark records a belief that Moyostung was once a man on earth who was worsted by a rival of the Lungkungr clan. He further states that when a wealthy man of the Lungkungr clan dies his relations will frequently blacken his face, lest Moyotsung should recognise him and take vengeance on him.

Life in the village of the dead is like life on earth, save that there is no sexual intercourse. Those who were rich here and rich there, and those who were poor here and poor there. After living out his allotted span there a man dies again and passes to an unpleasant, shadowy abode which goes by the curious name of "Dog fishing-village." Anyone who treated his dog badly in this world finds the position reversed; he is himself kept as a dog, with a dog as his master, and receives in full measure, pressed down and running over, all the cruelty, starvation and neglect which he meted out to his canine friend on earth. Many never reach this hell. Anyone who jabs his foot against a stone on the way to it from the first land of the dead is turned forever into stone, and anyone who jabs his foot against a stick is turned into a piece of wood. Even those who reach it do not remain there long. After a short time they just fade away and disappear.

Rarely does a Naga regard illness as due to physical cause. So used is he to blaming on Tsungram all the evils that happen to him that, should he in any case do not do so, he thinks it necessary to explain to the Tsungram that in this particular instance he does not hold them responsible for they naturally expect him to blame them and, unless reassured, are likely to be angry at the unjust charge they think he is sure to make against them. If, therefore, a man, obviously through his own carelessness, cuts himself with a 'Dao' while in his fields, he gets an old man to perform the Achachang ceremony as soon as he gets home. The old man goes outside the village fence and offers a little chicken and an egg and says: "All the men of this village are blind, and careless with 'Dao! It is this man's own fault that he cut himself., You Tsungrem are not to blame. Do not be angry with him." He leaves the chicken impaled on a stick with the egg by it, and hangs on the outside of the village fence a carrying-band or some such inexpensive article which the man had with him when he was hurt.

The way in which a man can be brought by spiritual forces to sickness or even to death are numerous. Only a 'medicine man' can diagnose a case correctly and select the proper ceremony to be performed. A man's soul may be retained by a Tsungrem; or his celestial Mithun-soul may be sacrificed; or his dead relations may draw his soul away; or a kitsung may harm him; or careless words spoken by someone in all innocence may cause him to sicken; or the soul of game he has killed may take vengeance on him. With this formidable catalogue of ghostly perils before one, one marvels that a Naga is ever healthy. But he generally is. Once he is ill, however, sacrifice after sacrifice is offered. Probably at one time the supreme sacrifice was that of a human being. A relic of this practice lasted till three generations ago in the custom, in case of desperate illness, of formally offering a slave to the Tsungrem, but instead of killing him, cutting off one of his fingers and letting him go.

It is after a man's own Tiya which causes him illness. It may refuse to bring him good fortune, or it may even sell the man's celestial Mithun-soul to another Tiya for sacrifice, or propose to sacrifice it itself — obviously a very serious thing for the man. In case of childlessness, therefore, or wasting sickness a 'medicine-man' recommends that a sacrifice to the Tiya be made. This must be taken to the Tiya by a 'medicine man.' An ordinary old man may be capable enough of making an offering to a Tsundgrem, but it requires someone with special powers to go to the sky world. Sometimes the 'medicine man' goes into a trance as soon as the offering is ready and sometimes he waits for night fall to send his soul in a dream to the country of the Tiya. One way of performing the ceremony is as follows: The sick man, or one of his household, calls in the 'medicine man' and makes up an offering consisting of six Chabili (or five if the patient be a woman), a small brand — new pot which has never been used, a cock with no white feathers, three leaf parcels of rice for his ancestors, one for Anungt-sungba and one for his doorkeeper.

The 'medicine man' is handed a leaf-cup of Madhu, a little of which he sprinkles on the ground saying: "Whether this man's Tiya be in the first sky or second sky or third sky let me reach it." He then gazes at the surface of the 'Madhu' till he goes into a trance. In about half an hour he recovers, drinks some 'Madhu' and eats soiree ginger; and reports the result of his journey. He takes the offering in a basket to his house and in the morning announces what dreams he has had.

A man who has a stomachache often blames the Kitsung of some friend whom he has visited frequently of late. He goes to the friend's house tells him of his trouble. The friend then holds a 'Chunga' of 'Madhu' in his left hand and waves a brand over it, saying: "May my Kitsung not torment this man." The afflicted one drinks the 'Madhu' and is cured, or he may go to the friend's house, eat a little rice and place three little heaps of rice on the three stones of the hearth. Or again he may get his friend to stroke his stomach and tell his Kitsung not to afflict him.

The dead are believed sometimes to draw away the souls of the living and so cause them to waste away. A dead parent, it is held, will try to attract to himself the living child for whom he longs. It is a bad sign if the dead appear often in dreams, for it means that their souls are visiting the earth. A 'medicine-man' who diagnosis a case of illness is due to the influence of the dead recommends that a present be sent through another 'medicine-man' who is known to have the power of reaching the dead. This ceremony is known as "going to the dead." The 'medicine man' is given a present of food and the dead man's ornaments to take away for the night.

In the morning he returns the ornaments, having kept the food as his perquisite, and reports on his visit to the next world. Usually he says that he met the dead man and persuaded him with the aid of the present to release the patient's soul. Sometimes he frankly admits that he has failed. It is not always love that causes a dead man to draw a soul away from earth. Sometimes a man's illness may be due to the capture of his soul by a dead enemy. As he is almost always unable to obtain the loan of the dead man's ornaments for the rite, he sends an extra large present of food as a ransom. If this does not have the desired effect the patient dies.

Witchcraft

Though the influences of the spirit world so frequently injure his soul, and through his soul his body, it is very rarely that a Naga attempts to direct these powers against an enemy. True, as a rule he takes care not to leave the trimmings of his hair and the paring of his nails about but it has never been heard of anyone trying to work magic with such leavings. Bewitching through models is very rare now, but was apparently commoner once. The old custom was to make a wooden image of an enemy in another village and spear it and end but off its head.

An old way of injuring a village with whom one was at war was somehow to place in it through a benevolent neutral, an egg on which you had blown, with an appropriate prayer that the enemy be struck blind and deaf and become feeble. The Konyaks, Phoms, Rengmas and Changs have a similar custom. Sometimes black-magic is used for the public benefit to punish an unknown offender. For instance, if granaries are maliciously fired by some one unknown the village priest will throw some of the burnt grain into each of the village springs, with a prayer that the incendiary may die if he drinks of that water.

Morung

Morung is a very old institution of the Naga tribes. It however, has vanished from most of the educated social groups. Angami is perhaps the only tribe in which Morung system was never prevalent for marriages. Morung is a club for youth (boys and girls) in which they sleep in the night.

In the opinion of some social anthropologists it is a training and guard house as well as a club house. In Naga villages it is constructed near the main gate of the village. In front of the Morung there is a big platform on which the boys and girls sit out and talk. In dimension it is about 16 metres long and seven metres wide. It is too high to step over and too slippery quickly to scramble over, so that an attacker, even if he got through the door, would have to jump on to it and down the other side and would be bound to expose himself while going so. There are sleeping benches around the walls and two hearths on the earth floor. Out of the two hearths the nearer to the door is reserved for the senior inmates and the back one for the youngsters.

One of the reasons for starting these boys, and girls, dormitories could be to give greater freedom to the parents to perform their worldly duties when the children are grown up. When the first child attains the age of puberty the parents are still young and capable of making love. The house being of a rather open construction and with almost no doors to bolt from inside, it might have been embarrassing for the parents to share the same bed when their grown up children could easily walk in through inadvertently.

But the main reason for setting up dormitories must have been to ensure that the children were brought up in a disciplined manner with the fear lurking always in their minds, it was essential that young boys grew up to be good warriors and the girls capable of supporting their husband and by nourishing good healthy children for the protection of the community.

Some of the anthropologists are of the view that Morung is an effective economic organisation for purposes of food quest, a useful of seminary for training young men in their social duties, and an institution for magico-religious observance calculated to secure success in hunting to augment the procreative power of the young persons.

Some of the tribals say that the Morung began because we did not Know what to do with these children. We were tired of setting their quarrels, and we did not want their noise. So we said "You all go off and play whatsoever game you like and spend your time together. You can do what you like provided you do the work we want from you, bring wood and water, tend the cattle and nurse the babies. "The dormitory among the tribals is a school for social training. It is also an open place for love marriages which are normally successful.

In Nagaland Morung is used for different purpose. There are Morungs in which only boys can sleep during the night. Sometimes one finds different houses for girls of the village. Community functions are also celebrated in these houses. During a marriage ceremony when the bridegroom's parents eat, drink and take rest, the bridegroom goes to the Morung and spend their nights, there.

A boy or girl who enters the respective Morung at the age of about seven years continued till he or she got married. When the young girls and boys join these clubs, they are absolutely innocent of, and unfamiliar with, love episodes that circulate there. Gradually they learn the ways of life by seeing other boys and girls of older age group.

A youth possessing relatively better physique, more efficient in agricultural work, dancing and singing is elected as the leader of the Morung. He is to be obeyed by every inmate of the respective Morung. It is the responsibility of the youths of the Morung to organise the village youths for jhuming, raids and wars in consultation with the village head. In the girl's Morung, the head girl trains the young girls in the art of cooking, nursing, weaving, use of cosmetic and agricultural operations.

The girls also receive the training in handicrafts like basket making, wood work, pot making and the preparation of some other household goods. The young boys and girls visit their parents, homes only at the time of lunch and dinner. On special occasions food is prepared in the Morung. On certain special occasions the senior people of the village are also invited in the Morung. The folklore is handed over by one generation to the other in these Morungs. In case a culprit surrenders he is customarily given shelter and protected from those whom he had offended.

The most interesting thing associated with the girl's dormitory was the liberty given to the young girls to choose their partners for life. It is quite customary and proper for the young boy to visit the girl's Morung after sunset and the elders never look upon this as an immoral practice, for they did the same when they were young. During these visits inmates of boys' hostel develop relationship with the members of the opposite sex. A girl is permitted to be friendly with the boys but she is expected to have intimate relations with only one boy with whom she is ultimately expected to get married. This courtship may continue for any length of time.

There had been cases when the girl found herself in the family way without being married. But it is not frowned upon by the villagers. In Morung the courtship is a period of adjustments and trails, at the end of which the two are in a position to conclude if their permanent union would be a success. By mixing in this way they learn about each other's habits, way of life, likes and dislikes, physical fitness and sex potency. If at any stage one found that the prospective partner would not fulfil the requirements, a break in the relations could take place — but this is not considered a stigma either for the girl or the boy.

They just continue their life as normal and start looking out for other suitable partners. In case the girl conceives during this period of trails and adjustments which is of course not without sentimental and emotional attachments and due to some reason the boy is not prepared to marry her immediately or at a later stage, a fine is imposed upon him to compensate for not concluding the affair.

The real life in a Morung starts at night. A central fire is lit in the hall. Around the fire the young boys plan their defence, offence, attacks and Jhum operations. After sometime they start singing the folk songs. The moment they start singing, the girls in the nearby Morung also start the music. On many occasions there are reciprocal songs from both sides. This pleasing programme ultimately exhausts the youths and sends them to sleep. Those of the young boys and girls who do not go to sleep may be in love with each other and might be waiting all others to fall asleep so that they may find peaceful time for love making.

Morung as stated earlier is not a universal phenomenon in all the tribes of Nagaland. The Angamis and Semas for example, who are more orthodox in their attitudes do not send their girls to the dormitories. The Aos, Lothas, and Konyaks are more liberal and permissive.

Through the institution of Morung, love-marriage is a quite common affair among the Nagas. Usually the boy and the girl after having had a period of courtship get their decision conveyed to their parents, who in turn negotiate among themselves and arrive at some conclusion regarding the gifts to be presented by the boy. The amount of gifts could be just nominal in case the boy came from a poor family. A few baskets of rice, rice-beer, a few pigs and one goat could be the entire bride price — But in case the man is of high status or belong to a very rich family, the gifts could include a number of Mithuns in addition to many other articles.

The practice of staging a mock fight between the two parties still exists in some remote areas of Nagaland. This was done to fulfil the old standing tradition of kidnapping the girl. After this fight which sometimes take a few hours, the girl's parents throws a lavish party to the boy and his relations and other associates who accompany him. They are all entertained with good food, meat and rice-beer being the two main items. There are a number of other interesting details connected with each tribe.

Marriage to the Nagas is quite a ceremonial affair in case it is a maiden attempt, otherwise the two could just settle down in a hut and start living as a married couple. This is done without much frowning from their neighbours. At the same time there is no restriction to the number of wives a man could have. It all depends upon the disposition of the man, the size of his pocket and his social status.

The greater the number of wives a man possess, the better status he attains. A poor man can hardly afford to pay gifts for one wife and then after his marriage he has to work hard to maintain the family. Given one wife, the husband's opportunities to make love with her are limited because of the various taboos and restrictions imposed by the society on various occasions like pregnancy, childbirth, death, etc. A man with a moderate economic status has to exercise restraint during such periods of sex inactivity, but a man who is economically well off and exercise great social influences over the community takes another wife to fill in the voids.

Some Nagas have as many as six wives. Polygamy seldom produces any ill feelings or jealousy amongst the wives. In fact, many wives suggest to their husbands to take other wives in addition to themselves as the new ladies would considerably reduce their load of work and at the same time add to the social status of the husband. Polygamy further increases the number of offsprings which no doubt is an asset for a community where there is no hired labour. The boys when grown up assist their parents in the cultivation, while the girls on getting married bring them gifts and thus help to increase household belongings of their parents.

Another way of acquiring a wife for those who are too poor to pay the bride-price is to serve in house of the would-be in-laws for a period that is mutually agreed upon. After having paid the bride-price in terms of services, the man can get married to the daughter of the master and later start his independent married life.

The illicit sexual relations between married or unmarried people, separations, divorces and widow-marriages are not uncommon. It is true that there is a great deal of sexual laxity permitted by the unwritten Naga marriage code. Variations do occur from tribe to tribe. A wife can get rid of her husband by just paying back the bride-price that her new husband pays for her. Then as a separated women she can cohabit with another man without any ceremonial initiation. Later she can leave him also and another man can get married to her by paying her bride-price. In certain cases there can be no end to such relationships.

The Aos appeared to, be rather liberal and pre-marital relations are quite a normal affair with them. Among some tribes, a son can marry his stepmother. This system came into existence probably to avoid the family going through the ordeal of lengthy procedure of inheritance. Also, if the stepmother gets married to someone outside the family, their is the fair of children not getting good treatment at the hands of the stepmother. This also saves the house from the trouble of fixing a bride price.

With the tremendous increase in literacy and education and conversion from tribal religion to Christianity, there is a substantial change in the lifestyle of the Nagas and their marriage pattern. The educated families, especially in the urban areas do not send their sons and daughters to the Morungs. The fruits of education are percolating down to the remote and unaccessible villages. Now there are schools in almost all the villages with a population of one hundred.

The parents send their children to schools instead of admitting the Morungs. Consequently the institution of Morung has died out in most of the villages. The educated Naga youths are behaving differently from their forefathers. With the transformation of society many of the traditional institutions are losing their importance and their places are being taken by the new practices and organisations. The preachers have been relently advocating that for a Christian Naga it is not good to have more than one wife at a time. Therefore, the Christian Nagas do not practice the polygamy and the traditional Morung life.

Modern influences have permeated through the society for which changes in the indigenous system of marriage have become inevitable especially in urban and Christian societies. The system of marriage price still exists, but perhaps relaxed among Christians. For among them, marriage is solemnised at the church which lays more stress on the spiritual aspect. These days feasts, sometimes on a lavish scale have featured out in the urban area, when in the house of the bride, a party is entertained before they retreat to the groom's father's house.

But at the latter a more restricted group may also have been entertained. The construction of a hut where the couple were to settle on generally is not prevalent except in the deep interior areas, where their usage and practice still keep their ancient colours. It is left to the couple to decide the convenient time to form an entirely separate family.

Tattooing

Tattooing is also an important ceremony in the life of Nagas. All the girls and the warriors used to be tattooed. The pattern of tattooing varies from tribe to tribe and from region to region. Tradition has it that formerly Ao warriors who had taken heads had circles tattooed on their backs. Some Aos tattoo on each side of the back near the shoulder blades. The conventional curved design on their chests. Prior to the spread of Christianity and Baptist Mission, most of the Naga girls used to be tattooed. The pattern varies slightly from group to group but consists of four vertical lines on the chin, a chain of lozenges from the throat to the bottom of the breast bone, inverted V's on the front of the shoulders and stomach, lozenges and solid squares on the wrists, lozenges on the lower part of the leg, and a sort of arrow pattern on knee.

The elaborate ornamentation of body by tattooing usually requires five years to complete. When a girl is about ten years old her legs are tattooed up to the bottom of the calf, the next-year her chin, chest and fronts of her shoulders are completed; in the third year the pattern is done on the calf, and in the fourth year her knees are tattooed in the final year her wrists and stomach are ornamented. All the girls of an age in the village are tattooed at the same year. Once a girl is married the only addition which may be made to the tattoo already done is that on the wrist. The tattooing is a sort of Rite de Passage. Once a girl has undergone her first year's tattoo she is regarded as a full-fledged member of the community.

The operation of tattooing is carried out by old women in the jungle near the village in privacy. This work is absolutely forbidden for a man. Till the sores are healed the girl may eat nothing but rice, bamboo pickles and birds. A well marked, clean tattoo is much admired. The punctures are sometimes become infected, and terrible sore result, a girl occasionally ever losing her legs. But considering the dirt and lack of precautions against infection the proportion of septic cases in very small.

Village Administration

Each Naga village has a head-man. The head-man is called by different names. The Tangkhuls called their chiefs 'Awunga'; the Anganis 'Kemovo'; the Aos 'Sosangs'; the Lothas 'Ekyungs; the Semas 'Akekao'; and the Konyaks 'Kedange: The chieftainship among the Konyaks and Semas is hereditary. Aos elect their chief, the Angamis call the village chief

'Kemovo' which means that the practice is prevalent among them but the office of the Angani chief is a very temporary business and may last single meeting, though in the past it could be just one head-hunting; campaign, or just one battle.

Wherever the village headmanship is hereditary, the Chief to deserve the dignified office must possess certain; physical and moral qualifications. In some of the tribes in the past a particular person by dint of strength and courage seized the chieftainship of a village and retained it by virtue of the same.

In some tribes the Chief plays a dual role being both the secular and religious head of the village. This is so among the Tangkhuls, Semas and Aos. The Chief has thus two sets of functions, one secular and the other religious and ceremonial. The latter he has to perform in spite of the existence of a village priest. The religious functions were usually shared by both or performed by the Chief in consultation with village priest. The actual sacrifices worship, etc. may be conducted by the priest but the presence of the chief in necessary and he takes a prominent part in the proceedings. Ceremonies may well be void without his participation. As the first man in the village he inaugurates and presides overall village festivals: He is the first to sow seeds, first to plant and first to harvest. He is also expected to give the Cenria signal.

The secular duties of a Chief are, however, manifold and far outnumber and outweigh his religious duties. Negligence of secular duties may cost him the Chieftainship.

A Chief is responsible for the effective defence of the village. In the earlier days of constant animosity among villages and the practice of head-hunting, the question of village defence was a matter of great-importance. Peace and property of any village depended on the ability of the village to keep enemies and attackers at bay. As such the village fence and the village gate were efficiently maintained and made impenetrable. The village braves had to be exported to remain vigilant.

He parcels out and allot the cultivable lands to the villagers in consultation with his councillors. He uses his discretion on the advice of the councillors in using the village funds to help persons in financial difficulties due to crop failure.

Visitors to a village must inform the purpose and duration of their visit to the village chief and pay him their respects. The chief in return would make the visitors welcome and guarantee their safety during their stay in the village. The Chief also remain in touch with the Morung meetings of the clan heads of the village are fixed and summoned by the chief and almost always held at his residence and presided over only by him. The larger meetings are held on the village lawn (green field) under his chairmanship. He opens the discussion and presents the case. He is responsible for the general well-being of his subjects and it is in his interest to keep them content and happy; as such he must have periodic consultations with his Councillors to get information regarding the problems of each clan in the village. In addition to these secular functions, he also act, as the judge.

In the olden days of head-hunting and wars, besides being the Priest, judge, and Leader of his people he was also the Commander on the battlefield. In those days his physical strength was more in demand than his sagacity or other qualities of head and heart.

It is also the duty of the village chief to send and receive messages to and from friendly or hostile villages and to disclose the nature of the messages to village councillors and the villagers.

He is the chief of all village gatherings of sports, dance and songs. The religious duties of the chief are mainly in connection with village Gennas or taboos and festivals. His presence at all ceremonies held in the village is necessary. The privilege of declaring a ceremony formally open is his.

It is however, difficult to state the extent of his powers as they varied from tribe to tribe and from village to village in the same tribe. Among the extremely democratic-minded Angamis the chief in the role of a election of the council differs from priest is an object of reverence and even awe because of the superstitious beliefs held by the Nagas and indeed all animists.

The Chiefs, however, do not exercise unlimited powers because the Nagas are highly individualistic. They may command respect because of personal qualifications and consequently wield considerable authority but that is an entirely different matter. The powers of the chief are in most tribes curbed and controlled by the village Council. Folk songs and stories tell of how a particular chief was looked upon as father because of his benevolence, feared by all because of his physical prowess and revered by all because of his many abilities and qualities.

Chiefs who deserved and command respect were obeyed, respected and loved. Villages were eager to display their gratitude and affection by deeds, and would till his fields, do other odd jobs for him, give him the heads of all animals killed in the village, etc. Where the chiefs are powerful, as among the Konyaks, it is neither easy, safe nor possible to be indifferent to the chief or defy his authority by ignoring his existence or presence.

Village Funds

The Nagas assess and collect village funds. They manage the village funds without quarrelling. The village funds are called *Saru*. After harvest the Tamtenyemr of every Minden, with as many other Tatar as like to come meet in the Tatar Ungr's house and reckon up what has been spent by the 'Khel' as a whole during the year. There are numerous items — pigs bought for Aksu, animals killed for sacrifice, pigs killed to provide the Tatar with pork at important debates, and so on. All these animals have been paid for on the spot as a rule by some councillor, who recoups himself from the funds when collected. The Tamtenyemr keep a tally of the cost in rice of each item with little bundles of bamboo sticks.

The expenses incurred in the year are totalled at the meeting, and the amount of rice required to cover them is estimated, leaving a very good margin on the safe side: To provide the rice each household is assessed at so many baskets. This is collected after harvest, when payment is easiest, and those who have paid animals are recouped. With the balance the councillors buy meat and 'Madhu' and recompense themselves for their labours with a feast. If the balance is too big the village objects with an exceeding great noise.

Besides the village Saru, each clan similarly collect Saru to pay for the collecting a fund from its members to meat consumed at their feasts pay for clan Aksu, and the 'Morung'

Village Council

Besides the chief every village has a council. It is the principal organ of the village. The members of the council are either elected or nominated. Women do not have the right to be elected as councillors. The method of tribe but all Naga tribes have some sort of a village body in which the entire village is represented, usually clan-wise.

The Angamis do not have a council. Any matter dispute is taken before a meeting resembling the ancient Greek democratic meetings. An eloquent elder of the village usually opens the proceedings and he is usually the 'Kemovo' or the head of the village. The discussion is joined by other elders but every villager has a right to speak.

Among the Aos councillors are normally the representatives of the various clans residing in the village. A person who is able to speak up boldly far his clan and is also otherwise, the fittest will be sent by the clan to be its representative on the village body.

The Councillors must have certain qualifications. Any married person — marriage being a sign of maturity — is eligible to hold the office of a Councillor. But he must be able to speak well and boldly. Councillors are elected for a term which varies from tribe to tribe. Among the Aos it expires after three or five years. The councillors are deemed and referred to as 'the wise men' of the village and must be honoured by others.

The Council decides private and public disputes. The execution of the decisions is also done by the Council. In case a person or a party fails to abide by the decision of the Council, it takes necessary action against him, and sees to it that all its decisions are carried out effectively. The Council does not tolerate defiance of its authority. The Council punishes the guilty of breaking any time-honoured law of the land. Every Naga is conversant with the traditional laws, customs and usages. Ignorance of the same is no excuse. It must punish the wrong-doer.

The administrative function of the Council include the maintenance of the village water supply and footpaths. Construction of new paths and bridges across streams and rivers which are swollen during the rainy season or are otherwise very difficult to cross. The bridges must be built well in advance. Dates of all village festivals are fixed by the village Council Priest and the Village Chief. The Council then proclaims the date.

The council also arranges and looks after the village market. There is no such thing as a regular market in the village, all transactions being effected personally and from house to house. But on special occasions, and especially before and during certain festivals, large markets crop up, resembling fairs, at which all conceivable items are displayed and sold: all kinds of goods which grow in the hills — rice, sesamum, soya beans, other beans, dried maize, and colourful Naga shawls and cloths, jewellery, head dress, etc. which attract the young men and women; spears and Duos for the warriors; buffaloes, cows, Mithuns dogs and even cats; fowls and poultry; earthen pots, tobacco pipes, mortars, plates, mugs, cane-baskets, mats and rain proofs. It is a noisy, colourful and crowded place and the infrequency of such markets increases their importance and fun.

The Village Council is also the custodian of the village fund for finance. The village Council utilises this village "Pool of Rice" and uses its discretion to distribute the same. The Council also assist the Chief matters of defence of the village and is expected to cooperate with him in all other matters relating to the administration of the village. The Council is an effective check on the powers of an unscrupulous or tyrannical chief.

Settlement of Disputes

Minor disputes between villages are often settled at a meeting attended by the village council members and the elders of both sides. Cases which cannot be settled in this way are brought to the legal courts. But in the old days some powerful village would be called in, which would be able to arbitrate on the matter and to enforce its findings. The only other alternative was war.

There are general exceptions also in the crimes and punishment in the Naga tribes. Little boys till they enter the Morung and little girls till they are first tattooed, are children in the eyes of Naga tribal laws. They are regarded as incapable of committing crimes and therefore no fine or punishment is given to them. Civil and criminal disputes between grown-ups are heard by the councillors concerned. More usually all the councillors of the 'Khel' or even of the whole village will be called in. They either come to a finding and fix the penalty or instruct the parties to take oath and so leave the decision to God. In the old days disputes which were particularly difficult to settle were often presented to the leading men in powerful villages.

Most disputes were settled by the payment of a cow or pig. But for certain offences particular punishments were assigned. In the case of homocide, for instance, whether deliberate or accidental, the relatives of the dead man would have been deemed wanting in affection had they not loudly and at length demanded the life of the slayer.

But public life would not allow the village to be again defiled with blood; the aggrieved party had to content themselves with wrecking the murder's house, looting all his property, and driving him out of the village. In case of injury the punishment was retributary, i.e. eye for eye and hand for hand. In practice most of the injuries were covered by fine. For theft the value of the property stolen had to be restored and a pig paid to the elders.

Many disputes are settled by oath. The usual procedure is for each side to deposit an agreed amount as a wager, together with the price of pig, the fee of the elders for the part they play in the proceedings. On the appointed day the parties, accompanied by a deputation of elders to act as referees, go to the place at which village tradition ordains that oaths must be sworn. Should either party trip or suffer any similar little misfortune on the day he is non-suited at once; all return to the village and his wager is forfeited. Should all go well each side takes the oath.

Sometimes it can be determined at once who has lost, but usually a reckoning is made at the end of thirty days. If either side has sickness in his household during that period, or loses any property, he is declared to have sworn falsely and the decision goes against him. If nothing happens to either side any property in dispute in divided and the case is dismissed. The actual oath can be taken in innumerable ways. A very common method of oath taking is by cutting off a fowl's head. Each of the parties declares he is telling the truth and beheads a fowl with his Dao.

The neck must be cut clean through between the base of the skull and the crop. A cut which does not go clean through, or which is not in exactly the right place indicates guilt, and very often truly so, for the hand of the nervous liar cuts not straight. If land was in dispute the oath would be taken on the spot, otherwise it is taken just outside the village fence. A very serious oath is that on a human skull picked up from the wreckage of some corpse platform. An accused man bites it and swears that if he be guilty, may him spirit join that of the owner of the skull. Should any misfortune happens to him within thirty days he is known to have sworn falsely.

This oath is very rarely taken and is believed to be the swearer, even if he is innocent. A commoner oath is that as tiger's or leopard's skull. This an accused man sometimes demands to be allowed to take. It is his business to go to the place outside the village where the bodies of tigers and leopards are displayed on platforms and fetch the skull. In fact, some Naga tribes like Sangtam, regularly keep a tigers skull in the village for the purpose of taking oath.

If he finds the skull in the jungle, he brings it into the village, and biting it, pray that he may die a horrible death if his case be false. He then hands it to his accuser, who bites and swears on it in turn and takes it back to the place where it was found. Parties between whom a case has been settled in this way may never till death eat or drink anything brought from each other's house, or cooked with fire from each others hearth.

Fishing disputes between villages are often settled by oath. Sometimes a representative of each side beheads a fowl in a way described above, thus settling the matter at once, or man on each side will throw a stone into the disputed water, or each will give the other to drink a 'Chung' of the water mixed with chicken's blood. The usual prayers are offered in these, and should either champion suffer misfortune within thirty days the other side gets the fishing rights.

In land disputes each party eats earth from the field in question and prays that he may swell up and die if he be speaking falsely. Here too thirty days reckoning is kept. If the ownership of a bamboo clump cannot be settled by argument each disputant cut a length of bamboo from it and returning to the village, stands in front of his opponents, house. He bites his piece of bamboo and prays that his corpse — platform be made from that clump if his claim false.

With these words he throws the bamboo into the house. The other picks it up and with the same prayer, hangs it up in his house as witness. Any loss or illness in the course of a month settles the dispute.

An Angami Oath: "I am now not speaking falsely; if I am lying between the sky and the earth, let me not live like others but let me be completely ruined.

A Tangkhul Oath: A serious Tangkhul oath runs as follows:

"If I die, may — I and my family (or clansmen or co-villagers) descend into the earth and be seen no more."

Domestic Life

Nagas know nothing of boredom. The Nagas never feel the lack of something to do what leisure he has from work he is quite content to spend gossiping, or just sitting and thinking. Most of the Nagas even without the aid of opium can sleep like a log for long stretches in the day, but whose hands are never idle when he is awake — he always seems to be making a mat or a basket or an ear ornament or something.

The awful monotony therefore, which is the chief feature of village life, does not worry the Naga. For the greater part of the year his fields need constant attention and one day is much like another. Before dawn the family begins to stir. The wife blow up the fire and the husband probably has a drink of Madhu. Water is brought up by the wife and children from the village spring and the morning meal of rice and relish is cooked and eaten. Then the family goes down to the fields, taking a gourd of 'Madhu' and the midday meal of cold boiled rice and relish wrapped up in leaves. This is eaten in the shelter of the fieldhouse when the morning's work is over.

After a shorter spell of work the family sets off up the hill home, probably carrying a load or two of firewood with them. The wife has no time to sit down and set when she gets in. She goes down to the spring with the children and brings up water again in hollow bamboos. The rice for the evening meal is set to cook and the wife or one of the daughters husks the paddy for the next day. After a supper of boiled rice and reish friends drop in for a chat. But no one is inclined to sit up late, and sleep soon comes.

During the day, when nearly everyone is down in the field working, the village is almost save for old people, very young children, and a few men whose turn it is also to stay in the village and watch for an outbreak of fire or carry urgent messages to the next village. The time passes quickly and pleasantly enough for those left behind. The old men sit about gossiping or making mats, keeping meanwhile a watchful eye on their grand children playing near. The old women talk and dry rice or seed cotton. The men left as watchers for the day sit about talking and sipping.

Madhu or occupy themselves with odd jobs. After harvest life is more varied. The men often go off on trading expeditions and the women have more time for spinning and weaving. Festivals and feasts are frequent. On the morning of a dance there is much visiting and drinking of Madhu. Ladies bedeck themselves with ornaments. There is no "scrambling into dress clothes." The finery has to be put on with care, and wives do not eat, their husbands go to the dancing ground till they have seen that they are properly turned out. The women too have to put on their best things, and it is a curious fact that an Ao woman takes as long to put a hornbill feather in her hair as an English woman does to put her hat on. The festivities begin between three and four and often the singing, dancing and drinking go on till dawn. The village is a sleepy place next day.

Adoption

Adoption is not a common phenomenon among most of the Naga tribes. Wealth is pretty evenly distributed and it is not often that a man is so desperately hard up that he will go to another man and call him father in the hope of being supported. Nor, as there are no heavy marriage prices to be shared, is there any incentive for a man to go about seeking whom he may adopt, as in sometimes the practice of Sema chiefs. Nor does the adopter necessarily inherit any property the adopted may accumulate. If A adopts B and B dies without heirs A gets B's property. But if B has a son or even an unadopted brother D, C or, failing him, D would get the whole of B's property, save a very small portion which would go to A. Should B's descendents die out, after no matter how many generations, A's descendents would inherit the property if his line were to become extinct.

An adopting father receives the same shares of meat from his 'son' as a real father. These consist of a portion of all sacrificial meat and the head of all game, including monkeys. In the case of game the father returns the skull after removing the meat, and often adds to it an egg and a prayer for continued luck in hunting. The son hardboils the egg, offers six little scraps to the skull, and eats the rest.

There is another form of adoption, which is common among the Ao tribe especially among the Chongh Aoso A man, who wishes to make a particularly ostentatious display of wealth, can, provided he has done the Mittun and a big present of meat, usually at least three or four entire cows and pigs. He is then entitled to were cane leggings. In return for this present his adopted son must call him 'father' build him house for nothing if he gets burnt down, and come to work in his fields for nothing occasionally. Should any Morung, 'Khel' or village consider that they have been adopted by so many 'fathers' that they cannot conveniently fulfil their duties to them all, they can break the tie by providing a pig, which they share with their 'father' This recompenses him for the very slight services he loses. His glory remains undimmed.

Friendship

The Nagas attach great importance to formal friendships, which are of various kinds. The closest tie is that with a friend called *Atombu*. The two parties must belong to different phratries and different villages. If two men, A and B, agree to become Atombu they first exchange gifts of a Dao and spear. A year or so later A kills a pig. Half he distributes in his own village among men of his clan and the husbands of women he calls sisters. With the other half he goes and visits B, accompanied by a large party of friends. He gives B the half pig, some handsome ornament, and a cloth for his wife, and spends the night drinking in the houses of B and a cloth for clan's men. In the morning B in turn kills a pig, and gives half to A, together with some money in cash or a live cow. Then again about a year later A revisits B and gives him half a pig and two cows. Such friendships are often hereditary, the children of Atombu reviewing the tie each generation. The children of two Atombu may not intermarry, and a man addresses his father's Atombu and his wife as 'father' and 'mother' A man could not take Atombu's head in war. If it were taken and brought in by someone else he would put a little rice and 'Madhu' into its mouth and lay a small offering of food under it as it hung from the head-tree. The Atombu must help each other in misfortune and sickness.

Ashibu or Khaoba is a friend of different party, but of the same village. Two Ashibu will exchange gifts and give each other large shares of meat at feasts of merit.

Besides being bound to help each other whenever need arises, formal friends have special duties to perform on certain occasions.. For instance, when giving a feast of merit a man receives constant assistance from such friends. Or at a man's first marriage his friends will make his door, the trays above the fire, and the bamboo 'Chungas' which the newly-married couple must use for six days instead of ordinary cooking pots. They will light the fire with a fire-thong and have thing ready for the bride and bride groom when they come.

Again in many villages if a man brought in a head it was the duty of one of his formal friends to go and fetch the bamboo from which to hang it from the head-tree. A man addresses as Tinu a friend of his own phratry to whom he is not related in any traceable way. Such friends usually exchange little gifts of tobacco and so on when they meet. A lady-love is addressed by name, but is spoken as Yingachir. She must, of course, be another phratry. Women friends of different phratries give each other small gifts and speak of each other as Atongla; if of the same phratry they address to each other as sisters.

Folklore

Like all other Indian languages and dialects, the Naga dialects have also numerous folktales, folk songs, and proverbs. Since Naga dialects have no scripts, the folklore is inherited by the successive generations in oral form. The Morung life, the festivals and other such occasions throw opportunities that help in the richness and revision of folk songs as well as folktales. Some of the folk songs and folktales have historical background but many of them are based on mere myths. There are however, folktales depicting human and animal character interwoven and remind of Aesop's Fables or Vishnu Sharma's Panchatantra.

A story deals with the Wax Girl which states that in the days when our ancestors lived at Nungkamchung (the oldest Lotha Village), there was a girl of the Ezung clan whose name was Yensali, and she was a wax girl. Her parents did not wish to marry her to anyone, but Tsontsotsu promised never to let her go out in the sun anywhere, so her parents gave her to him in marriage. He was careful to keep his promise. Now he built his house near the path which the villagers used to go to their fields, and as the villagers went to and from their fields they kept saying, as they passed the house, how good Tsontsotsu's fields were. Because she always heard Yensali said to her husband "We will go together and see the fields tomorrow."

So the next day they went, and when they reached the field Tsontsotsu said to his wife "You go down the track and look at the field from that big rock there. Then go up the field-house and wait there." And she went down along the edge of the field and got up on to the big rock to look. But when she climbed up the rock she melted. Then Tsontsotsu went up to the village and said to his father-in-law about it and he asked him whether he has touched her clothes and ornaments, and when Tsontsotsu said he had not, he said "Go down early tomorrow morning and sprinkle Nshi leaves on the place." So Tsontsotsu went and sprinkled Nshi leaves over his wife's remains and swarm of bees appeared and turned into his wife as she was before. She brushed her hair back with her hand and went home with her husband.

After this he never let her go anywhere, but always made her stay in the shade of the house. And in due course two sons were born to them. The elder son was called Champomung and the younger was called *Shishanga*. They were so called because Tsontsotsu spent all his time in the Morung (Champo) and because he did the Shishanga ceremony. That is why to this day the descendents of Champomung are called Champomungdri and the descendents of Shishanga are called *Shishangdri*. This is a story of what happened about seven-eight generations ago.

Another interesting folktale is about Humchibilio. This story is also from the Naga tribe. Once upon a time there lived two brothers, of whom the younger was always luckier in everything than the elder. However, carefully the elder cultivated his land the crops were always bad, or if he married a pretty wife she always turned ugly. One day these two went down and looked at their fields to see how they were doing, and exchanged their land, the younger giving his elder the fields he had prepared so well, and the elder giving his younger brother his bad fields. But the fine fields which were given to the elder brother grew poor crops, while the poor fields which the younger brother received did splendidly.

Then the elder brother desired to take his younger brother's wife, who was very beautiful: so meaning to lay a trap for him he went with him into the jungle, taking a cock with him. As he led the way in the jungle the elder brother kept asking "Do you know this place or not?" and the younger brother would answer "This is where father and I gather fuel wood" or "This is where I set traps for birds" or "This is where I set traps for squirrels" or "This is where I look for game" or "This is where I fish." At last they arrived at the edge of a cliff and the elder brother asked "Brother, do you know this place," and the younger brother replied "I do not know this place."

Then the elder brother said "We will sleep in the night there," and when they had a meal he cut a length from the stem of a plantain tree and wrapped it in a cloth. Then putting the cock at their heads the elder brother lay down by the plantain stem and made his younger brother sleep behind him. At night when the younger brother was fast asleep the elder brother stole quietly cock away. But the cock called out "Cock-a-doodle-do," your brother has run away; "Cock-a-doodle-do, your brother has given you the slip and gone."

Then the younger brother woke up and thinking about the plantain tree wrapped in a cloth was his brother said "Brother, it is cockcrow. It will soon be light, and gave the plantain tree a push, so that it went rolling down the cliff." My brother has rolled down, my brother has rolled down" he cried, and climbed down after it. Then when he saw that it was the plantain tree he hacked it into little pieces and threw them away, and called to his brother and said "A Tsangon bird is caught in our spittle. We will share it. Wait for me," and after his brother, but could not and him. His elder brother, when he heard his younger brother calling, scratched over his footprints and spittle with his spear but so that his tracts would be lost, and with a shout "I am going this way. Come along" made off.

The young brother tried in vain to catch up with his elder brother and in the evening came to a tree loaded with big red Zowoti fruit. Up this he climbed and slept in the branches. That night the Zowati fruit ripened and in the morning he picked and ate some of these. Now there came to that place a tiger carrying on his back a Sambhur (deer) it had killed. His carrying-band was cobra, and he had a barking deer for a pad in the small of his back and wild boar as a pad behind his head.

In his hand was a very bright long bladed spear which he twirled and flourished, chanting "Ho, ho, ho" as he bent under his load. When he came to the Zowoti tree he said "I smell something alive" and looked up into the branches. Then the man said "I am keeping watch over this fruit of yours, grandfather tiger, in case some stranger should come and pick it." Then he kept picking the fruit and handing it to the tiger to eat, till there was only one fruit left at the very top of the tree. Then the man said "There is a fruit at the very top of the tree which I cannot reach.

Give me your long bladed spear, father tiger, and I will cut it off for you. You stand down below with your legs wide apart and your mouth open and your eyes shut and I will pick the fruit and throw it right into your mouth." Then the tiger handed up his spear and stood as the man told him. And the man hurled down the spear and struck the earth at the tiger's feet without touching him. "Hullo," said the tiger, "What are you up to?" "I am only a boy, father tiger," he replied. 'I could not hold your spear properly and it fell out of my hands. Hand me up your spear again and be careful to stay as you were before." The tiger did as he was told and the man speared him right through the mouth. Then he kept picking and throwing down leaves on the tiger to see if it was dead or not, but it was not dead, for its ears twitched when a leaf hit it. At last there was only one leaf, and when he picked this and threw it down on to the tiger its ears did not twitch for it was dead.

Then the man came down from the tree and picked up the body of the tiger, and, chanting as the tiger had chanted, went on his way till he came to a village spring. Now there were some maidens bathing at the spring, and one of them was very beautiful, whom when he saw he greatly desired to take to wife. So he threw the long-bladed spear, and 'tong' it stuck in the wooden fence below the spring, but he lay hidden behind a worm-cast. But the maidens were frightened and ran up to the village and told the men what had happened. And the men came down and wondering who had done this thing tugged at the spear but could not pull it out.

Then the wanderer from his hiding place laughed at them and said, "Cannot you even pull the spear out? I will put it out 'top' for you it you will give me the beautiful maiden, who was bathing here to be my wife." Then the men of the village said," who was that?" and even searched among the fallen leaves looking for him, but could not find him. Now the maiden whom the wanderer desired was the chief's daughter, and her father called out "Whoever you may be if you can pull out this spear, I will give you my daughter as your wife. Come and pull it out." Hearing these words at wanderer came from behind the worm cast and pulled out the spear.

'Now when the wanderer was going to take his bride the maiden's father dressed up his slave girl in fine clothes and beautiful ornaments and put rags on his own daughter and threw rice husks over her. But the wanderer was too clever to 'be deceived in this way and took with him as his bride the real daughter.

Putting his bride into a carrying basket he set off to carry her to his village, but when he came to where the paths met below his village he found the load too heavy, and leaning the basket up against the bank he went up to the village to call his relations to help. Now an ugly woman called Humchibilio on her way to the spring to fetch water saw the basket and she opened it and peeped inside. And finding the maiden in it she dragged her out and tore her to pieces with her hands. Then throwing the remains away below the spring she got into the basket herself and waited. When the bridegroom's relations had carried up the basket for him they opened it and looked inside and said "Is this the kind of bride you call us to carry up" and mocked him. And he, knowing that this was not the bride he had brought, was full of shame.

After a time from the pieces Humchibilio had thrown away there grew up a very beautiful bamboo shoot. When the bridegroom saw it he said "That is like my lost bride." Then he broke it off and peeled off the outer skin and brought it home and put it in the pot to boil. When he was present it only boiled "bubble, bubble, bubble," but when Humchibilio was watching it alone a voice came from the bamboo as it boiled "Humchibilio tore me in pieces. Bubble, bubble, bubble." Then Humchibilio said to her husband "Husband, listen to the noise this bamboo makes as it boils." Then he listened and heard a voice come from it as she had said, and took it off the fire and threw it out behind the house.

After sometime this too grew into an orange tree with a single orange at the top. When Humchibilio went near the orange was high up at the top of the tree, but when her husband went near it bent down towards the earth. Then her husband said "That is like my lost bride" and picked it and put it in a carrying basket.

Then the orange turned into a maiden. When the husband and wife had gone to the fields she said "My beloved will be angry if I do not clean the house. He has no proper wife," and with a tinkle of ornaments she jumped out of the basket and set to work. She defiled Humchibilio's bed with filth and took ashes and poured them on it, but she dusted carefully her husband's bed. Then she swept out the house thoroughly and prepared a meal. When the husband and wife came in they said "who has got all this ready for us? Even if we go without food ourselves we must give him something." So they went and asked their neighbours. But their neighbours only answered, "We cannot get through our own work. Who would do so much work for you?" The one day the husband pretended to go out to work, but came back quietly and kept watch. And when the maiden jumped out of the basket her husband exclaimed. "Eh, where have you come from?" and caught hold of her. Then the maiden told her husband the whole story of how Humchibilio had torn her in pieces and how she had become first a bamboo shoot and then an orange.

Having heard the tale her husband sharpened his Dao and waited for Humchibilo, intending to kill her. After a little while Humchibilio came up from the field with a load of wood and wild taro and called from outside to her husband within the house, "Husband, come out and lift down my load for me. "At these words her husband came out and killed her with one blow, and as she fell she gasped "Wild Taro." That is why nowadays if you eat wild Taro which has been sliced with a Dao you get a sore throat.

After this the bride was wedded to her husband but whenever she went out she pricked herself on Humchibilio's bones till the last she could not leave the house and her wounds swelled up and sloe died.

This is the end of the story:

A story reveals with the friendship between man and tiger and the circumstances that led to animosity between them. It is believed that in the very beginning man and tiger were fast friends. They lived in the same den and cultivated the same field. There was a pig also who used to play havoc to the crops in the field during night besides creating hollows in front of the den that caused tumbles to man and tiger in the early morning. Tired of this nuisance man and tiger killed the pig. Both of them cooked the pig's flesh. Tiger went to the well to have a bath and fetch water. In his absence man thought of not giving cooked meat to the tiger fearing that the latter would develop taste for meat and might kill man sometime for meat. Thus he hurriedly cooked some wooden logs for the tiger when he was away to the well. After sometime tiger came back. When tiger and man started eating in their respective bowls the tiger found it difficult to chew the wooden logs but he noted the man enjoying his dish. Smelling something foul, the tiger asked for more meat. When man went inside the den to bring more, the tiger tasted the dish of the man and came to know about the reality.

When man came back he saw the tiger eating from his dish and the idea that now tiger would not spare him, shuddered his entire body. Man took to his heels as he had seen the burning hot eyes of the tiger and his itching paws. However, he was chased by the tiger. Finding no way out after covering some distance man forced himself in a rabbit burrowing. Though man succeeded in entering the narrow burrowing, one side of his waist belt continued to hang outside. The tiger tried his best to pull the man out with that end of the belt but failed. When the tiger got tired, he retired to his lair. After sometime man came out and instead of going to his old dwelling searched another shelter for him. Since then Nagas believe that man and tiger are unfriendly to each other.

Another folktale reveals that man, spirit, and tiger were the sons of the same mother in the beginning of the creation. In old age when the mother" fell ill, she was looked, after turn by turn by her sons. Whereas man and spirit looked after the mother properly, the tiger in his turn used to lick her only and it turned her more sick. This way the condition of the mother became critical. Man and spirit apprehended that in case mother died in the presence of all, the tiger may devour her dead body. Thus they wanted to keep the tiger away from the cottage. They gave a cracked gourd to the tiger and asked him to bring water from the mother.

The tiger went to the stream and filled the gourd with water but found that it leaked out while he had covered half the distance. The tiger went again and again. Meanwhile the mother died and they buried her beneath the furnace as they were sure that the tiger would dig up the grave if set up anywhere else. In the evening the tiger came back and found no mother. On enquiry he got only evasive answers. He ultimately realised that the mother was dead and her corpse has been buried. He sniffed here and there to find out the location of the grave but did not succeed. Thus the dead body of the mother was saved. Consequently, there is no taboo among the Nagas to erect a house over an old grave.

After mother's death, brothers distributed their belongings and decided to establish separate dwellings. Man and tiger both wanted to live in the village and none wanted to go to the jungle. The spirit suggested a way out. She fixed a target and said that whosoever touches it first would remain in the village while the other shall have to go to jungle. Spirit and man knew that the latter would never succeed in the race. They connived and hit upon a plan. A bow and arrow were prepared for the man. When competition started man instead of running the race shot at the target and the spirit declared that man had won the competition. Finding himself cheated and ashamed of not being tactful, tiger ran to the jungle. The Nagas believe that since then man resides in the village and tiger in the jungle.

There is another tale which explains as to how dog became a faithful animal for the man. In a fight, a bitch was killed by a deer. Her two pups wanted to avenge the death of their mother. They went to the elephant and asked for his help. He asked the pups to stay for the night with him and in the morning he would accompany them to chase the deer. During night the pups started barking.

The elephant thought that the noise may invite trouble to his hideout in the form of lion. Therefore, he threw out the pups. The pups then went to the tiger. He also replied in the same way. However, during the night when pups started barking he also apprehended danger and threw the pups out of his lair. In the end the pups approached the man. In the night when the pups started barking, man encouraged them to do so. Thus the pups decided to stay with man. The dog is ever since believed to be faithful to man.

The Pantho Raja (Brinjal King) story gives an insight in the Naga life and the tactics employed by them in solving the problems. The folktale narrates that there was an old widow who had six sons. One day when they came back from the Jhum land they were served with a vegetable dish which was very tasty. On enquiry their mother talked in light vein that the dish had been turned so tasty by the urine of Hasiring cobra.

The boys thought that the flesh of the cobra must be much more tasty when cooked and they decided to kill the reptile who was notorious for his ferociousness. Their mother tried to dissuade them from this venture but they were determined in their mission. With a load of Lao-Pani, Jowar, breads, salt and Daos they started their journey to hunt and kill the cobra. In search of the reptile they reached a cottage in the evening where they met an old lady, and they asked the way leading to the hideout of Hasiring Cobra. That mysteriously looking old lady a test to the youths. She gave them to eat the steel-grams which they could not chew. She thought that the youths were foolish but even then pointed towards the way. By the next evening they reached the hut of another old hag. She also gave them a test by way of giving a cracked gourd to fetch water from the pond.

But they again failed in the test. This lady also thought them foolish but showed them the way. On the third evening they again reached the hut of yet another old hag. This lady pointed towards a thorny bush and asked them to bring its flower without touching its branches. But they failed in this test also. After treading the path shown by this lady they in the end reached a rock on which Hasiring cobra was seated. He challenged the young men who told him that they had come to kill him. The cobra drew a long breath in which he gulped all the six brothers.

Their mother waited and waited for her sons but in vain. One day while she was picking brinjals, a thorn of the brinjal plant ran into her palm. It is believed that after sometime the widow gave birth to another son who was named Pantho Raja since he was born of a Pantho (brinjal). He grew up in a sturdy, tactful and brave young boy. One day his mother narrated him the story of her earlier six sons. Pantho told his mother that he would kill the Hasiring and free his brothers. He assured her mother that he would essentially succeed. He set on the journey and get through the tests given by the three old ladies. He remarkably chew the steel grams, put a thick banana leaf in the cracked gourd and fetched water in it. He also pinned a hook on a bamboo stick and picked the flower from the thorny bush without touching its branches.

On being challenged by the cobra he threw spears in his eyes and blinded him. Thereafter he immediately cut the stomach of Hasiring and freed his brothers. All of them came out as if they were arising out of their beds. When Pantho told them that he had freed them, they did not believe and instead severely beat him and tied him with a tree.

When they reached home, their mother asked them about her seventh son. They were still talking about Pantho when the latter arrived in the courtyard of the house as he had been freed by one of the old ladies. He asked his mother that all her six sons were not only fools but ungrateful too. He asked his mother to bring a cotton thread ball so that he could go to the heaven and also take her with him. He caught hold the one end of the thread and threw the ball in the sky and it linked the earth with the sky. He started climbing it and asked his mother to follow him and not to look back.

Seeing this strange thing the other six youth started crying and requesting through shouts to take them also along with. Pantho warned his mother, "Do not look back. The dwellers of the earth cry like this. Everybody wants to go to the paradise but they have not performed good deeds so that they could not go to the paradise in soul and body like you." But the mother could not resist the temptation of glancing over her crying sons. The moment she looked back the thread broke over her head. Pantho marched ahead and mother continued to hang in between. The Nagas believe that when the mother turns sad, she starts shedding tears which reach the earth as rain drops. The thread around her becomes lightning and rainbow.

Naga folktales also have casanavos in Gakripu and Zosheto. Gakripu, a horse rider started helping an old mother and her young daughter in crossing a river. He promised the old mother that after dropping the daughter on the other side of the river he would come back to pick her up. Instead he flew away with the young dame and the old mother kept on crying.

Zosheto is remembered in a folktale for voluptuous hilarity. He once took all the young women of his village for fishing in the stream. He told them that he would go upstream and mix some poison in the water and they should stand downstream hold King their skirts to catch fish. He is said to have used Ayirha root powder which leads to irritating sap when mixed with water. The sap entered the women's sexual organ and made them mad for a sexual intercourse desire. They begged Zosheto to satisfy them. He is said to have possessed wonderful powers and he was able to satisfy all but one girl. She was left untouched because she preferred to obtain her father's permission to have connection with Zosheto.

So great was her desire that she immediately left for her home to seek her father's permission. But the shrewd and cunning Zosheto went up by another way and arrived at her house first. He found her father out, and thus hid himself in the inner room. She came into the outer room and called out and said "Zosheto has had connection with all the other women of her Keel. May he have connection with me tool. Then Zosheto who was hid in the inner room answered in a feigned voice and said "Zosheto has had connection with all other women, so you must let him have connection with you too. "Then he went at once straight down to the river again. But again Zosheto went quickly by another way and was ready waiting for her. He asked her what her father replied and when she told him the words he had himself uttered, he satisfied her too.

Folk songs also contain such lyrics that extol feelings of love, pathos, heroism, etc. The inhabitants of Vakching village in Konyak area claim that their village was the first village of God's creation. There is a folk song about it, that speaks:

Since when the earth came into existence,

Water sprouted and rocks were formed,

And we in the lineage of Young Bern Aou Niou,

Our sons are healthy and sturdy and number similar to stars,

Sun rises and goes higher in the sky,

Oh the sons of Yana and Shayong you are also as high,

Oh the tall trees of the original garden of Yana and Shayong.

You are great.

Bring thunderous and darkness piercing light.

A love song sung by Angamis reveals the following feelings

I will grow as beautiful as you are, When I recollect the sweet memories of our past,

It touches my heart so deeply, my darling,

When you are young, I loved you ten times,

Even today my love for you has not diminished.

There is another Angami song which reveals the feelings of pathos:

Thou were like Jupiter, the year we were wedded,

One morning you went to check the traps in the jungle,

My darling, the enemy killed you in an ambush,

On receiving the word, I reached there,

Covered your dead body with a black cloth.

You did not leave me when I was simple and you innocent.

Then why did you depart when our minds were out.

There are folk songs that throw challenges to other tribes also:

Hear our songs with your drum-like ears,

Oh you the elders and wretched dwellers of that village,

Raise your dog-ear like ears and listen,

The greatest songs of our distinctly-revered village,

Oh thou rascals who think ill of us.

Standing on the cross-road near a rubber tree,

You declare that you settled Kongan village,

Where flows the might Faeeliang,

And then you start murmuring.

Oh go and seek shelter in your mother's lap,

Go and seek a hideout in your houses.

What ill can you bring to our settlement.

There are reciprocating folk songs by boys and girls expressing each other's futility.

Oh girls of that Morung, Oh our friends,

There are jewels and coins in your mother's hands,

There is very little or nothing in your husband's hands.

Once you have borne two or three children,

Your physical charm vanishes and you are attractive no more,

Better to love your friends, the childhood playmates.

Music and Dance

Though the Nagas have a good enough ear for a tune, they possess very little in the way of musical instruments. In every 'Morung' are to be found one or two buffalo-horn trumpets which the bucks blow for their amusement. There are two types of bamboo flute. One, about twelve inches long, is used by boys and has two stops. The other, which is played by bigger youths, has three stops and is about thirty-six inches long. Occasionally small bamboo instruments are to be seen in Mokongtsu in which the sound is produced by a vibrating tongue. The Ao classes them as flutes and says they are copies of Gurkhal toys seen in the foreign settlement. The Jews' harp of the Aos is precisely similar to that of the Angamis. Both girls and young men use them, but only after nightfall. It is not the custom to use them in the day.

Every Morung possesses a small drum consisting of a hollow cylinder of wood with the ends covered with cow hide. Such a drum is invariably the property of the Morung as whole and never of any individual. The drums are repaired every year at the Moatsu festival. Before the hide is stretched on these are put inside a few grains of rice from the house of a good singer and the tooth of a barking deer, "because the bark of a barking deer carries very far." Unlike the changes and Konyaks, who use their big log xylophones on such occasions, the Ao custom on the death of a rich man is to beat a hide drum outside his house and sing of his wealth and prowess. These small drums are also invariably used at dances. A drummer, with his instrument slung across his chest, walks up and down with the dances and slaps the time with his fingers, a double beat being the signal for them to turn. The instrument can be used for death-singing and dances of any time of the year, but except for these purposes, it may not be beaten between sowing and harvesting, "because the earth (fields) is pregnant."

Dancing plays an important part in all ceremonies, but the steps are monotonous in the extreme. At Mithun sacrifices the men and women dance a dance called *Tsungsang* is Mokokchung District inside the house of the giver of the feast. It consists of a circle of alternate men and women with linked arms chanting and moving slowly round in time to the singing. No Naga dances are silent, all those taking part chant continually. Dances in the open air, such as those which take place at the Moatsu festival, give more scope for variation. First the performers walk slowly round in a body chanting and showing off their finery. From time to time one will break away and give an exhibition of jumping and spear-twirling. This opening procession is called *Sangbangtur* because the men are "as beautiful as Sangbang berries.

The next dance is usually that called *Ango Kazu* in Ao tribes of the Nagaland. In this dance the dancers move in a column of fours, formation is quick time to the tap of the drum, the column wheeling about in all directions, like a fish swimming. Among the Chongli Nagas there is another dance called *Moya Yari*, imitated from the Semas. This too is danced in column to a quick step.

When the drummer gives the signal with a double tap the dancers move backwards instead of forwards. The prettiest dance of all is the chang dance called *Miri Yari*. The dancers, all men and boys, from a ling line with the leader on the right and the best dancers next to him, trailing off to small boys at the left end. The leader holds a Dao in his right hand, and with his left hands holds the right hand of the man on his left, who in turn joins hands with the next man and so on. The usual step in a step to the right, a short step back, a flex of the Knees and two stamps with right foot. A drummer near the leader gives the time.

The line goes round in a circle and is led in all sorts of curves by the leader. Finally it winds itself up into a spiral and unwinds itself. While the men are dancing, the women dance too apart. This dance called the 'Moon Dance' is in some villages only danced at might, though in other villages it may begin as early as three in the afternoon. It is a very dull affair. Two lines of girls form up face to face, each girl with her arm round the waist of those on either side of her. Each line in turn moves two steps and a jump forward while the other line moves back. There is no drummer in attendance, a subdued chant giving the time.

Arts and Crafts

The rich arts and crafts of Nagaland portray the artistic calibre and creative imagination of the local craftsmen of the Northeastern State of India. It has several small-scale cottage and medium-scale industries that produce fine products of the traditional art of the state.

The art of weaving is primarily the domain of the female folk. The weaving industry is one of the important industries of the region that has added to the financial strength of the state.

The women design beautiful patterns on pieces of cloth to make them colourful and attractive. The excellent design patterns on the Angami Naga shawls bears relic to the unique artistic skills of the artists who have inherited the art from their forefathers.

The men folk produce excellent pieces of wooden work. The artists carve exquisite designs on the wooden pieces. One of the traditional arts of Nagaland, the woodcarving industry produces beautiful products that have an internationally acclaimed status.

The local indigenous inhabitants master in the art of making baskets which are decorative and functional as well. The baskets of different sizes and shapes are used for variety of purposes.

The traditional ornaments reflect the rich cultural heritage of the place. The native population love to wear heavy jewelleries on days of special festive occasions.

The local citizens draw beautiful pictures of animals and birds on the walls of their houses to make them look attractive. The state is famous for producing several beautiful items of bamboo and cane work.

Nagaland is famous for producing excellent pieces of pots from mud. The pots are used for storing water. The metalwork is another industry that has flourished in the state.

Embroidery

The beautiful embroidery of Nagaland portrays the rich artistic calibre of the local craftsmen of the state. The local indigenous population design unique patterns on their shawls, clothes and other decorative items made up of cloth which reflects their cultural heritage. The splendid embroidery of the Angami Naga shawls has an internationally acclaimed status. Most of the tourists who visit the Northeastern State prefer to buy the beautiful shawls as relic of the rich artistic creativity of the native population. Designed with colourful threads or wools, the Angami Naga shawls reflect the old glory and grandeur of the state.

Popularly known as Sami Lami Phee, the Angami Naga shawls were gifted to the valiant fighters by the ruler of Nagaland in recognition of their service during the ancient times. The Angami Naga shawls are usually embroidered with unique design patterns of several wild animals against the black base of the shawls.

The exclusive embroidered cloths are an important part of the rich arts and crafts of state. Most of the local indigenous inhabitants have mastery over the traditional art of designing beautiful patterns of animals on the pieces of cloth.

The unique embroidered items help the state to earn huge revenues and have helped in the economic and social development. The State Government has taken several landmark steps to improve the small-scale and medium-scale cottage industries for further enhancement of the traditional art of embroidery.

Woodcarvings

The Nagaland woodcarvings are known for their elegant designs and excellent quality. It earns huge revenues from the woodcarving industry of the state. An integral part of arts and crafts the beautifully designed wooden works portrays the rich artistic calibre and imaginative skills of the local craftsmen.

The tribes of Wanchos, Phom and Konyaks are known for their splendid mastery over the traditional art of carving beautiful products from woods which they have inherited from their forefathers. The excellent pieces of wooden work have internationally acclaimed status. Most of the tourists who visit Nagaland make it a point to purchase the pieces of traditional art as relics of the unique cultural heritage and artistic creativity of the place. The wooden pieces of artwork are primarily used for decorative purposes.

The woodcarvers produce unique pieces of wooden work from traditional instruments of adze, chisel, dao and axe. Wooden figures of human beings, elephants, hornbill, mithun head, tiger and other animals are the main products of the traditional industry of woodcarving. The woodcarving industry has led to the strengthening of the economic base of the state.

The woodcarvers of the area of Konyak draw inspiration from the Khajurao artwork and carve excellent figures of human beings. The State Government has taken several steps to improve the traditional industry of woodcarving in the form of extending financial help and moral encourage to the craftsmen.

Basketry

Nagaland basketry can be used for a variety of purposes. Most of the local indigenous inhabitants know the art of making baskets from bamboo and cane. Bamboo and cane are easily available in the neighbouring forest lands. An important part of the traditional arts and crafts of state the aboriginal tribes of the Northeastern State make beautiful and usable baskets for daily use.

The art of making baskets have been mostly mastered by the men folk of the region. Basket making reflects the rich mythical history and folk culture of the state. According to the unique folk culture of the Ao tribe the local indigenous inhabitants had inherited the art of making baskets from the magician, Changkichanglangba on the sixth day of his death. Prior to his death, the magician had instructed the native population that after six days of his death, they would find out some interesting things in his grave. As per the direction of Changkichanglangba, the local inhabitants did find several beautiful baskets of different sizes and shapes. Thus the art of basket making was introduced among the tribal communities of Nagaland. The baskets vary in size and shape. While the Angami tribe make cylindrical baskets, the Ao are proficient in making conical shaped baskets. An essential household good of the local inhabitants the baskets are generally used for keeping vegetables, clothes, and crops. Baskets also serve as decorative items. Most of the tourists who visit Nagaland prefers to buy the beautiful baskets for imparting an ethnic look to their house.

Traditional Ornaments

The Traditional Ornaments of Nagaland are worn by both men and women specially during festive occasions. The ceremonial metallic bell necklace of the tribal people is very famous. A number of small bells are attached to a string. Multi-stranded jewellery is very popular in state. The Classical Naga necklaces that are worn by tribal men and women, often consist of a number of beaded strands. The necklace-ends are completed by wrapped threads, small sheep horns, or knitted string. The hook of the necklace is generally carved into a horn or bone, or a button which is made from a small bead or coin. The Naga warriors pendants are designed in the form of miniature trophy masks in order to symbolise their bravery and courage. Colourful glass beads are generally strung on chords and lightened by coins.

The traditional ornaments are multicoloured with simple designs and very beautiful. A necklace made of coloured beads is generally worn by the natives around the neck. The beads are made from variety of paraphernalia-like stone, bone or shells. They also wear armlets made of ivory or brass. The most common ornaments used by the Nagas are necklaces, earrings, armlets and bracelets. The Naga ornaments are usually designed from ordinary to semi-precious stones, ivory, metals boar's teeth, etc., and are a hallmark of the high degree of creativity and dexterity of Art and Crafts.

Paintings

Cloth painting is a very popular form of painting of Nagaland. The natives belonging to the Lotha, Ao and Rengma tribal communities practice this highly skilled art of painting on clothes. The Ao art of painting is quite similar to that of the Rengmas even though the basic pattern is quite different. The famous warrior shawl of the Ao tribe is painted in white. Only a warrior who has headed a war or performed some feats of merit is allowed to wear this shawl.

On the white median band, figures of various animals like elephant, mithun, tiger, cock and even Dao spear and human heads are painted with black colour. The colours used in these painting are natural colours that are prepared by mixing the sap of a tree, with very strong beer and the ash of the leaves. Fine chiselled bamboo sticks are used in the form of brushes. Sometimes, instead of the ash of Tangko leaves the ash of bamboo leaves are used. This results in the formation of a gray fluid. The old men of the tribes who have perfected this art over the years work on the intricate paintings. They paint the motifs in free hand on the lines of thread. The Rengmas also use the same medium of painting.

The Arts and Crafts of Nagaland are a hallmark of the consummate skill, expertise, talent and creativity of the tribal craftsmen.

Handicrafts

Nagaland's handloom and handicrafts own a reputation for their quality. The beautifully hand woven tribal shawls of various tribes, Naga mekhelas (Sarongs), Naga hand bags, which are exquisitely and intricately designed, have won worldwide appreciation. The new generation of Nagas have ventured into fashion designing on a commercial scale, reproducing fabrics that represent the past, fused with modern taste. They have handicrafts like beads, cearlands and baskets, made of cane and bamboo.

Textile

Textile of Nagaland had always carved a niche for itself in the country. The textile consists of locally spun thread and natural colouring. Every woman is supposed to be skilled in the art of textile making. Textile making is an integral part of their tradition. It has been rooted deeply into the Society and Culture from time immemorial.

The texture of the textile made in the state is different from the fabrics that are woven in the other states of India. The loom, which every house possesses, is a simple tension loom. Weaving, spinning and dyeing have always been the three important industries. The Lothas, Rengmas and Aos grow surplus cotton that they not only met their own requirements but also offered it to the neighbouring tribes.

With the introduction of mill-made yarn, which is easily available and inexpensive, the locally spun thread will face stiff competition, unless and until the Nagas do not find an alternative or if they do not switch over to the modern techniques. There are weaving training and production centres in Mokokchung and Dimapur. Two cottage industries, training and production centres have been set up in Mon and Aghunato.

The textile of Nagaland and the indigenous techniques of spinning and dyeing:

- Technique of Spinning in Nagaland;
- Dyeing Technique of Nagaland;
- Weaving Technique of Nagaland;
- Painting on Cloth in Nagaland;
- Nagaland Symbols and Design on Textiles.

Style of Living

So far as the standard of living of the peoples of Nagaland is concerned, the Naga tribes in general are having a poor standard of living. There are however, inter-regional and intra-regional variations in the standard of living of the rural and urban populations. The undernutrition and malnutrition may be observed among all the tribes of people of Nagaland. Most of the people are having a bare sustenance and during the winter season the quality of food further deteriorates as there is hardly any crop which harvests in the winter months.

Lifestyle

The existing social scenario of any ethnic group, tribe or subtribe or a macro or meso region is the direct outcome of its physical personality, historical processes, economic requirements and social institution. The cultural ethos and social organisation of Nagas are no exception to this. Despite technological advancement and progress under the Five Year Plans, the Nagas are living very close to nature, and the gamut of their life is closely controlled by the prevailing environmental conditions.

Naga tribes have got their own individual and distinctive approach towards life. The mode of life in way indicates that they are backward in culture, religion, and social organisations. Some of the aspects of the Naga life, especially those pertaining to site of settlements, food, clothing, tools, family life, communal life, festivals, dances, games and sources of recreation have been briefly described in the following lines.

The most striking feature of the location of villages and settlements of the entire Naga tribes is their location. Almost all houses, thatched huts are constructed on tops of steep hills or sharp slopes. This practice is not in conformity with the settlements of other tribes of the neighbouring states. For example, the Apatanis of Arunachal Pradesh, the Garos and the Khasis of Meghalaya Plateau prefer to stay close to rivers and roads in the fertile valleys, while the Nagas prefer the hilltops and ridges.

The primary consideration for such a selection of site is the basic need of defence. In the historical past, the Naga Hills were attacked by various outside invaders resulting in the subjugation of original inhabitants. At the same time when the period of comparative peace prevailed, there always occurred inter-tribal and inter-village disputes which in some cases continued for generations. The simple act of clipping off a one metre bamboo stick from the territory of a neighbouring village or accepting of an invitation of a village-headman; and then not attending the feast or function could lead to an inter-village dispute.

In such disputes, after, many heads were lost. The strategic setting of the village settlement was, thus, of utmost importance, which was invariably a place difficult to reach. Under such a situation of permanent enmity, hill tops with steep climbs, giving an all round view of the surrounding areas were the preferred sites. For settlements a ridge with steep gradient and a spur with a steeply-rising slope from which one could observe movements of the enemy were naturally attractive locations from the defence point of view.

Apart from defence, other factors are also taken into consideration before a place for the establishment of a Naga village is finally selected. For example, preference is given to a place which is in the proximity of water springs and has fertile tracts to be brought under Jhuming or terraced cultivation. Since the settlements are developed away from the rivers and streams, the presence of a water spring is a must for providing water for the domestic needs. To fetch water from the rivers at hilltops is time-consuming and cumbersome. Consequently, the Nagas are economic on water. At the occurrence of long rainless intervals, they use the stored water of rains for the domestic and drinking purposes. Consumption of stored water for cooking and drinking is one of the main reasons for the spread of various stomach and skin diseases.

The selection of site for the development of a village settlement is a difficult task which needs logical thinking and careful planning. Before a village site is selected, party of experienced and responsible members would go and stay at the tentatively selected place. They observe and examine if the site is safe and secure from the defence point of view. Subsequently, they study the texture and structure of the soils of the surrounding tracts to ascertain if the land is fertile enough to sustenance the population at a subsistence level. The allotment of land for the construction of houses is done on the basis of first come first serve. Some preference is however, given to the seniority and status of a particular family in the respective social group.

A new village settlement is generally the result of natural growth of population. Other reasons could be insufficient lands, depletion of soil fertility, fire, epidemic disease, or unfriendly relations with the neighbours. From the administrative point of view, a large village is divided into smaller sections locally known as khel. Ungma and Aliba — villages of the Mokakchung district are the typical examples of the rural settlements which have several khels each.

The name of a village is derived either from some peculiarity of the site or from the natural vegetation ground around. The gates of the village in the olden days used to be closed with wooden door hewn of a single piece of wood and ornamented with carved circles. The village fence, which was of wooden stakes, lashed together and bristling with Punji (a number of hardened bamboo spikes with pointed ends imbedded in the ground to obstruct the movement of enemy or entrap the animal) stretched around the village. A village relied mainly on its fence for its safety, advance lines of defence in the form of Punji, filled ditches being only really useful where the ground comes either side of the path fell away so steeply that they could not be outflanked.

A noticeable feature of the Naga house is the way in which variations in structures indicate precisely the status of the owner. The details vary from tribe to tribe and from village to village, but a man with knowledge of the local customs can tell by a glance at a house exactly what feasts of merit the owner has given. The variations are however, confined to the front part of the house and the decorations of the roof. The layout plan of the main structure is always the same.

The main structure of the house consists of a small front room locally known as chin, on the ground level a large main room 'kilung' on piles and at the back a sitting-out platform (Songlang) also on piles. In general the houses vary little in size. The size too, in the crowded villages are so restricted that even if he would, a man cannot expand his house much. An average house measures eight metres by five metres with a platform at the back measuring about four metres long and five metres in width.

The back and the front of the house are generally square and the roof is made of the thatched grass or palm leaves. Planks are not used at all, the walls and the floors of the house being made of strong bamboo matting, save the floor of outer room which is of earth. In this outer room is kept the rice-pounding table (Sumki), bamboos for holding water (Tsushi), spears stuck up by the central post and an add assortment of baskets and other tools. In the middle is a hearth (Atap) furnished with three stones for supporting cooking pots. The roof is always slanting to drain off the water of rains quickly and the ceiling is of bamboo matting.

The simple house which the young man builds at the time of his marriage and hence before he has given any of the feasts of merit which entitle him to add further establishments will serve to illustrate the methods of construction. No particular orientation is favoured. The only rules about the orientation of the house are that a house may not be built exactly opposite to a house across the street. In case this rule is not followed evil spirits and their influence will be wafted out of the door of one house into that one facing it.

Moreover, the front gable of the house should not be lower than that of the neighbours's house opposite otherwise the owner will be subservient to him nor naturally would it be built is higher unless on the same grounds; otherwise it might invite a quarrel with the neighbour. The house must be so constructed that the sun cannot strike directly through the back door on the hearth obviously because it would seem to put the fire out, though no such specific reason is given for the custom.

As stated at the outset there is a marked variation in the construction, design and building material of houses of the different tribes. Houses in southern Nagaland are not Machang structures which were by form a great contrast of the house pattern obtained on the north of the state. The dormitory (Morung) is an exception because there is a raised wooden platform, the floors being lined up with wooden poles and sometimes with planks. In the very exceptional cases on the up-long hill side, the houses stilted are seen, supported by the wooden pillars which are stood erect. The Angamis, Kuki, Zalliangs and Rengmas use truncal posts, pillars, cross-beams and patterns. The roof is thatched where from the gable, the straw is distributed alongside the roof. The thatch is a sort of a typical shrub dried by basking in the sun. The porch however, is provided in certain cases, two layers of roof.

In an indigenous Angami house there are two main compartments with a porch. The porch through which the house is entered contains the pounding materials and a trough where the pigs are fed. The fuel wood and bamboo accessories are also kept there. The porch is further like a weaving shed where women laboriously process out their yarns and work at the loom. There, pigs, cattle and dogs are fed. Cows are tied for shelter at night near or in the porch. An outer room behind it, contains agricultural implements, uplong baskets of paddy, a weaving loom and other accessories. From the roof is seen the poultry baskets suspended on walls where hens laying on their eggs are sheltered at night, poultry being an important part of sacrifice and obsequies. The inner room behind it is a family hall serving a multifarious purpose as a fire place, kitchen, a bed room, and a store room, congested with food stuffs, utensils, earthen wares, bowls, saucers, gourd bottles, etc. Over the hearth, racks are suspended from the roof by which meat is dried by exposing it on the smoke. There is no chimney which makes the house smoke-stained.

An indigenous bed is of solid plank. At a small room on the rear, bears are brewed.

Nails are seldom used in the indigenous house construction as the people have cane robes and creeper plants for that purpose.

Among Rengma, a front room sometimes contain provisions of sleeping arrangements where beds with solid planks are laid. There is an additional hearth in it. The inner room constitutes another family apartment. Advanced people in the village have made out more elaborate partitions. A sleeping place may have been neatly screened or a portion may have been made. There might have been more than one fire place to meet the need of the smaller partitions. In villages, houses roofed with corrugated sheets have substituted thatched buildings at certain places and may have floorings with planks raised from the level of the ground. But many houses though roofed with corrugated sheets, and walled with planks, poles and logs still retain the indigenous form in the village.

Another common feature is the absence of barms where grains are stocked commonly noticed in the Sema, Ao, and Lotha areas. It is only Rengmas in southern Nagaland who have them. They are small sheds raised on poles, fenced with bamboo splits and the roofs are thatched. Such barns are laid out in a group near the village.

The indigenous style of furniture is simple. Hunters adorn their houses with horns, skulls, and beaks of game. They extract the horns, bones, beaks, hairs, hide, and skin and tusks for personal adornment. Beer bamboo mugs, bottle gourds, cane jugs and baskets, platters, saucers, mortars, scooped out of wood, locally made earthen wares, sets of costumes and ornaments, a handloom form universal articles of Naga furniture.

Seat arrangements are small wooden seats of about one to three feet of height standing on two supports. Cane stool (hula) afford seats. But rows of stone blocks scattered alongside the house are used for basking in the sun by the aged persons and for holding entertainment. It is interesting to see a happy folk gathering in the stones sitting and relaxing over them in the sunshine during the winter time.

Ivory-decorated spears, exquisite costumes are among the items used during the past as ceremonial and emissary presents among the Naga states and probably with their neighbours.

A characteristic feature of a wealthy Naga household is the occurrence of two crossed posts protruding from the beams over the porch so that they stretch upwards the roof, they stand as a symbol of wealth when the head of the house has given a party or feast to the village khel or has erected a stone memorial to keep his name alive. The posts at the porch have carvins, representing various animals and other forms of architecture abound on the pillars and walls.

There are several rituals and religious formalities before a new house is constructed. A Naga, after selecting the site for the construction of house, enquires from a 'medicins-man' whether it will be lucky one. The question, the 'medicine man' answers after gazing into a leaf cup of rice beer and enquiring of the spirits. If the answer is favourable the 'Medicine man' is asked to name an old man whose offerings of the customary little sacrifice would be acceptable to the spirits. The man suggested by the 'Medicine man' comes to the site and lays out six little heaps of rice and leaves, six little heaps of rice and ginger and six little leaf cups of rice beer.

Then plucking a fowl of either sex alive, he utters "Let this house site be lucky. Let there be no sickness or illness. Let there be no headache or stomach ache. Let fine boys and girls be born." He then cuts the throat of the fowl with a sharp piece of bamboo and slits its stomach; and from entrails foretells the general fortune of the builder and his bride. The site is then left vacant for three days. If during that time a village pig or jungle cat or other wild animal leaves its dropping on the site then another site must be selected.

When all is ready and the necessary ceremonies have been performed the builder and his friends set to work and generally finish the construction of the house in a day. On the day of marriage the final touches are put to the house by the owner and his formal friends. So far as the street and lane patterns of the Naga villages are concerned, the path running along the top of the ridge becomes the main street. This street at some places is so narrow that the gables of the houses on opposite sides overlap overhead; in others widening out into dancing ground where Mithun are tied up before sacrifice.

The houses are so close together that it is after possible to walk along the backs, stepping from platform to platform. Behind the two rows of houses flanking the main street are other rows, each row facing uphill towards the forest of bamboo poles supporting the platforms of the row in front. Every village has its park lane, usually the street on the top of the ridge where the rich man lives, poor people living in the houses on the slopes on either side, till you come to the squalid little hovels of old widows on the outskirt of the village.

Lower down the slopes, and sufficiently removed the ensure their safety should the village catch fire, are granaries, little miniature houses raised two or three feet above the ground or piles. In one of the open spaces of the villages or khel of a large village, stands a head tree. It is treated with no particular reverence. At the foot of this tree are placed round stones. These stones are brought from the river courses, and are considered as prosperity stones.

The water supply to the village is generally made from springs below the village. The water of this spring is allowed to collect into little ponds. Usually, little efforts are made to keep the water ponds clean, but sometimes they are fenced on all sides to keep out cattle and pigs and roofed over to prevent leaves falling into water. They are redug after every two or three years, a fowl or an egg being offered at that time.

Dress

The male and female dress and their patterns among the different tribes are more or less the same although there are trivial variations in the mode of wearing the dress. The principal dress of man are the kilt and the wrapper, while women have the skirt, shawl, bodice and apron. The female skirt consists of a piece of cloth about one and a half metre long and about half a metre in width, wrapped around the waist. The colours of dresses and skirts vary from tribe to tribe and it is very difficult to describe all the varieties. Generally, the women wear Tsotzgtem (Puttees) which are sometimes worn. Many old women always wear a pair of warmth, but at dance young and old alike often wear them as part of their full dress. Naga cloth of indigenous weaving are coarse, thick and durable and therefore congenial for the cold weather. They are woven of yarn although cotton cloths are used as bodice, aprons, under wears and other minor garments.

The Naga men wear Lengta. The Lengta consists of a strip of blue or white cloth some four feet long and ten inches wide with a pattern at one end. Boys, till they are five or six years old wear nothing. They are then given a little 'Dao' and 'Dao-Belt'. But from nine years in most villages they wear a Lengta, 'like a grown-up man.

In wet weather men wear slung over their backs rain shield made of thatching-palm or pandanus leaves. The Pandanas leaves are plucked and dried and are then boiled and sewn edge to edge with cane. Women wear large Shan hats. Men of position have their kilt decorated with two or three lines of cowries striped along its length and hemmed on the two uplong borders. They use a belt also for fastening it. A wrapper, suspended from a shoulder is worn outside a typical shirt or jacket but the latter is not a compulsory dress item.

A women's skirt is a sheet of cloth by rolling it along the waist which loops down to cover the legs. A bodice covers the breast. An apron is worn by fastening either on both the sides of the collarbone or one end is fastened along one side and the other is suspended below an armpit. This dress often keeps the hands bare but they girdle a shawl by suspending it from one of the shoulders. A ceremonial costume of Naga women may have multifarious colours.

Weaving and colour combination art differs from tribe to tribe, but the dress pattern is intrinsically the same. Many of the clothes are striped on the corners of their width and entire length; the stripes run parallel, but sometimes introverted with geometrical designs and embroideries within the stripes or outside. Each tribe have their own tastes of embroidery, zigzag, horizontal and geometrical patterns. Stripes are generally of different colours from the main background of the cloth. The ceremonial costumes have more complex colour formations on deeper linings.

Every Naga tribe has its own favourite colour. For example, the Angami's loin cloth is of a dark blue colour embroidered with cowries while those of Semas and Lothas is a combination of white and blue. The Aos are fond of red and blue colours and the Sangtam prefer embroidery word.

Many tribes wear feathers and skins of many birds and animals on their hats. The Aos in their ceremonial dress with their spears, wrapped in coloured hair and bows, arrows, swords and shields decorated in all combinations of primitive paints take great pride in their dances and songs. The young boys and girls dressed in their best often listen to their various mythological stories and battle scenes.

Dress without ornaments are incomplete. Nagas are very much fond of wearing ornaments. Skull cap of bear skin, red goats, hairs, broad circlets of bear's hairs are among the ceremonial wearings. The old custom was that a man was entitled to wear two horn bill feathers for each occasion on which he got first spear into an enemy, one for each successful raid in which he took part and one for each time he did the Mithun sacrifices. Nowadays he can wear three horn bill feathers as soon as he has bought the right to wear a warriors ornaments can add one for each Mithun sacrifice he performs.

Ornaments in profusion which men wear are derived from metals, bones, cowries, shells, cane, leather, orchids and wood. Neck ornaments are strings of beeds, shells, stones boar's tusks and horns. An opaque red stone serving as a necklace suspended by a thread on cane string is highly prized. A conch-shell worn with a chain of beads implies social status. An ivory gauntlet is a valuable ornament, leggings are blue-dyed cane rings. Women's ornaments are earrings, wristlets and bracelets of brass or copper, but sometimes of copper, lead or silver. They use copper earrings. Again ladies have their necklace, bracelets and an opaque red stone as a set of their ornamental dress while beads introverted with pieces of buffalo's horns are also the highly-valued neck ornaments. Aesthetic as they are, both male and female use further personal decorations of wild flowers.

Dancing dress is yet more colourful. Man's head-dress is a coronet of horn bill feathers, circle in shape, the feather positioning a convex canopy frame. However, these coronets vary in form according to the status of the wearer. 'They are fastened at the head by the white cotton robes, held out by a circular shingle. Ceremonial male body garments differ from tribe to tribe and place to place.

The hand-woven sashes or baldrics of mixed hues are worn as scarves which, wide enough, crossing on the chest, cover the body but make the arms bare. They may have been worn over a sleeveless jacket or ganji or a shirt. On the breast, badges especially made of cow's tail introverted with animals' hairs neatly polished are also worn. Among Chakesang an apron' suspended from the collar bone replaces the baldric, the apron looping down is enfolded at a waist forming a kilt below. Sometimes they substitute the feather's bonnet by a tight conical cane helmet which topmost fringes are decked with red-dyed small feathers; in other places they use horns in place of coronets, may be rhino, buffalo or Mithun type. Neck ornaments are sometimes introverted by twigs of hair or pieces of horns. Sometimes necklets are of a bone dyed with a bamboo decoration but with strings of red yellow and other colours and a pendant of conch-shell.

In the urban areas although scarves and blouses of modern designs are used as supplementary dress items of mill-made fabrics, ladies still keep intact their original skirts woven locally. In the urban places, men have used modern dress patterns although they still love to suspend from the shoulder their age-old mantle which shelters them from cold. In several schools shawls have been adopted as school uniform. In fact primitive, indigenous and modern dresses go side by side which provide a spectrum of the vast change. The Nagas wear a typical raincoat, covering the body in convex woven of the very soft, neatly polished fibres probably made of a sapper but the cancave is straw, the same type being used for the thatching roofs of houses sewn layer upon layer. It is rain-proof. There is also a rain-hat made of fibres suspended by a string. Both men and women use this type of rain shade at the time of various agricultural operations.

The ears of some of the male Nagas are pierced in three places. Ornaments and feathers are worn in the ears by the males, while the females normally wear brass rings. At the time of dance they wear brass chain, one horn bill feather at their heads, strings of beads, necklace of beads, conch-shells and alloy ornaments. The traditional dresses are being replaced by modern dresses. Many have given up their traditional shawls and the teenagers may be seen in slacks and jeans.

Food

Almost all the Naga tribes are carnivorous. They are ferocious eaters and relish meat for which reason domesticated animals are kept both for food and sacrifices. Excepting food that is forbidden the Nagas may eat almost everything. Rice is the staple food. Rice is eaten twice a day with fish, pork, mutton, vegetables and if he can obtain nothing else he contents himself with chillies, salt and jungle leaves. Beef, pork, game, dogs, fowls, birds, fish, crabs, beetles, spiders are eaten. Meat is preferred fresh but an animals long dead is by no means despised.

They appreciate the smell of dried fish very much. Meat and skin are often half-dried over the fire and will then be kept for a considerable time. A Chang Naga will boil and eat his shield when it goes old, having first soaked it to get rid of the dressing. The whole of an animal including the skin, blood, intestines and even the eyes are invariably eaten. Nothing much except the hair and bones is thrown away. Many a time the Nagas made raids in the Assam Valley to steal dogs.

Dog's meat could be a speciality and among certain tribes the flesh of a black dog is a delicacy. Eggs and hens are generally consumed during the innumerable ceremonies. During very important ceremonies, however, Mithuns, pigs, cows and goats are hacked or killed after they had been made to undergo an infinite number of sufferings. At the same time killing and eating of certain animals, fish and birds is a taboo among certain Naga tribes.

Nagas generally do not eat tiger, leopard, gibbon, wild dog, wild cat, civet, flying squirrel, bat, mole, eagles, hawk, owl, nightjar, crow, spotted dove, snakes, bull frog, and newt. Most of them refrain from pig's stomach, bamboo rat, frogs and crabs. Naga women generally do not like elephant, goat, bear, monkey, scaly anteater, fowls and their eggs, mud fish, locusts, white-ants and the kill of any wild beast.

Milk and milk products are considered as a taboo in some of the Naga tribes and it is because of this reason that Mithuns are not milched. Thus milk and its products are considered as impure foods. In the opinion of Scrrias "If we are going to eat the flesh of animal, why should we milk it." Butter, curd, butter-milk and cheese had never been known to some of the tribes.

Very old people, young boys and girls (before they tattooed) can eat anything they like, as they are hardly reckoned as the full members of the community. But if anyone else eats a forbidden food he or she falls ill.

Slices of meat with entrails of animals slain are dried by suspending on kitchen racks, meant for longer preservation. Fish both fresh and dried is taken.

By quantities of fish dried towards the interior villages are rather negligible, so that there are more imports from outside. Pork, beef, chicken, fish and mutton are prepared into various curries both in the indigenous and modern system. Meaty soups boiled with vegetables or herbs are the favourite traditional dishes taken with meals. They relish cooked, smoked and broiled meat. Games including wild animals, birds and fowls are all taken. Beers, deer, hares, rhinos, elephants, boars indeed almost all the available species are taken.

Bamboo shoots are prepared into vegetable curry is a favourite dish. Kachu and other vegetable herbs are common. Condiments prepared with wild vegetable salad and tuber roots are used. Dals (pulses) with the local pulse, and Til are rich. Generally they prefer hot tastes with chillies. Chutneys of beans, chillies, a bit of meat or fish paste are refreshing. Vegetables recently adopted have supplemented the indigenous ones.

Of the modern beverages adopted widely, tea is more relished. Tarnuls (arecanuts) and pans (betel-vines) though for the past, confined largely to the north as a social customary practice, have also been taken to the south. The dietary system of the urban dwellers is however, changing fast.

Nagas prefer to drink Madhu, also known as Yi, Pitha and Rohl. The Naga system of fermentation is everywhere almost the same. To prepare Madhu rice, maize or millets are boiled for about half an hour and then kept for cooling after which some indigenous fermenting material prepared from the local herbs is added. These contents are enclosed in some baskets or leaves and allowed to ferment for a few days. After fermentation the contents are poured into bamboo or cane tubes or waterproof baskets made of bamboo and a little quantity of water is added to it. After two to four days the mixture is ready for drinking. The rice beer so made must be consumed on the same day otherwise it may get spoiled. The fermented mixture, however, could be retained for a number of days in a covered container.

In the southern parts of Nagaland Rohi and Pitha are the special drinks. In the preparation of Kohi, rice first is cooked in a vessel and the rice thoroughly boiled is spread over or heat for sometime. Then the powdered yeast is mixed with the cooked rice. This being over, the preparation is exposed for about one hour or so before it is laid down in a basket, the latter being lined up within with layers of plantain leaves, the mouth thoroughly shut. The basket is again kept in a warm cloth before it is removed to a cold and shaded place.

Thus after two-three days, it is stained to another vessel by a cane net or a bamboo tube. It needs more fermentive power usually twice of quantity of that applied in the case of Pitha. And thus it becomes a strong liquor. Yeast is not the only fermentive agent, but sprout paddy ears (when thoroughly dried and powdered) and even certain wild berries are used. Crops comprising rice, millets, maize, job's tears are all brewed but rice is the beat. Rengma, Chakhesang and Zeliangroung use the common type of Rohl and Pitha but as regards to details in the methods of squeezing the liquid. Keeping of preparation, staining devices, there are minor differences.

Drink is a tribal way of entertainment. A weary traveller finds it welcome for quenching his thirst in a scorching heat and similarly for warming in the cold weather. Ceremonies cannot become complete without pouring of libations, a festival drink is a must at festive banquets, and arduous works and physical exertions are undertaken with its help. Tribal beers are said to be nutritious enough as they contain large proportions of proteins and vitamins. But intoxicating drinks have an evil in spoiling individual and national character; it has been found that extravagant addiction has put to waste many great talents which if, on the contrary properly channelised, could have been of great use to the community.

Tea is a popularly consumed beverage. But since sugar is an expensive commodity and cows are not milked, tea is generally taken without milk and sugar. Kowai (raw bettlenut) consumption is universal in Nagaland.

In the moist and cold weather conditions of Nagaland it gives additional heat to the body. Tobacco smoking in pipe is also universal among all the Naga tribes. It is quite popular with women, more so with the old ones. The local tobacco is quite strong which the Nagas consider the best and consumed in large quantities. Many Nagas also smoke opium in their long pipes. They produce their poppy seeds in spite of the fact that the government had been trying to discourage its cultivation.

Feasts of Merit

The Naga tribes are quite gay type and they enjoy every opportunity of achievement. For every success and achievement the Nagas arrange parties and feasts. The successful sowing, harvesting, in Jhuming, marriages, childbirth and death of a person in the family, Khel or village are celebrated. On such ceremonial occasions, parties, dances, music concerts, games, sports and feasts are arranged. Feast to the villagers are also given to achieve some distinctive status in the community and the society.

The Nagas are very conscientious of their social status. A well-off Naga is never satisfied with a large holding, a bumper crop, a rich wealth of cattle unless his distinct social status is recognised. For achieving this distinction the rich Naga first has to achieve the blessings of the village priest and the village elders, after that he selects two huge monoliths in the forest which would be planted at the cross-road of the village to mark his distinction. It is a fortnight-long festival during which the host Naga gives feast to the entire village with favourite and especial dishes including meat and Madhu. No one is allowed to go without food even for a single time in the village.

During the period of feast the host has not only to abstain from the use of meat and liquor but should also remain Genna. On the first day two Mithuns of male gender are tethered with the supporting pillars of the house. The elder of the family fondles one of the Mithuns for sometime and suddenly pierce a sharp-edged pointed bamboo stick through the heart of the animal. Simultaneously another person performs a similar act with the other animal. The animals are thus sacrificed. The host gets the horn and hind-legs while rest of the beef is cooked for feast.

Before the food is served the village priest is invited to initiate the feast. The host offers him Madhu in a leaf bowl. The priest sips the Madhu and utters "May God shower prosperity on you. You may have bumper rice crop, your rice been containers be not exhausted ever and may all the members of your family always be in good health. "Then starts the community feast for which four or five Mithuns, some buffaloes, pigs and several dozen of chickens are slaughtered.

After the procession of about fifty young men proceed towards the jungle to fetch the stones. The Genna host, his wife, the village priest and village elders lead the silent procession. On reaching the youth to the monoliths in cane fibre woven ropes and drag the boulders to the selected site where the monoliths are to be installed. The host offers the blood of the sacrificed animal to the stone, while freshly-brewed rice beer is offered by his wife.

The young men beat drum and start dancing. Once this ceremony is over the host is permitted to attach the horn symbol to his residence. Now onwards he earns the right to sit with the socially distinct personalities of the community. The person who hosts the feast of distinction gives the second third and fourth feasts after intervals of two to three years. On each occasion the entire village is served with meat, beef, pork and rice beer. The fourth feast known as Tsumatsu concludes the series of feast of merit.

Tool and Weapons

The armoury of Nagas is simple. The main weapons of attack are Dace and spear. Cross bows are mainly used for hunting rather than for war. Dao is the companion of a Naga throughout his life. The trees are fell with it and the forests are cleared with it. In the past he used to cut the head of his enemy with it. The second important weapon is spear.

The spear is generally taller than their own bodies. The spear can be used either for throwing or for thrusting. Made of wood, the spear has an iron point at the end of a sharp little blade. It varies in design and can be painted at either end. The spears of Aos, Anganis and Seynas are most colourful, leaving the points and a six inch portion for holding the spear, the entire length of the spears in muffed up in some animal's hairs in bands of different colours. With the hair many spears of different patterns are made. It is an exquisite piece of art, the colour combination always conveys a very high degree of aesthetic sense. Thus even though the weapon of war, the Nagas give expression of their artistic urges.

The other weapon for use at long distance is the bow and arrow. Made out of bamboo, it has many varieties, but generally the components are the same. A hardened bamboo and string are used for the bow. The arrows are very effective with pointed or iron heads. Occasionally, the arrows are accurately balanced by fixing a few leaves or feathers in the slit at the rear ends.

The arrows are made still more dangerous by applying some local poison at the point heads. This poison is so lethal as to kill a person within forty-five minutes after the arrow punctured the body. In some cases it took many hours for the case to prove fatal. At the same time life could be saved if the arrow is pulled out quickly and the ruptured portion of the body thoroughly cleaned. These days the Naga hunters also use. 22" rifle for killing the animals. The locally manufactured muzzle loaders are quite popular in the north and eastern parts of Nagaland. Swords are rarely used as its place has been taken by Ira o.

The defensive weapons of the Nagas are shields and helmets. The shield is a sheet of hide, an oblong rectangular shape. The hide in the concave position is nicely bounded to a bamboo support at the convex. Plumes also crown the shield decorated with white cowries. The hide is tiger's, or leopard's or elephant's or bear's. Shields scooped of wood or made of steel were not used in the Angani and Sema tribes as they are being used by the Aos, Lothas and Konyaks. The shields are generally made of bamboo and leather. They can be straight, concave, or bent along the central axis like a slopping roof. A few of the shields are covered with hide for greater protection. The helmets are made out of cane peelings and sometimes reinforced with bamboo or cane stripes.

Head Hunting

The practice of head hunting was prevalent in the past among the Naga tribes and for the last about fifty years not even a single case of head-hunting has been reported in Nagaland. Head hunting often used to be associated with the Naga warriors. The modern youths of Naga tribes are enlightened and they hate the word 'head hunting'.

The origin of the practice of head hunting is a matter of great controversy. According to the opinion of some of the anthropologists, the practice of head hunting originated from the superstition that the increase in soul matter led to agricultural prosperity and rise in population. According to these experts, it was the belief of the Nagas that soul lies in the head of a male or female. When a head hunter beheads a human being and takes the head to his village, it is believed that the soul would also be transferred to that village and would consequently bring prosperity to the people of the village. The Ibaris of Borneo, the Was of Burma and the Kagoros of Nigeria are still notorious for this game. In Europe also some of the primitive tribes dwelling in the Balkans carried on head hunting till the early years of the present century. Human sacrifice still heard in many parts of India in fact, in a degenerated form of head-hunting.

Up to 1940 head-hunting had been a very popular game of the Nagas. Though officially it is claimed that this detested game had been brought to an end long ago, yet it is possible that some of the remote and far-flung areas like Tuensang, the Konyaks carry on this practice. Apart from the collection of Aren (soul), head-hunting has been practised for displaying power and strength on many frivolous grounds among the Nagas. The refusal to pay the agreed price of the bride, shelter or culprit, insult to a village, abduction of a woman, trapping animals and cutting of grass in areas not belonging to one's own territory, acceptance of a challenge and the exuberant desire of the young men to prove their manhood their beloveds and wives are some of the provocations that led to head-hunting. Increase in population in the hilly region with poor resource base of the Naga hills might also have been the reason of the head-hunting so that the ecological balance is maintained.

The unhappy feature of this hateful practice has been indiscriminate chopping of heads. The women, children, old, weak and infirm have been the unlucky victims who obviously could not resist the ferocious invaders. As a matter of fact, a women's head was considered as a more prized trophy. This was for a variety of reasons. Women were given the maximum protections by the village folk; and taking a women's head meant penetration deep into enemies ranks, with all its concomitant risks. Possibly there was also the desire to reduce the enemy population by killing their women folk. Yet another reason could be the desire for women's hair was used for ornamental purposes. Many a time some community perform this act to prove their superiority.

In the year 1962, a messenger of Pangsha village (inhabited by Khunnuggan Nagas) was slain by the people of Neklak village. The Kalu Konyaks of Pangsha village announced to the beat of the drum that they will raid Neklak village and prove their strength. The date and time were announced. On the appointed day a huge procession of men, women and children marched to Pangsha. The men were made to drink by women and the children were excited to see the sight.

Many of them were enthusiastic to receive the initiation in the game. On the outskirt of the Neklak village women and children stopped, while men dancing, yelling and laughing entered the village with their Daos which had been sharpened by their women folk. The raiders collected forty-five heads mostly of children, women, old and physically handicapped people who could not escape to the jungle. The village was burnt to ashes. The invaders came back. The invaders came back with their trophies.

They were greeted with shouts of joys and jubilation by the waiting women and children. Every married woman offered more beer to her victorious husband. The bravery of the heroes was judged by the number of heads they had slained. The unmarried girls entertained the distinguished youths and many marriages were settled on that fateful day. Back in their village, the victory was celebrated for three days. The youth entering into adulthood were initiated into the game. They were given a Dao and make to strike the heads from the first to the last, and the performance of this formal ceremony listed them among the future head hunters in the community. The raiders were not satisfied and desired to reap a still more rich harvest of heads. The Neklak villagers were thus frightened. They ultimately yielded and sent apologies to Pangsha, recognising their superiority in the area.

The raids for head-hunting requires careful planning. Information is gathered regarding the enemy's strength, defence disposition, obstacles, and routes for escape. Intensive military training is imparted to the youths. The entire operation used to be put under the command of a warrior whose bravery and valour had already been put to test. Sometimes a number of villages pooled their manpower and force against a common enemy, and all these men acted under one leader who was responsible for this operation.

Certain ceremonies were used to be performed before a head-hunting operation was made. Some fowls were sacrificed and eggs were broken to find out if the omens were good. If the results gave negative indications, the raids were postponed. The execution was the most exciting affair. Raiding parties had sometimes travelled even beyond a hundred miles to avenge the enemy. An attack at dawn is generally preferred though raids at other times were not uncommon. A village could be surrounded from all sides or from two or three sides, depending on the topographic conditions. When the aim was to avenge an enemy, their entire village could be set on fire. Many were caught unaware before the flames leaped out, those who tried to escape were put to death by spears or hacked by Dao. Arrows especially with poisoned points were very popular and a warrior who used such arrows was not expected to miss the target. Sometimes the granaries were spared. It is reported that the prisoners of war were seldom taken and it was a matter of great shame to anyone to fall alive into the hands of the enemy. The prisoners on some occasions were sold to the richer strata of the community and there had been cases when the slaves were murdered in cold blood to quench the thirst of the skull-hungry master who while sitting in their huts wanted to swell there treasure of skulls with the aid of their wealth. The slaves could be sold and resold time and again. The slaves generally reconciled with their position and made no frantic attempt to escape.

When a raid is made for head-hunting the old and weaker people were swallowed by the fire before they could step out the doors. The young warriors while resisting, either fell fighting or killed a few of the enemies. The picture was that of a chaos, many men and women, lying scattered, burnt houses and deserted villages. With their booty, the heads with blood trickling down from the slashed portions, the attackers returned home triumphantly hoping to earn a name and win the affections of the beautiful girls of the village. It was a matter of pride for any young maid to be the wife of one who had gained maximum human heads.

The tradition of head-hunting, though barbaric, fulfils the basic human aspiration of standing superior to others. In an underdeveloped land there are very few other means of attaining the status of an overlord. Every community or nation tries to fulfil this inherent desire of moving a step further than the surrounding neighbours, militarily, politically, economically, culturally and even in the field of religion. But in the case of Nagas these forces are every weak or not properly developed and a substitute has to be found.

Also to gaps in the above aspects of life, energies of people had to be directed to some other sphere. The shape of this new sphere of activity depends on the background of the community, their actual heritage and the prevailing conditions of terrain, climate, weather, plus the nature and stage of development of the surrounding communities. The Nagas kept themselves in perpetual preparedness for any military engagement. Also their social institutions, community life and other religious ceremonies did not remain uninfluenced by the honour and the privileged position which a head hunter earned. This very art which was a source of inspiration has now gradually come to a dead end, which has brought peace to the people.

Throughout the pre-Independence history of Naga tribes, the main concern of the Nagas was to slay and avoid getting slain. The entire life of an individual, his family and his village evolved around this. It is not just a matter of pleasing themselves with physical achievements, it combines the spiritual satisfaction with the abstract supposition of fertility and of a happy future in the world of the dead. This practice though harmful for the peace of the land and though barbaric, fulfils the basic human aspiration of standing superior to others.

In an underdeveloped land, there are very few other means of attaining the status of an overlord. Every community or nation tries to fulfil this inherent devise of moving a step further than the surrounding neighbours, unitarily, politically, economically, culturally, and even in the field of religion. But in the case of Nagas these forces are very weak or not properly developed and a substitute had to be found. Also due to gaps in the above aspects of life energies of the people had to be directed to some other sphere. The shape of time new sphere of activity depends on the background of the community, their heritage, and local physical environmental conditions and the stage of development of the surrounding communities. The end of head-hunting has brought many blessings to the people, the greatest one being peace.

Health Care

The Nagas when they feel ill usually do nothing or consult a 'medicine man' as to what sacrifice they ought to offer. They had small faith in modern medicines. 'Any medicine of which the first dose does not have an immediate effect he regards as useless. He will neglect an ulcer for months and only come to hospital when his life has become a misery. He then expects to be cured in a few days. Just as illness, according to his ideas, comes upon him suddenly through the agency of an evil spirit, so, he thinks, will be instantaneously cured when the evil spirit is duly appeased.

Now the situation has changed. The educated and forward looking Nagas are no longer superstitious about the modern medicines. This change in attitudes occurred mainly after the Missionary work.

In fact, public health started with the opening of a charitable dispensary at Chumukedima which in 1875 was declared ' to have attained a popularity with the local population. In 1878-79, about 450 outdoor and 152 indoor patients were receiving treatment in it. In this connection, it may be worth-noting to recall Mr. Cooper, renowned for his proficiency in handling delivery cases. Mr. Cooper won the admiration and love of many Nagas who paid him glowing tributes as the father of public health in their country. In 1905-06, it was reported that the dispensary at Kohima was ten-bedded while Wokha was four-bedded. But the hospital (when upgraded from dispensary) at Kohima was running short of surgical apparatus while Wokha and Mokokchung dispensaries were hard-pressed with accommodation problems. Another dispensary was opened at Henima in 1906-07 while a hospital camp was also set up at Piphema.

During the Japanese invasion (Second World War) hospital camps were scattered all over the district in the charge of both military and civilian doctors for extending medical relief to the wounded soldiers and sick evacuees.

Vital statistics have not been available as regards birth and death rates owing to the disturbances which raged the district from 1955 to 1964. As early as 1905-06, Allen wrote thus "In the absence of all statistics it is difficult to say whether the death rate is high or not. The Nagas do not increase rapidly in numbers, but this may possibly due more to a low birth rate than to a high mortality. Hutton, J. H. is of the opinion that the occupants of Naga house seldom exceed five in number.

A man and his wife perhaps with two or three children, perhaps an aged and widowed parent, perhaps a younger brother still unmarried — such is the usual family. Children are not numerous, and owing to a high death rate among infants, it is exception to see more than three children to a family. There is no denying the fact that in the hills the birthrate is low which accounts for a poorer rate of density of population in the plains.

Men of Medicine

Medicine men may be a male or a female. A female, however cannot be a priest. A medicine man will say what sacrifice is necessary in a certain case, but a priest or a private person acting temporarily as a priest, offers it. The medicine men are called to deal with the abnormal situations and cases. A medicine man is also known as 'extractor of dirt' and refer to their pretended power of sucking out of man's body bits of stones or wood, or lumps of hair or whatever may be causing pain. The part of the body where the 'dirt' is supposed to be has first to be rubbed with wild mint and is then massaged and sucked. The powers which a Naga 'medicine-man' mostly advertises are those of taking omens by certain methods, travelling to the next world either in a trance or in a dream, or even taking with spirits in his walking state.

The usual method of bringing on the trance state is to gaze into a leaf-cup of Wadhu'. The 'medicine man' falls back unconscious and his muscles become more or less rigid. After a time he is brought to by his friends; a kind of wild mint is put on his ears, his nose and the top of his head, and his arms and legs are rubbed with it; some of the powdered leaf is blown up his nose. On recovering consciousness he describes his journey to the patient's soul which lives in the sky-world.

The first sign that a person is endowed with the powers of a 'medicine man' is a tendency for him or her to talk incoherently and converse with spirits, especially at the new or full moon.

Diseases

Up to 1900 there were reports of the incidence of epidemics such as smallpox, fever, cholera, and anthrax. Most of the disease originated in the foothill areas and in the valleys with their insalubrious climate. Sometimes disease were spread by contagions from the plains. For instance, up to the Second World War, malaria was described to be endemic in Dimapur area and around and was very much feared. But it subsided when the soldiers cleared the swamps and marshes by heavy counter-medical operations. But malaria still survives elsewhere.

The lower hills have more incidence of smallpox, dysentery, cholera, malarial fever ad influenza with regard Chumukedima and Dimapur areas, frequently reported in the Dimapur Hospital. Pneumonia, anthrax, chicken pox, measles, dysentery and enteric fever are the other cases reported in the hills. Sometimes such diseases cause high infant mortality rate. Goitre and veneral disease are not so common in Nagaland. Malarial fever and lung disease before the First World War caused considerable proportion of the total casualties but the large number of deaths was caused too by measles and influenza. Other ailments in Nagaland comprise of black water fever, respiratory, stomach, eye and ear disease, inflammation and ulceration, and tuberculosis. But such cases are not too many. Among other disease, leprosy has more occurrence in the southern tribes of Nagaland.

The Kohima Hospital also known as Naga Hospital, are treated cases comprising anaemia, bronchitis, broncho-pneumonia, fever, malaria, pulmonary tuberculosis, tuberculosis on other organs, joints and bones, typhoid, fever, infective hepatitis, diarrhoea, and dysentery, intestinal parasites, eye and dental disease, injuries, skin disease, goitre and others. Such diseases have become more perceptible perhaps due to the growth of population.

Standard of Sanitation

Health services are being appreciated amongst the village people day-by-day. Medical sciences attained popularity as early as 1875, from which date, the local people were taking themselves to vaccination rapidly as safeguards against epidemics. In 1902-03, it was reported that 76 persons per mile of the population were successfully vaccinated every year from 1897. But sanitary conditions have not been improved in the villages unless their living conditions are ameliorated. Some villages are heavily congested with houses which have no compounds and no proper ventilation system. Villages have no adequate latrine provisions. In 1961-62, a team of personnel comprising rural health inspector, sanitary inspectors and vaccinators was constituted to promote better sanitary conditions amongst the mass of village people.

Hospitals

Foremost among the present hospitals is the Kohima Civil Hospital generally known as the Naga Hospital. It is the gift of the government to the Nagas of the district in recognition of their assistance and cooperation with the allies in the defence of India from the Japanese. It is situated on a hill side at the town's exit on Dimapur National Highway. The hospital is well equipped and is one of the standard institutions inside the state. The hospital is in the charge of Civil Surgeon. Major and minor operations are conducted and some cases are brought from other medical institutions. The hospital has residential buildings for the staff.

A new Tuberculosis Hospital was opened in 1969 is situated at Khuzuma on Manipur border. It has a capacity of one hundred beds. There is no denying the fact that health services have made enormous progress. There is at least one good hospital and several dispensaries at Mokokchung, Phak, Zunheboto, Mon, Tuensang and Wokha. Under the present pattern arrangements have been made that one medical unit covers 40 sq km and one bed covers about 450 persons.

Nature of Health Services

The programmes mainly include promotion of health by opening hospitals, dispensaries and primary health centres which total 30, 92, and eight respectively in March 1988. Schemes have been laid down to promote training of medical personnel outside. Moreover, national programmes such as eradication of malaria, tuberculosis, small pox and leprosy have been taken up, the efforts which have received appreciation everywhere. The response is gratifying, for the public have been extending cooperation in the construction of hospital buildings and lands for building have been acquired, free of cost, from village people. The fullest use of medical advice has been taken up by the people and medical services have been highly appreciated.

Emphasis should further be laid on the implementation of health drive programmes of small pox and malaria eradication schemes and BCG vaccination campaigns. The National Malaria Education and Smallpox Eradication and BCG Programmes have been launched in the state.

In addition Leprosy centre was opened in the District in 1966-67, the team investigating and taking up leprosy cases. Moreover, the District School Health

Advisory Board has been constituted to assess physical fitness of student community and ameliorate health conditions.

Major Festivals

Nagas have a number of festivals and numerous occasion of communal dances. Naga festivals aim at fertility corresponding to the different agricultural seasons. The festivals among all the tribes are similar to each other and rest upon a common background of beliefs. The simple, sturdy and industrious Nagas celebrate their festival with great festivity and jubilation. On the occasions of fairs and festivals special prayers are made to express their gratitude to the supreme power. Some of the occasions are also remindful of the events and incidents found their legends. Below are some of the typical instances of festivals.

Angami Festivals

Tsiekanyi: A seed sowing festival, observed annually in the month of Keno (February), while anterior to it, no sowing of seed is done by any household. Two days Ganna (a ceremonial household observation in which no work is done) is observed in which a first sower (Tsikrau) neither joins any feasts and drinks offered by his neighbours, nor touches any insect, as if that were done, the crops are liable to destruction by pests. During the village Pennie (suspension of business) two days long, each household partake in the feast prepared for Mithuns, pigs and other animals and the home-made beers. The Genna being over, the people then are free to sow the seed in the field.

Ngonyi is another important festival performed during the month of Kera (April) at the close of the seed sowing observance. It is five-day long with which the entire village celebrates the strict Pewrie. Each household has plenty of boiled meat and rice beers to take. Kerunnyi which falls during the month of Kechu (May). The ceremony conforms to the transplantation system of paddy seedlings in the terraced fields. It is two-day long Pennie. Feasts are not at lavish scale as during the other festivals.

Tsunyi A. millet harvest festival after Tsu which means millet and Anyi which means festival. It falls either during the last part of July or the first part of August. It is a two-day long Pennie.

Theyuukhupfu falls during the month of August. It is a children's festival when all the children exchange cooked meat among themselves. This is also known as 'giving the toad his rice festival'. The festival rests round a story which suggests that at the beginning of time, a man, a mouse, and a toad who were bosom friends found out rice which they managed to distribute. But the mouse finding it difficult to carry the rice, requested the man that she may be allowed to eat it in the corner of his field.

The toad refused to take any rice but prayed man that it (the toad) may be offered rice once a year in its name, hence the festival of giving the toad its rice. It is interesting to note that when the festival opens, a mother in the household performs a special rice-giving ceremony by giving a little rice wrapped in the plantain leaf saying 'take your share, toad and place it somewhere under the bed'. The Genna lasts for four days.

Chandanyi: A path-clearing festival observed during the month of Chadi (July) and five day long. On this occasion all the village paths and grave yards are cleared; the people are not allowed to have any intercourse with strangers.

Thekenyi: It is two-day long Genna. On the first day Liedfu Lied, a woman reaper goes to the field and cuts a few heads, she will tie the stumps of rice (hays) and have a piece of mud, worm-cast pasted on them. At home she has brought them, she opens her month to taste. This ceremony marks the opening of the harvest. Next day is Mechu Lied (Mechu = public) and Pennie (holiday) for every one, and on the following day it is open to every one in the village to reap as he pleases.

Liekhwenyi: This festival centres round the reaping of Theke, a species of Ahu paddy which thrives in the Jhun fields. It is a five-day Genna when on the first two days, household festivals are held with a meat of slain animals and rice-beer. But the three days which follow are spent in clearing the village paths leading to the field.

Vate or Tekede or Kava Kete

This festival centres round the preservation of grains. Grains recently reaped are cooked, women taste the food in the leaf plates and distribute it from the baskets, and not from pans. Meat is forbidden, but they go on rice and Dal (pulse) made of beans only.

Terhunyi: This festival is celebrated to please the spirit Tehro-nyi. The legend goes: One day while returning from field a Tehroma (spirit) called *Ziesuo* followed her (a woman) and put his hands over her eyes from behind.

The women asked him to go away but Ziesuo refused to let her go until she promised him her daughter in marriage. She promised and got her released but saw no one. A few days later the same thing happened again, and again she promised, and went home with a sad heart. One day her daughter went to the field with her companions, and as she was coming home she lagged behind the others. Suddenly Ziesuo caught hold of her and took her to his home and she lived with him as his wife.

"After sometime she came to her mother and said that her husband was very handsome and a wealthy man; she asked her mother to come with her and ask of him whatever she wanted, and she would receive it. She advised her mother to ask a small basket hanging on the right corner of the middle room, in which all kinds of animals are kept. They took some husks of rice and set out for the daughter's house, dropping husks along the road for fear of old woman's losing her way home again.

"Staying some days with her son in law, the old woman said she must go home. Then Zeisuo said to his mother-in-law to ask for anything she liked. The old woman answered that she liked many things but since she could not carry it she would only ask the little basket hanging in the right side of the room to keep her heart in. This troubled Zeisuo and he requested her mother-in-law to ask something else. But the old woman stuck to her request by saying that she could not carry heavy things. So Zeisuo had to give her but requested her not to open the basket until she reached home. He further advised her to shut the door when she opened that basket and not to go out for five days.

"So the old woman started home with the basket. But about the middle of the way the old woman found the basket heavy, and herself longing to open it. When she opened, behold, animals of every kind, every sort of beast and those which were able to fly or run swiftly came forth and fled, and those unable to get away were again shut in by the old woman. Then she came to her house, shut the door and opened the basket and found the domesticated animals which she kept then in the house with the door shut for five days and they all became tame.

"Next year the daughter and the son-in-law came to visit her and found her house filled with domestic animals. Zeisuo asked his mother-in-law to kill some fat bulls and eat them in his name. And so this festival is kept every year and called *Terhunyi* (the spirit fest)."

This is the second-most important Genna to the Angamis. Complete thirteen days Pennie is observed by Kohima group, but seven-day long Pennie by the southern Angami group. Ceremonial dresses are worn while pounding Paddy for Zhathoma. Everyone enjoys in festivities with flesh of Mithuns, dogs, pigs, etc. along with rice-beer.

Sekrenyi: It falls in the month of Rude (December) in case of southern Angani group and Keno (February) in case of Kohima and western Angami group. This is the most important Genna as regards festivities as maximum flesh of Mithun, pigs, dogs, chicken and rice beer are taken. Five days Genna is strictly observed.

The ceremony is to ensure the heath of every individual during the coming year. On the first day, in the morning every male member goes to the village wells to wash himself and his clothes and returns with a jar-full of water. They will then prepare a separate hearth. Every male member will have to make his own fire, produced from a fire-stick and cane of an indigenous system. Then every one will strangle a fowl and if the right leg crosses over the left leg, then omen is said to be good. The men must remain chaste for the first two days.

Sekrenyi connected with the renovation of the village gates is a colourful celebration centering round the bearing a wooden door carefully hewed of a tree and designed in a traditional style. The tree cut off at the sacred grove is turned by the carpenters into a beautifully carved out door and laid near the Ministers' Hill in Kohima for a few nights. The day is fixed for bearing it to the site where the gate is situated. That day sees the ceremonial marches of the different groups of people from the Khel, all male, to the Ministers' Hill.

The congregation assemble and make ready the robes with jungle creepers, elastic enough to pull out the wood while the priest mutters words of prayer to the deity of gates. The procession sets off in pompous manner, with two lines of man in a grotesque fashion holding and pulling the rope with which the wood is held out and dragged from the rear of the procession. Men are in the very best of their traditional dress unfurling with their feathered canopies, hairy badges, cowry-hemmed kilts and the multi-coloured leg guards like the sea of wave of diverse colours enchanting the eyes of the spectators.

They wear the dress in different fashions according to the rank and age. Pulling in the rope, they raise incantations in duet sonance along the way against the sounds of gun-shots right from the sight where the tree was removed until they emerge to the Khel. They have lots of drinks to tipple and meat to enjoy the ceremony at their village.

Khilunyie, at Phek, an eight-day long harvest festival, is observed towards the last week of November. The ceremonies are serialised as follows - the first day conforms to the ceremonial closing of the harvest: during the second day the rice-grains are arranged, and made ready for husking. On the third day before sunrise batches of the house wives, girls and boys set out to the streams to catch fish, snails and other insects which when brought home are cooked and eaten.

The whole lot is taken before sunset, nothing is spared. Men just sits waiting for the return of the fishing parties. The fourth day is complete rest. Men and women sit down on their parlours and sip on their drinking mugs. The fifth day is a fishing celebration when women bring home small fishes from the muddy terracing grounds. The sixth and seventh days are spent in sports and games. The eight day, which does the festival, witnesses the group of people collecting at the groves and plucking thatched grass, straw, creepers and bamboo for innovation or construction of houses.

Therine Another Chakesang festival is rice-husking. Its noted ceremonial feature is the throwing of cooked rice grains or pouring of libations on the floor of the house, an invocation being made to the deities to bless the household. The next two days see the ceremonial bathing of men folk on the first and of the women on the second well, at the village, a sort of a purgatory rite before a new season is entered. On the day are performed the paddy-husking celebrations. It is during this season that new house constructions are resumed. The Chakhesang Sakrinyi like Angani Sekrenyi is one of the biggest of local festivals, a ten-day long in which fowls, dogs, pigs, and other animals are butchered, Khel feasts arranged. This festival is associated with birds' hunt and performances of sports including wrestling. The festival closes down the old year and opens out a new agricultural season.

The Rengma Nagadah is a harvest festival, of nine days duration. The day that inaugurates sees every household brewing the county beers and keeping ready the herds of cattle for this great association of festive joy; on the second day the animals are butchered household-wise.

The third day provides a spectrum of villagers rejoicing over the harvests reaped by the community, singing dancing and toasting of rice-beer with each other. From the third day onward, all the celebrations become shifted to the Morung-a cultural centre; on this day they organise the forthcoming programmes and arrange a Khetal feast which comes in the next day. This is a children's celebration when all the village children partake in the feasts at the Morung with food provided from their respective households. The programme which follows conforms to the special feasts distributed to every house by village women at morning. Another principal Rengma festival, Tsichye, performed in the month of March, is a one day feast held to inaugurate the tilling of the soil at the Jhun field.

The Zeliangroung main festival is Meleingi, the paddy-husking celebration. The preparations in advance are chalked out when at the four council sittings, the village male population sit down together to discuss and decide upon the vital programmes of the pig affair. The festival is both household and Morung celebration. On the day of festival, each household makes large-scale fermentation and keeps in stock festival beers to last during the festival.

The household members are entertained at a sumptuous meal. During the second day, the people take their dogs, best in the breed, for butchering and feasts are held out. The third day up till sunset is passed in leisure eating and drinking but after the sunset, all husband men prepare special meals which they present to their respective father-in-laws while wives accord courteous reception to their respective mothers-in-law. The latter in turn present costumes to their respective daughters.

On the fourth day the married couple exchange dainties and wines which the husband and wives have cooked separately. The day also witnesses the games and sports among boys with long jumps, singing and incantations in a duet sonance. On the fifth day from each household donations are collected by women group to meet the expenditure for a Khel feast. On the sixth day separate batches of household collect fuel at different groves which home they bring while husbands perform collection of donations from various households.

The seventh day which closes the festival is passed in the Khel feast taken at the Morung. Nitsokhu is a Sangtam's festival, relating to the burning of Jhums during the month of April. It is a three-day long festival. On the first day, when the Genua is performed, one notices the different household groups gathering on their respective houses and passing out their time idly. The second day is the sowing festival when every family is busy sowing the seed in the field. It is during the third day that dainties of meat are prohibited but the fish locally caught is taken at the family feast.

Nizakhu Festival

In the month of May when supplications are held to the deities and sacrifices are offered in a five-day long festival. On the first day the people wake up, will not touch any food or drinks but first hurry up to offer the sacrifices with meat and rice. This vital ritual finished, the household can take the meals. On the second day, fermentation and slaughter of cattle one a large scale is performed, so that the drinks and meat so much prepared will last during the remaining days of the festival.

On the third day, when the dawn breaks forth, various households attend their respective fields where they sow the seed. No on should eat and drink until after he or she has returned home. The next day, it is a Germa, the household sipping out on their mug and eat the meat. The fifth day opens out sowing of seeds.

Rasa: when the ceremonial plucking of the young crops is undertaken. It is at this ceremony that boys and girls are freely mixing out. This festival held in the month of July is five-day long. On the first day, batches of boys go out into the jungle for collecting bamboo and sticks which when they are brought are distributed to girls awaiting their return. The entire performance is jovial. Boys hum their traditional tune and chant when attending the jungle. The second day provides a sight of young people's social meet when boys are entertained with drinks by girls, especially fermented alongwith the boiled skin of the pieces of meat.

Towards evening it is the time when the old village men at the village site are entertained with fish and boiled corn. On the fourth day, the infant crops extracted from the ripening and green stalks are brought home ceremonially. In the evening simple meals with fish and ginger are taken in every home. Genna follows on the next day.

Tsatekhu — a harvest rite, observed towards the month of August, it is three-day long. During first day the housewives are collecting sheaves of millet, which are packed with a piece of fresh fish inside a Chunga (a bamboo pipe with mouth opened but the contents well closed with a shutter of leaf), suspended from the main post of the house. The second day is passed by the villagers in the cleaning of all the village wells and paths. On the third day there are lavish feastings.

Khuthei festival is held in the month of November. There are no elaborate rituals but on the first day, new bamboo tubes are designed and moulded to serve as water containers for the next year. On the next day, feasting celebrations are held.

Kate is a festival, celebrated in November or December which closes the harvest-season. Women are busy wrapping rice and fish together in the plantain leaves which next are piled up in a basket, full of rice. It is presumed that the doing might help the household to preserve such harvested crops much longer. They refrain from drinks on that day. But on the second day they have their meals and drinks prepared only from the newly-husked paddy.

Nazhu conforming to an Angami Sekrenyi, the dying of an old year. The festival is connected with the feeding of the deceased ancestors and other dead persons, the festivals of games and sports and the construction of platforms on the village paths for affording rest to the farmers returning from their fields. The first four days are preliminary preparation. The most part of the performance is the fifth day when the deceased are called to partake at the food and drinks offered to them. Men are fasting that day but women can eat and drink. The seventh day called *Khuchi* is passed out by the village men in the jungle who try to find out a creeper where the village teams will pay a tug of war but women at the early morning hours take bath at the village wells and will not eat until that is finished.

The eight is the marriage anniversary performance. The ninth day is spent in the construction of wooden seats in the village paths. On the tenth is performed a tug of war between men and women. The game will not stop until the creeper is broken. On the eleventh day the trees are felled and jungles are cleared. Pieces of iron are scattered in the field to divert the evil spirits, plight.

Tuluni festival is celebrated by the Sema Nagas of Zunheboto region and it is generally held in July every year. Saghu and Awona are two other important festivals of the Semas. All these festivals coincide with one or the other agricultural operation. Tuluni, however, is the culmination of these festivals which coincides with the ripening of the crop. The festival spreads over five days. The day of initiation is fixed by the village priest which generally falls in July. On the first day of the celebration nobody is permitted to leave the village.

On the second day the men who earned social distinction get rice beer brewed for a community feast. Rice beer brewed for this occasion is called *Azhichoh*. On the third day a grand community feast is held in the everybody takes pork. On the fourth day prayers are offered to the Litsba deity who is thought as the deity which protects crops and brings agricultural prosperity. The prayer is offered by the married couples in their respective dwelling at the foot of the frontal post of their house. The fifth day is spent in giving a face lift to the village.

Tokhu Emong is the festival of the Lothas of Wokha region. In order to carve unity and uniformity among Lothas inhabiting different ranges of the region, the Lothas elders decided to celebrate this festival simultaneously in all the Lotha villages. It is also a harvest festival. After reaping and thrashing their crops of paddy, etc. the Lothas find time to rejoice over it. On this occasion past rivalries are forgotten and new ties of friendship are forged. Friends and relatives are invited to participate in the month-long rejoicings. During the celebration no one is allowed to leave the village. If by chance, some stranger happens to come to the village, he has to stay in the village throughout the festival period and he enjoys the lavish hospitality of the villagers.

Here again the priest initiates the ceremony. He heads the party that moves from house to house for collecting unhusked rice. When a house holder contributes his share, the priest shower blessings on him and then puts the grain in the basket. Out of the collection, a part is spent on buying a pig while the rest is brewed into rice beer. The pig is slaughtered on the first day and its flesh distributed among the villagers and it is considered as a contribution to the general prosperity of the settlement. A grand community feast is held which is followed by group songs, dances and fanfare for rest of the days. During this period prayers are also offered for the welfare of the departed souls. Those families which lost some near or dear one in the recent past also perform the last rites during this period. Many young boys and girls are engaged during the course of celebrations and immediately follow their wedding. On the last day the village streets, wells and surroundings are renovated.

Amongmong, Meteriinco, Mia, Tsokum, Monyu, and Naknyulum are the important festivals celebrated by different Naga communities living in Tuensang district. The largest and comparatively less developed region of the state has many tribes who are still very close to nature and very much fond of celebrating festivals.

The Sangtam festival of Amongmong falls in September and starts after the crop has been reaped. The festival is spread over six days. Each day is specified for a particular job. The priest of the village gives the signal of starting the function. The first day known as Jartsika is supposed to be the last day of the field work. On this day the oldest woman of the family starts the day by offering worship to the three stones of the furnace and offers meat, beer and rice to these stones. All the inmates of the dwelling including the animals are not permitted to take food before these offerings. As the sun rises the youth rush to the Morung and there the young lads as well as lasses engage themselves in collective singing and dancing. The songs generally narrate the bravery and prowess of the youth. On this day maize is not consumed. There is a superstition among the Sangtam Nagas that consumption of maize on this day leads to the outbreak of smallpox in the region.

On the second day fuelwood from the forests is collected. On the third day all the members of the family worship the three stones that make the furnace. On the fourth day roads and paths are cleared. Fifth day is spent for collecting the material for feast which is enjoyed by everyone on the sixth day.

Hunapongpi is another sentimental festival of the Sangtams. It means to display affection to all the near and dear ones. Prayers for the departed soul are held. In this festival children are the prominent participants. The young boys and girls display a cock fight. The winner is crowned as king cock. In the evening the young children enjoy a chicken feast. They preserve the leg pieces for next days feast. Before starting the feast the children send the cooked liver and head of the birds to their parents alongwith a tumbler of rice beer. The parents offer prayers for the long, happy and prosperous life of their children.

The Phoms of Tuensang district celebrate four festivals in a year, but the festival of Monyu is celebrated comparatively with more gusto. The festival falls in the month of April soon after the sowing period ends. Offerings and prayers are offered to the spirits and God for prosperous harvests. The festival spreads over a dozen of days. Half of this period is spent in community singing, dancing and feasting while the latter half is devoted to the community work related to the renovation of the settlement. Fuelwood is collected, new clothes are prepared and rice beer is prepared for rest of the year.

The festival commences with the head of the family sacrificing a chicken. The blood of the chicken is sprinkled on the floor and walls of the house. Taking out the intestine of the bird he predicts a prosperous and happy future for the family. The chicken meat is cooked with ginger, chillies, dried bamboo shoots and fish. The cooked meat is packed into leaf bundles and tied with the posts that support the house. After this ritual is over, the entire family enjoys a lavish dinner consisting of special dishes. On this day white rice, signifying prosperous living is taken in the food.

Naknyu Limi is the festival of Chang Nagas of Tuensang district. This festival is celebrated for six days in the month of August. Marriage ceremonies are a taboo during this period. Even the married men keep away from their better-halves. Prayers are offered for departed souls. The village priest is given offerings of cereals and other things. The God of Sky is also appeased through prayers. It is a ranly month and a thunderstorm is taken as a misfortune for the rest of the year. Central fire in every household throughout the night is a special feature of the festival. In the mornings the young boys and girls participate in day-long rejoicing. Apart from songs and dances the youth also arrange a feast in which elders of the village are invited.

Mia and Tsokum are the two important festivals of the Khemunagns of Tuesang region. The former is celebrated before sowing while the latter is celebrated after the harvests. Before sowings, prayers for bumper crops are offered to the deities. Sacrifices are also made in this connection. In October harvesting starts. The farmer desires to express his gratitudes to God for giving bumper crops and for his expression man takes recource to songs, dances, and music. Feasts are held by man to share his pleasure over his success in farming with his fellow travellers.

Metmneo is the festival of Yinchunger Nagas living in the Tuensang district. This festival coincides with the harvest of millets. This is a five-day festival. The festival is opened by an elderly man of the village by offering prayers to gods of spirits. On the first day the entire village brooms the streets, cleans the village and decorates the houses as well as outerwalls and gates of the settlement. On the second day the paths leading to Jhumlands and damaged during preceding rains are repaired. On the third day the inter-village roads are set to shape. On the fourth day water wells and springs are cleansed.

On the fifth day villagers engage themselves in the harvesting of millets. The entire village accomplish the work in a single day through collective as well as cooperative efforts. After the millets have been collected, friends and other near and dear ones are invited to participate in the community feast as well as in music and dance. Gifts are also exchanged on this occasion. The newborns taking during the festival period are said to be the harbingers of agricultural prosperity. If the newborn baby is a male, his parents offer six pieces of neat to the priest otherwise only five pieces are offered. It is believed that boy has six soul-while a girl has only five.

Ming Monyu is a six-day festival in 75 Konyak settlements of Mon district. These villages finish their sowings by the end of March. Aoling Monyu marks the end of winter and heralds the spring which coincides with a variety of flowers. Konyak is probably the richer Naga tribe as far as their cultural heritage and work efficiency are concerned. The slim, trim, neat and delicate Konyaks are very fond of orchids which abound in Konyak region. They are also fond of tattoos. They not only get their bodies and faces tattooed but also wear tattooed clothes.

The Morung leaders lead the song parties during the festival days. The songs revolve around the prayers offered to Sky God for bestowing bountiful crops and also for protecting their crops against the attacks of pests, weeds, beasts and birds. Every house hold prepares special dishes and the same are exchanged with one another. Older generation is shown special respect by the younger ones. Brothers with gifts visit the married sisters.

Aos of Mokokchung district celebrate Moatsu after the sowing period. The festival of Moatsu is spread over six days. On the evening preceding the day of beginning of Moatsu the village priest throttles a chicken at the foot of the main post of the Morung. On the next morning different Morung organisations pool together to buy a Mithun or pig or cow for sacrifice. After the animal is sacrificed the head of the slaughtered animal is given to the Morung Priest. Rest of the animal is divided into two halves. One half is given to the Morung inmates and the other half to the village elders. The elders in turn share it with the priest. In the afternoon a gala feast of especial dishes is enjoyed by everyone. Songs and dances continue on the following five days.

Tsungrem Mong is yet another festival of the Aos of Mokokchung District. It is a harvest festival. Men and women, young and old all attired in colourful costumes participate in songs and dances and through these activities express their gratitude to gods for bestowing bumper crops. This occasion also provides an opportunity to the younger generation and village stalwarts to demonstrate their intellectual skill and physical powers. A group of young boys holds the stage and narrate the funny instances related to the lives of the older people. Peals of laughter break in the audience. The festival concludes with a tug-of-war between men and women. Being chivalrous towards fair sex the men choose to pull uphill and allow the women to pull downhill. Ultimately men lose to women as a good gesture.

Oee Nivu is a festival that is celebrated in different parts of Nagaland with slightly different nomenclatures. In most parts of Nagaland crops are ready for harvest in the month of September. On an auspicious day fixed by the village priest, sky god is propitiated. He is thanked. A feast arranged and then harvesting starts.

The elder of the founder family in the village picks seven ears of different paddies and hang the same in his house. This festival also starts with animal sacrifice. Before sun rise two to three pigs are tethered in a common yard of the settlement. The two youngmen catch hold of the pig and the eldest man of the village pierces a sharpened and pointed bamboo through the heart of the animal. While he performs his job he utters "Oh pig; we are not sending you on to a wrong place. You are being sent on a good cause. Do not be annoyed with us." The man who kills the animal is given the kidneys of the animal. On this occasion steel weapon is not used to kill the animal as it is considered ill-omenous. Moreover, even the pointed bamboo weapon is new and used for the first and the last time. Thereafter some more pigs, Mithuns and chickens are slaughtered.

The relatives exchange gifts on this occasion which invariably include the flesh of the sacrificed animals. People run race in offering gifts. The girls pound the rice and prepare a cake out of it can be eaten either by their boy friends and lovers or fiancees. On the other side the male youths organise dance and go to houses of their beloveds to get cakes. In old days the youngmen used to present their female friends with human skulls to be used as drinking bowl. After day-long rejoicing the youth go to snoaring sleep since they have to engage themselves in the strenuous job of harvest next morning.

The site in the field is also attractive. The young girls in a row cut the paddy and hand over the sheafs to the young boys who take it to the storehouse. There some girls thrash the grains. By evening straw is separated and grains take the form of small heap. The Nagas use rice as food as well as drink. Rice beer is an important drink of the Nagas taken on all important occasions.

Thus the Naga festivals are so designed by their originators that they have both household and Khel implications, and are connected with Jhuming operation. On these occasions communal dances, fishing trips, sports, games, war-dance, hunting, singing, and incantation, house construction, are performed which are necessary for furtherance of the ties of friendship, corporate understanding which to the Naga are the indispensable traditions and ways of Naga life. Through these festivals he learns at his mother's laps and nurtures as he grows about the mode of life and the gamut of Naga culture. All the sacrificial rites are in the hands of the priests. And the jovial gestures, the sportive spirits, the humours and jokes — all these are much in store of the leading festivals.

Sports

The picturesque state of Nagaland is home to numerous tribes, who possess a fascinating wealth of vibrant festivals and traditional songs, dances and games.

The most popular sport in the state by far, is an indigenous form of wrestling. The bouts start with the contestants holding each other's waist girdles. As soon as the signal is given, both the wrestlers try to throw off each other. A combination of various leg tricks and sheer brawn are employed to achieve victory, but the use of hands on an opponent's legs is considered a foul, though hands can be used to hold other parts of the body, waist upwards.

A wrestler is declared the winner if he can throw off his opponent, and in the process, get the trunk of the opponent to touch the ground, taking care not to let his own trunk do so. The wrestler who succeeds in pulling or thrusting down his opponent, or forces him into a kneeling position with both knees and one hand, or one knee and both hands touching the ground simultaneously, also wins. It takes three bouts to decide the result. Naga wrestling is quite popular amongst the Angami, Chakhesang, Zeliang, Rengma and Mao tribes. The sport has acquired an all Nagaland sports status, and each alternate year a competition is held.

The other prominent sport in Nagaland is cock-fighting. This sport consists of kicking, solely, with the legs, and is quite similar in technique to Tae kwon do. The contestants stand apart on their marks and exchange kicks. The use of hands to hit or catch is absolutely forbidden. The barrage of kicks goes on until one party or the other surrenders. The kicks can be inflicted on any part of the body except the groin. This game, most popular amongst the Sema tribe, demands superb strength and agility, speed and awesome leg work.

Popular Sports

The common sports comprise high jumps, long jumps, stone weighing and javelin. The spear is a main weapon although it has got religious significance during any practices of exorcise, when the evil spirits are awarded off. It had more religious significance in the good old days of head-hunting. In the interior areas cultivators still use it for fighting with the wild animals and protecting their fields from the brute's damage, and no occasions for protecting themselves from the robber.

Spikes are further used in large number when traps and pitfalls are set to the game. Peg-tops is the favourite game of the village boys. Wrestling is a man's championship. During recreational hours both men and women play bean games. Schools have introduced various athletics. Slings with stone, an indigenous game used for birds' hunt.

Fascinating games range from elephant or rhinoceros to squirrel and small birds. Corporate system of hunting big games such as tigers, hares, deers, wildpigs, bears exists. It is a system of picketing the hunting ground at respective locations by groups of men; dogs smelling the trace give the sign of the game's whereabouts and yells, shouts and cries raised by picketeers, provocative enough to an animal, thus instigate it to come out and face the challenge, which when it has come is speared and speared from one position to another until it is fallen out.

The hunters thereby save their fields from the ravage of the brute. Elephants likewise are hunted corporately but hunters take up position from over the trees, who shriek at the animal which when irritated, sets himself at random, upon which, the hunters spear or shoot it till it succumbs to the injuries. The tusk, horn, and feathers are valuable items of the game. They also use pitfalls to trap the animal. In hunting, Nagas are experts, stories being told of adventures in hunting, their skill in circumventing the game. Morung-wise expeditions are ceremonial. They perform divination to ascertain whether the expedition is worthwhile.

Nagas use several devices to catch fish. Fishes of hill streams although small are considered to be more tasty than those available from the neighbouring places. The experts in the game use wires for small catches. Fishes both dried and fresh have religious importance in connecting with the observance of certain fertility rites, but less commercial importance, except in the eastern Chakesang area of the banks of Tizu, Doyang and Dikhu where fishes are caught, dried and transacted on a small commercial basis.

One device used in fish catching is by tossing the pebbles and small fishes are then caught by hand. In the larger catches, a more popular device is by damming the river bed so that when the river bounds away over the diversion, fishes laid stuck in the mud are caught. Another way is by driving away the fishes to a net, the barricades with ferns having been made that fishes do not move beyond it. Aconite plants available locally are also used for poisoning which accounts for an easiest and a largest catch.

There are many ceremonial hunting and fishing expeditions. On such expeditions fishing is undertaken on a truly corporate basis. The expeditions being pre-planned, elaborate arrangements are made in advance as regards the distribution of work and other allied matters. The hunting party on return celebrate their victory in a jovial manner. Hunting is one of the most popular games among the Nagas. The shares are distributed in accordance with the age and rank of the fishers or hunters.

6

Education

Education is one of the supreme elements in developing the abilities of an individual. In India, education is one of the priorities of the government especially in Nagaland. Education in Nagaland gives an emphasis on providing opportunities for the various fields such as commerce, culture and information technology. Despite the problems in their economy, Nagaland is boasts with colleges and universities. When you want to join the number of professionals in this place, University of the Nagaland is the place for you to enrol. This university offers quality of leaning and state of the arts facilities as well. Here you can find degree courses such as law, engineering and IT.

The 2001 Census Report on Nagaland education pointed out that only 67.11 per cent of the total population in Nagaland were literate. Such a low Nagaland education rate is obviously a cause of concern. The Government of Nagaland is working towards increasing the level of elementary Nagaland education. In order to make sure that Nagaland education percolates down into the masses, the government has introduced a policy of free and compulsory education for all children below the age of 14.

The schools in Nagaland are the base of the Nagaland education system and there are a number of schools in different parts of the state. The most popular schools in the state of Nagaland includes:

- Jawahar Navodaya Vidyalayas.
- Assam Rifles Training Centre High School.
- Little Flower School.
- Vivekanand Kendra Vidyalaya.
- Assam Rifles High School.
- Kendriya Vidyalaya.

There are a number of colleges in Nagaland and they offer different kinds of courses. These colleges are a major boost to the system of Nagaland education. The types of colleges in Nagaland include:

- Research Institutes.
- Computer Colleges.
- Engineering Colleges.
- Hotel Management.
- Law Colleges.
- Polytechnic.

The final level of Nagaland education is the Nagaland University which is a Central University. Established by the Government of India in the year 1994, the University of Nagaland has it campuses in Lumami, Medziphema and Kohima. A total of 47 colleges are affiliated to this university and there are almost 18,000 student who study under this University.

The Backdrop

The history of education and growth of literacy are not very old. Christian Missionaries were the harbingers of education in Nagaland. E. W. Clark of the American Baptist Mission was the first man who came with headquarters in 1874 at Mulongyimchen in Mokokchung District. P. T. Carnegy, a Government Official wrote in 1876 that 'he is well satisfied with the progress he has been making amongst the Nagas there. The Nagas of the neighbouring villages have not attempted to interfere with him or show any displeasure at his continued residence in the hills. The Mission station later on was shifted to Impur which became the Ao Christian Centre later on.

The veritable Mission work in Kohima started in 1878 when Rev. C. D. King was deputed to Kohima; the District Headquarters was then being shifted to Kohima from Chumukedima. But being refused permission, King had to confine himself to Chumukedima; his work there was never successful. There was opposition to mission work both from the public and government. One Missionary wrote: "The greatest difficulty which the missionary had to face was perhaps over-cautiousness on the part of the government officers, as they were opposed to the missionaries." The missionary was obstructed from visiting Kohima as the Angamis had taken up arms against Government, for which in 1879, the Angama Freedom Struggle was subdued; during this war King fled for refuge to Mulongyimchen hitherto known as Deka Haimong and from there to the plains but returned when it was calm and was allowed to work in Kohima.

Prior to the coming of the mission, a few schools were opened by Government. A school at Chumukedima headquarters Station in 1876-77 was attended only by the officials' children as the local Angamis then were apathetic to any system of education. Children were helpful mates in performing both domestic and field works and were even earning. The industrial school at Chumukedima also failed and closed down. In 1878-79, three more Government Schools were started.

While mission in the Ao area had begun to bear fruits, it was not so in Kohima. King encountered opposition and worked in the face of risks and dangers. But in 1884, his efforts had begun to meet success when a first school was opened at Kohima. He put down Angami to the Roman alphabet and taught school children to read and write in their language. King left Kohima in 1886 and the Mission charge was taken over by Hr. Rivenburg.

Rivenburg was a highly qualified medical man. He was at first trained in theology and later was specialised in medicine for the purpose of providing medical assistance to the local sick persons. Moreover, he was gifted as an orthographer and educationists. It was he who successfully adapted Angami, to the Roman alphabet by which he produced Angami alphabets, arithmetic and some versions of the holy scriptures for the use of school children. When the administration had become settled, opposition to the mission also became mitigated and later on, village people extended their cooperation to the mission in respect of school building. They furnished labour or materials and handed over lands for the purpose of school buildings.

It was the valued cooperation of non-Christians, to great extent, which was held responsible for the success of the earliest mission educational enterprises. As else where 'the Christian Missionaries were harbingers of western education. When their efforts had borne fruits, they were emulated by the government which started to open schools and educational institutions'. An instance is exemplified by the fact that in 1911-12 out of 22 schools, 12 belonged to the mission against 13 which were Government. After 1910 one mission training centre was opened at Kohima. A High School in Kohima upgraded from the mission M. E. School was the only highest school institution in the Kohima Sadar subdivision before independence which became government-managed school afterwards. It was recognised as High School Institution about 1939-40.

Increase in Schools: In 1908-09, there were 21 Government Schools, the total number of pupils being 561 boys and 550 girls. In 1909-10, schools increased to 25 but in 1911-12 they dwindled to 22 in number. In one Baptist report, it was mentioned (in 1912-13) that 14 village schools which the mission handed over the government some six or eight years ago had closed. A few of these were responded by the mission. At present, 'villages are asking for teachers... the Nagas want education'. In 1913-14 schools went up to 24 in number.

Meanwhile the mission and the people started more venture schools. The technical school was one of the most renowned in Assam. The public was enthusiastic about having more schools of higher standard. In 1931, there was a total of 42 schools at the Kohima Sadar subdivision alone.

But the greatest impediment to the spread of education was an absence of higher standard schools and the middle schools were few, for which up to Independence, a large number of Naga students were compelled to pursue high school and college studies at Guwahati, Jorhat, Golaghat, Imphal, Shillong and other distant places. In 1906-07, a, few Naga pupils were granted scholarships for study in Berry White Medical School, Dibrugarh. In 1907-08, scholarships were provided to Angami students to study at Guwahati.

In 1931, Mission M. E. School of Kohima had 180 pupils on its roll, two-thirds of whom were non-Christians, the school had hostel accommodation. There was no mess system but boys cooked their own meals and undertook social services such as cleaning and fencing works in the school compound. The Government M. E. School at Kohima had in October 1930, 142 pupils (10 were girls). The Missionaries had asked for Government permission to start high Schools and with their persistent efforts, the M. E. School was later on elevated to High School. In 1937, a Government hostel was also opened at Kohima.

School Inspectorate during those years devolved on the Deputy Commissioner and the Inspector of Schools, Assam Valley and Hill Districts.

In 1931-32, it was pointed out that 'the disadvantage of having to learn a second language in all classes at the primary stage and to pass Assamese for the M. E. and High School examinations handicaps the Naga pupils in their race for higher education. In the Mission schools, Assamese was excluded from the school curriculum but it was taught in the Government Schools.

Post-independence: Many more schools were started after independence, but during the disturbances, schools, could not rum well and some temporarily closed down. Yet despite disorders, enthusiasm was not waning on the part of the local people for opening more schools. After the interim Government was set up, schools went on increasing by leaps and bounds, many of which started as private institutions, which later on were taken over by the government. Institutions ranging from primary to college had existed in the District by 1961-62. Up to 1963, Kohima District had one science college, eleven high schools, fifty middle schools, 255 primary schools, one basic training centre and one polytechnic school. In 1967, there were three colleges, 16 high, 66 middle and 268 primary schools. That many schools sprang on self-help efforts or began as privately organised is noted in 1961-62 when 5 high schools, 17 middle and 16 primary schools were private institutions, unrecognised yet. Below is given the list of Government High Schools.

- Kohima Government High School.
- Pfutsero Government High School.
- Tseminyu Government High School.
- Dimapur Government High School.
- Peren Government High School.
- Viswema Government High School.

In 1967, the following were added to the already increasing number of High Schools.

*   Chiechama Government High School.
*   Thinuovicha Memorial High School.
*   Chazoba Government High School.
*   Phek Government High School.
*   Railway High School Dimapur.
*   Christian English School, Dimapur (Private).
*   Baptist English School (Private).
*   National English School, Kohima (Private).
*   Rughoboto Private School.
*   Ghathasi English School (Private).

To cite instances on enrolment, the Phek High School had 180 students while a total number of 178 students read in the Peren High School, both in 1967. Headmasters of standard High Schools are graded as class 11 Gazetted officers. Many schools have libraries. Hindi has been included in the school curriculum. In the leading institutions, local dances, sports and games, carpentry, arts, crafts, and social services are also taught. A few schools have brought out magazines such as Peren High School magazine published in 1966-67.

Drills, scouting and cadet corps were also been introduced and guides for girl's section have been formed. Social service programmes consist of school compound and access road cleaning by the school communities, this being the vital school tradition which has continued since the days of the British Government. Liberal provisions in aid of construction and maintenance of schools have been made.

Over ten lakhs Rupees was (as an exemplary case) sanctioned in 1961-62 for the establishment of L. P. School not to speak of middle and high schools in Kohima District alone. Persistent efforts simultaneously having been made to meet the dearth of teachers during the previous years.

Teachers' Training Centres were opened in the state and many teachers were deputed for training outside also. All the public ventures for opening of schools were taken up by Government which provide CGI sheets along with other forms of financial assistance.

Schools

There are a number of Nagaland Schools and all of them maintain a certain level of quality and standard. Most of the Nagaland Schools are affiliated to the NBSE, that is the Nagaland Board of School Education but there are also some schools that follow the

Central board or the CBSE. The Nagaland Board of School Education which was inaugurated in the year 1974 is the nucleus of all Nagaland Schools.

The Nagaland Schools usually comprises of classes 1 to 10 and some of the schools also have the 11 and 12 classes. Education at the Nagaland schools are very class room oriented and the teacher tries to provide the students with an all round idea of the subjects. Games and sports are also a part of the curriculum of the Nagaland schools and the students are often taken out for picnics and excursions. Secondary School Leaving Certificate Examination in class 10 and the Higher Secondary School Leaving Certificate Examination in class 12 are the two most important exams in the Nagaland schools.

There are a number popular Nagaland Schools, these include:

- Jawahar Navodaya Vidyalaya.
- Little Flower School.
- Vivekanand Kendra Vidyalaya.
- Assam Rifles High School.
- Kendriya Vidyalaya.
- Assam Rifles Training Centre High School.

Famous Schools

- Baptist English School was started in 1960 at Kohima by the local Baptist Association which was begun with one teacher and forty pupils only but expanded now to the High School with more than 600 pupils today. The Church Council has been providing hostel buildings and furniture.
- National School-at Kohima, a proceeding High School standard.
- Town English School at Kohima M. E. School standard but proceeding to High School level.
- Little Flower School at Kohima Catholic M. E. School but High School proceeding.
- Chakhesang Baptist English School at Pfutsero which was started about 1963, with separate hostel accommodation for boys and girls, it is M. E., but proceeding High School. In 1967, the number of pupils was 120. The school is managed by the Chakhesang Baptist Association.
- Chizami English School with a hostel; the school has imparted instructions with kindergarten and lower standard only.
- All Saints, Home Cambridge School at Peren (residential with about 50 boarder) under the Catholic Management and 100 pupils on the roll.
- St. Joseph's Cambridge School (residential) M. E. Standard with forty-three pupils at Puruba under the catholic management.

- Baptist English School at Dimapur with boarding accommodation. It is a High School with more than three hundred pupils.

- Holy Cross Cambridge School Catholic in Dimapur.

It is learned that many more English Schools will be instituted by the different public bodies. Mention may be made of Christ King School Schema, attached to the Catholic Centre in the town of Kohima.

In a few schools, the local language is adopted as one subject in the curriculum.

Curriculum: Includes mother tongue, English, Arithmetic, General Knowledge, Hygiene, Geography, Drawing, Handwork, Garden work, Physical Training and Games for class III to VIII. History is prescribed for class III onwards. Cultural activities are included for class IV to VIII. English school course starts with Kindergarten and lower standard.

Colleges

Nagaland Colleges are an integral part of the education system of Nagaland and there are a number of colleges spread all over the state. There are different kinds of Nagaland colleges and all of them specialise in particular courses. The Nagaland colleges offer different kinds of courses which includes:

- Research Institutes.

- Computer Colleges.

- Hotel Management.

- Commerce Colleges.

- Law Colleges.

- Engineering Colleges.

- Polytechnic.

- Art Colleges.

- Medical colleges.

- Science Colleges.

- Music Colleges.

The oldest Nagaland College is the Fazl Ali College in Mokokchung. This Nagaland Collage houses a total of 13 departments of Arts and Science subjects. The Patkai Christian College is another premier Nagaland College and it has been rated as the best in the state by the National Assessment and Accreditation Council.

Besides these two Nagaland colleges, there are many other Nagaland colleges that are popular and provide a standard level of education, these include:

- City Law College.
- College of Agriculture Medziphema.
- Dimapur College.
- Science College.
- Selesian College of Higher Education.
- Mountain View Kohima Christian College.
- Nagaland College of Education.
- Oriental College East Ciralare.
- Salt Christian College.
- Regional Institute of *e*-Learning and Information Technology Lerie.
- Dimapur Government College.
- Sao Chang College.
- St. Joseph's College.
- Institute of Communication and Information Technology.
- Government Polytechnic.
- Kheloshe Polytechnic.

Major Colleges

- Kohima Science College — was started as a private recognised institution with 52 students in Sept. 1961. In 1964 it became Government College. Instructions are imparted in Mathematics, Physics, Chemistry, Botany, Geology, and Zoology (English and Alternative English are included for Pre-university Course). It is now a science graduate college. It has also hostels with permanent buildings.
- Dimapur College — started by the public in 1966. It is a private recognised college. The subjects of Arts and Commerce are taught.
- Kohima College — started by the public in 1967, the college in parts instructions in Arts subjects — English, Alternative English, Political Science, History Economics and Logic. It was started with evening classes but now extended to day classes.

University

In the year 1989, the Parliament Act No. 35 passed the Nagaland University Act. However, although the Act was passed in the year 1989 it was only in the year 1994 that the Central Nagaland University was established. The Nagaland University is a teaching cum affiliating university and a number of colleges in Nagaland are affiliated to it.

The headquarter of the Nagaland University is in the city of Lumami and it has a jurisdiction over the entire state of Nagaland. There are a total of 39 collages that are affiliated to the University of Nagaland and the total student strength of the university is around 18,078. The University of Nagaland has campuses all over the state including, Kohima, Lumami and Medsiphema.

The Nagaland University offers different kinds of courses and also has a number of schools of studies. Overall there are a total of 4 schools of studies and 25 departments under the Nagaland University, these include:

- Department of English.
- Department of Geology.
- Department of History and Archaeology.
- Department of Commerce.
- Department of Education.
- School of Agricultural Science and Rural Developments.
- Nagaland College of Teacher Education.
- Department of Linguistics.

Adult Education

Efforts but not on intensive scale had been made by the mission previously to set up adult education centres in the interior places. The changing governments revitalised adult education programmes among the masses for which 30 adult education centres have been opened in Kohima, Mokokchung, Wokha, Mon and Zenhoboto, graded as Government night schools equipped with teaching aids and other stationeries. The course covers one year. There are adult education centres of the blocks also.

Scholarships vary from Rs. 25 in the case of middle school pupils to Rs. 150 at post-graduate level while meritorious students get additional benefits and facilities. Education is free up to High School stage, except English medium schools which take school fees and other charges. Stipends one granted to girls and students who prepare for technological studies. There are two teacher's training centres at Chiechama (Kohima District) and Mokokchung which run basic training courses. By the close of 1985 there were 1250 trained teachers against 1810 untrained. Teachers have been deputed also to the centres outside the state for training.

Teacher Education

Nagaland is the 16th state of the Indian Union measuring a total of 16,579 sq km. It is home to 16 major tribes, in 11 districts. In 2001 census, it had a total population of

19,88,636 with a population density of 120 per sq km. The state is still predominantly rural, 82.26 per cent of the population living in as many as 1,278 villages. Naturally, agriculture is the chief economic activity. The history of formal education in Nagaland may be traced back to the arrival of the American missionaries to the then Naga Hills in the 1880s, almost simultaneously with the advent of British colonial power. The first school was set up in 1878 by Mrs. E. W. Clark at *Molungyimsen*. It was a school for girls only. Most of the students later became teachers.

Genesis of Teacher Education

The Nagaland College of Teacher Education was established in 1975, by the State Government, in Kohima. This was the first such institution. After twenty years, in 1995, Salt Christian College, Dimapur, started its Bachelor of Education (B.Ed.) course. This was followed by the Bosco College of Teacher Education, Dimapur, in 2003. The latter two are private institutions. It is gratifying that the prestigious Indira Gandhi National Open University began offering B.Ed. course in 2002 and Certificate in Primary Education (CPE) in 2005. There are presently 6 Government managed DIETs and 2 private run institutes providing Two Year Pre-service/In-service Teacher Education Course for primary school teachers. Three of the government-run DIETs at Chiechama, Mokokchung and Tuensang were established in the year 1997; the other three at Dimapur, Mon and Pfütsero were more recently set up in 2006. In this field the private sector has stolen a march on the government. St Paul Institute of Education at Phesama began primary teachers training in 1977. The Salt Christain College, Dimapur, has followed suit in 2006.

Types of Teacher Education

As mentioned above, the number and types of teacher education have risen in recent times with the rise in number of three more DIETs. However, as we all know, sheer numbers do not ensure quality. It may be noted that there is still no Master of Education (M.Ed.) course in the state. Two of the institutes have women principals. It was found that the government institute had the most number of teacher educators with B.Ed. and Ph.D. qualifications as compared to the other two privately managed institutes. While there was uniformity of salary for the teacher educators at the starting point, there was better incentive in the Government Institute.

The two private institutes also had part-time teachers who were, naturally, paid less. In case of Govt. institution, majority belong to inservice category and in case of private institutions, majority belong to fresh category. The number of B.Ed. trainees in all three Institutes ranges from 76 to 100 student trainees in a class. While the most of student trainees in Government Institute were in-service local people, majority of the student trainees from the other two Private Institutes were fresh candidates from outside the state. Of the three institutes in the state, the government institute provides hostel facilities to girls only. Of the two private institutes, one has a hostel for boys while the other provides residential facilities to both girls and boys. All the institutes, happily, have library and laboratory facilities even if access to computer and Internet facilities are limited. Some of the institutes were understaffed with only five teacher educators each, while one institute had as many as twenty-five teacher educators.

It may be noted that these were newly opened Government institutes. There is scope for improving the staffing pattern in the DIETs. Perhaps exposure to additional orientation and motivational programmes would add an element of purpose and mission to the teaching profession. Total number of enrolment for the in-service/pre-service teacher education is 349 in the first year in eight institutions and 110 in the second year in the four institution. It may be noted that three new Government DIETs were established in the year 2006 and one private college introduced the course only recently.

IGNOU B.Ed. course Contact Centre is located at the Nagaland College of Teacher Education, Kohima and the Centres for the CPE course are located at the District Institutes of Education and Training at Chiechama, Mokokchung and Tuensang as well as the privately run St Paul Institute of Education, Phesama. The annual number of applicants for the IGNOU teacher education course is gradually growing in recent years. Learning via mass media, both electronics and print, without daily interaction with faculty is still an arrangement many have not got accustomed to.

The fact that many probable aspirants are not computer/Internet savvy is a barrier. Inadequate Internet and television connectivity particularly in the remote regions of the state acts as a 'deterrent'. However, IGNOU Regional Centre Kohima has already achieved impressive results despite the bottlenecks that distance education is confronted within the state. The IGNOU instructional materials and learning packages are much sought after by the student trainees of the conventional system and its own students. The practical aspects of the programmes also need serious attention as much depend on the hands on experience to become effective in teaching. The limited face-to face interaction between the academic councillors and the student trainees and among the student trainees themselves deprives them of the rich experiences their counterparts in the conventional institutions enjoy.

The State Council for Educational Research and Training besides managing the teacher education conducted at the DIETs, also organises short and medium term courses and trainings from time to time. The District Centre for English is a five-year project, 2005 to 2010. The centre conducts a ten-day programme, from time to time, for in-service graduate English teachers in schools. A certificate is issued after completion of the training. This is a programme sponsored by the Ministry of Human Resources Development. All learning and instructional materials are provided by the Central Institute for English and Foreign Languages, Hyderabad. Another noteworthy programme organised by the

SCERT during 2002-2004 was titled 'Educational Quality Improvement Program' – popularly known as 'EQUIP'. It was directed towards overhauling education especially in the areas of curriculum development, teacher training, textbook writing and capacity building. 'EQUIP' was sponsored by the UNICEF. As many as 42 programmes were conducted in the form of workshops, seminars, training sessions and the like. EQUIP culminated in an adaptation of pedagogy called Activity Based Learning (ABL) approach. It also resulted in the development of 17 textbooks for Class I to Class IV and integrated learning.

Teacher Training Curricula

The B.Ed. course provided at the Nagaland College of Teacher Education was recently reviewed on the basis of the model provided by the University Grants Commission (UGC). The new course of study included four core papers, which are compulsory, two optional papers (method papers) and one elective subject (special paper). Evaluation scheme for the theory is 75 per cent external and 25 per cent internal. The total marks for the theory papers are 700.

Practical work consist of field-based experiences including practice in teaching (micro and macro), peer observation, community work; work experience (food preservation, campus beautification, painting/art, knitting/embroidery, envelop making, toy making, paper cutting, candle making, cookery skill, decoration items, etc.) and co-curricular activities (physical, health education). Scheme of evaluation for practical is: Field-based Experience — 300 Marks (External 62.5% and Internal 37.5%); and Co-curricular Activities and Work Experience — 100 Marks (External 50% and Internal 50%). Total Marks of the B.Ed. course is 1,100 marks.

The course structure of Pre-service /In-service Teacher Education conducted at the various institutes for primary school teacher preparation included: (a) foundation course, (b) content and methodology, (c) practicum and field work — internship: micro and block teaching. Report writing of one project work is also included. Evaluation is done on the basis of essay type questions, short answer questions, very short questions and objective type of questions. A scheme of 75 per cent external and 25 per cent internal is followed.

The programme structure for IGNOU B.Ed. Course consists of core courses (20 credits), content-based methodology courses (8 credits), special courses (4 credits), practical courses (16 credits). IGNOU CPE course structure consists of four theory papers with 10 credits — teaching language, teaching of mathematics, teaching of environmental studies and understanding the primary school child. The practical component has 8 credits, which covers school-based activities, workshop based activities and practice teaching. The main aim of the programme is to cover the backlog of a large number of untrained teachers working in primary/elementary schools in the North- Eastern States and Sikkim.

Summary

Recognising the need for quality improvement is not the same as dismissing teacher education as a non-beneficial programme. It is taking cognizance of the potential of teacher education to transform the quality of school education in the state.

Nagaland is changing and teacher education cannot remain out of sync with the changed and changing aspirations, needs, values and preferences of the people. It is the responsibility of teacher education institutions to make proactive contributions to the emergence of finer values in the sociocultural-political life of the people and to take 'strong measures' to raise the bar of performance and productivity in a creative way. The consequence of not doing anything is certain to be serious.

7

Language and Literature

Naga linguistics have not received adequate attention as they ought; apart from Grieson of, Linguistic Survey of India, the other contributions in this field is flimsy. A conclusive view point, however, is that Zeliangroung, Sema and Renga are Bod languages and are assigned with Garo, Kachari, and Koch of the Assam-Burmese (Sino-Tibetan) form of speech. Angami is also attributed to the same class irrespective of the more compound 'morphological and lexical features which it abounds. Kuki belongs to a different family and is classed with Burmese-Chin, sub-stock of Sino-Tibetan. Chongli and Ao languages belong to the Central-subgroup of Naga languages.

Grierson has included the Nagaland dialects in the Tibeto-Burman family of languages. He further subdivides these dialects into Western, Eastern and Central subgroups. The Angami, Rengma, Sema, and Chakesang dialects come under the western subgroup. The Central subgroup includes the dialects spoken by Aos, Lothas, and Phoms, while the eastern subgroup is made up of the dialects principally spoken by the Changs and Konyaks. All these dialects appear to have originated from the same stock and are highly tonal as well as agglutinative.

Excepting the Nagas minor ethnic groups who are living in the areas of isolation most of them are bilingual or multi-lingual. The following Table shows the mother tongues and subsidiary languages of some of the important Naga tribes.

Tribal languages have been put down to the Roman alphabet, but it is Angami Rengma and Ao languages which have had a small corpus of a written literature in the form of school textbooks and Christian publications. Next comes, Rengma and Lotha which have Christian publications and a few books for elementary classes. Angami is the language recognised up to matriculation standard at the secondary level.

Name of Tribe	Mother tongue	Subsidiary language
Angomi	Anganu	English, Nagamase, Hindi, Seliang, & Sema
Chakhesang	Chak	Hindi, English, Assamese & Sema
Rengma	Rengma	English, Hindi, Assamese, Angami, Sema
Sema	Sema	Assamese, English, Hindi, Angami, Sangtam,
Zeliang	Zeli	Assamese, Hindi, English, Angami,
Aos	Chongli, Mongsen	English, Naganu
Lothas	Lotha,	Assamese, Hindi, English, Nagami
Konyaks	Konyaki	English, Nagami, Assamese

The other tribes while using Angami and Ao as a medium for primary and middle standards, have simultaneously made efforts to develop their respective alphabets. Bible translation work has been done in Chakru (Chakhesang), Lotha, Zemi, Konyak and Zemi (Zeliangroung) groups.

Local Language

Ao Language

The Ao language, which Sir George Grierson places in the central subgroup of Naga languages, is apart from the differences in pronunciation found in various villages, divided into a number of distinct dialects of which the chief are Chongli, Mongsen, Changki, Yacham and Longla. Of these dialects by far the most important are Chongli and Mongsen. Roughly speaking Chongli is spoken on the Langbangkong and the latter on the Asukong; Changkikong and Chapvukong. But the areas merge into one another, and in many villages such as Sangratsu one 'Khel' speaks chongli and the other Mongsen. Of the two Mongsen appears to be the more closely allied to Lhota which is dissyllabic, while Chongli tends to be monosyllabic (stone – lung c; Alung M; "Dad" – Nok C; Anok M).

Of the two main dialects Chongli is the dominant, and shows signs of gradually becoming the language of the Ao tribe. Most Mongsen-speaking individuals know Chongli, while comparatively few people whose natural dialect is Chough can speak or understand Mongsen. The spread of the Chongli dialect has received great impetus from the work of Mission. All translations have been done in Chongli by the Missionaries and it is used for all Mission work. The result of this is that few Aos can express themselves on Christian subjects in the Mongsen dialect. A Mongsen-speaking pastor, probably, ordinarily thinks in Chongli when he thinks about his religion; certainly he almost always uses that dialect even when preaching to a Mongsen speaking congregation. There are five vowels — A, E, I, O, U in Chongli but variations in their sounds make them into eleven vowels. There are twenty-four consonants in this language.

Nagamese Language

Nagamese is the most popular among the spoken languages in Nagaland. Widely spoken by the tribal people of the state, the Nagamese language is a mixture of different Naga and the Assamese languages. It has also been enriched with some contributions from Bengali and Hindi languages. It is the *lingua franca* of the Naga population.

Nagamese has gained its popularity due to simplicity of the language. Since the language does not have any written scripts, it does not follow any grammatical complications. Nagamese has no use of gender classifications, which makes it more easy. Nagamese is popular as the language of communication. Although there are many languages in the Nagaland, the Nagamese acts as the interlink between these languages and helps in better communication.

Tenyidie Language

Tenyidie is one of the common languages in Nagaland. The Tenyidie language is also known as the Angami. Mostly spoken by the natives of the Angami tribes, Tenyidie have a number of dialects like:

- Dzuna,
- Kohima,
- Kehena,
- Chakroma,
- Khonoma,
- Nali,
- Mima,
- Tengima,
- Mozome.

The Tenyidie is considered as the standard dialect among the Angami dialects. It has emerged as the most popular language among the Angami tribes. It falls in the Sino Tibetan language family.

Literature

Religious Literature

A popular legend among the Nagas explain the multiplicity of Naga dialects in Nagaland. In the beginning there was very little prose and poetry in the various dialects and languages of the Naga tribes. The advent of Christianity and conversion of the tribals into Christianity transformed the cultural life of Nagas appreciably. Angami, Naga, Lotha, Sema and the Konyak are the dominant languages of the Nagas.

In the later parts of the 19th century, a special stress was laid on the development of local languages and literature. Three Angami was reduced to writing in the Roman alphabet; it was Dr. Rivenburg who produced the gospel according to St Mathew printed in 1890, the first book in Angami. In 1829 a hymnal came out in print comprising selected pieces translated from English by Rivenburg. Before 1904 the other publications in Angami were the Gospel according to St Luke, Rivenburg's translation came out in print.

The service of the Rev. Dr. Rivenburg was manifold, by him a dispensary was started by him at Kohima for the benefit of the local sick people, he built up the first Angami Mission School, he organised Christian Mission work at their area and in being the father of the Angami Alphabet, Revelation in an Angami rendering was printed in 1918. In 1924, the books of Philippians, Colossians and Ephesians were edited in the Angami language. But progress in the translation work of the Bible was rather, slow for it was not until 1927 that the New Testament was printed, while the version of Genesis was printed up to 1923.

In 1927 and 1937, respectively the second and third edition of the New Testament came out. In 1960 the next edition came out. Much of the translation was done by Angami Collaborators. A Bible Translation Checking Committee was constituted to accelerate the work, by which 30 books of the Old Testament have been translated and the version of Deuteronomy got prepared. The Complete Bible in Angami was published in the Seventies.

Apart from the Bible translation work, the Christian centre also published a number of booklets and translations from the English classics, the most significant being the version of the Pilgrim's Progress which came out in print in 1953. Yet much of the work not yet completed by the missionaries has been brought to the completion by the Angami translators themselves with an object in view of making the revised portion more authentic.

The two Angami Christian journals in wide circulation are Ketho Mu Kevi and Kohima Mission Leshu distributed from the Kohima Christian book room. In Chakhesang, a journal entitled Chakhesang Christian Leshu was in large circulation in 1959-61 distributed, from Phek, the Christian Centre which had later shifted to Pfutsero where there is now a Baptist English School.

The other Christian publications worth mentioning comprise Christian Kehou Dze (for the use of vernacular Bible School) edited in 1958, Pastors' Handbook (mimeographed), Dieliekovi Tsalida (Gospel-Song) and Parables, also Church History and Way of Salvation in Angami renderings in addition to a hymn-book.

The Catholic Church also produced leaflets recently in the form of prayer book and a bible story.

Secular Literature

The primer and arithmetic by Dr. Rivenburg had been in the use of schools, which from time to time were revised. In 1904, A Way to Health in Angami by Rivenburg was published. In 1905, was published Rivenburg's work English and Angami Naga Phrases. In 1915, Tanquist revised the primer whilst in 1930, supple made a new edition of the first reader. Angami-English Dictionary by Dr. Haralu (in 1933) in another notable contribution, complied with the help of other Angami collaborators. The dictionary was revised by Mr. J. E. Tanquist, an American Baptist at Kohima. Angami interpreters of the Deputy Commissioner's staff namely Neihu and Lhouvisielie of Kohima, Neikhriehu of Jotsoma, and Thepfushitsu of Khonoma also assisted a lot in giving modification. The Kohima at variance with the Khonoma dialects are used. The preface has amply been brought out by Dr. Haralu with an autobiographical sketch. It was called Dr. Hutton who recommended it to the press.

It is worth to note that other secular publications in Angami by the church were Kephruda Kerieu (an arithmetic), and Words, Divisions and Spellings.

In pre-Independence, there had been reports of dearth of standard books and the need for literature was felt. As early as 1897, reports go to suggest that the 'enthusiasm for education has perceptibly increased that there has been a marked revival in letters — a sort of Naga Renaissance' and simultaneously the need to perpetuate the Naga thought, musical expressions, incantations, folktales, and oral traditions in literature.

It may be relevant to point out here that for sometime during the pre-independence, Assamese was read side by side with mother tongue in the government schools. But afterwards Assamese was abandoned. The well-known authors of Nagaland are:

> Alemchiba Ao who has written 'A Brief Historical Account of Nagaland. Several historical accounts of Nagas have been written by J. H. Hutton, V. Elwin, J. Mill, Haimendorf Furer, C. Von. there are several young social scientists who are contributing in the field of literature and fine Arts.

Contemporary Literature

Literature in other forms also evolved during the post-independence. Among the textbooks which the Textbook Production Branch has produced, mention may be made of the following:

- Kephruda Kesau I, 1963.
- Kephruda Kesau II, 1963.
- Mahaphruda I, 1963.
- Mahaphruda II, 1963.

They are school readers suitably amended of the old ones used in the schools up till the inception of the Interim Government. Ruzhukhrie Sekhose is the most notable literary figure among the Angamis. He is a versatile writer so much that the subject matter which have received considerable treatment in his hands are varied. On linguistics, he has produced the following works in Angami:

- Angami Idiomatic, 1958.
- Spelling World Division, 1962.
- Initiatory Grammer, 1959.

These works are expected to go a long way towards enriching vocabularies. On folklore, his contributions comprises the following:

- U Kenei dze, Part I and II, 1954.
- Angami Naga Folklore, 1954.

In addition he has written a book entitled Gandhiji published in 1962.

In respect of lexicon, a book entitled Angami-English-Hindi by Benjamin was published in 1962. Miss Beilieu's Angami mu English, Anglo-Angami Phrases is another contribution. The Aesop's Fables adapted of English by Hisale pinyu was published in 1964.

In addition an outline History of India by Lhoulienyu was published in 1962. Kumbo Angami's work entitled Miavimiako dze with materials drawn from Assam's history is considered to be an addition on the study of history printed in 1948.

On hygiene and health; the following are important:

- Keshurho dze da — Printed in 1955 by R. Zhavise Angami.
- Umo Kevida — Printed in 1958 by Dr. Uzielie Angami.

Geographical topic is comprised of the following: Kiju dze by D.D. Phewhuo (1962). On education, the following is available: Mhasidie (1963) by R. K. Neihulie. In addition there are Short stories complied by Dino and Viswedel which came out in 1963 there is a little corpus of a written literature but there are prospects of its future growth.

Angami, Ao, Sema, and Lotha tribes languages have been reduced to writing the Chakhesang, the Rengma and the Konyaks are trying to develop their respective alphabets. As regards Bible translation, it has been translated into several Naga languages. Some of the tribes like Chakhesang and Konyaks have further pressed to include one qualified expert in the Bible translation committee for safeguarding their linguistic interests.

The only publications in Rengma are the Four Gospels and the Acts in addition to a hymn book and a few other booklets. The Rengmas also use Angami in the Church and as medium of instruction in their schools. But at present Rengmas have attempted to accelerate Bible translations in their language. Even in Zemi, small publications such as Poster's Handbook by H. K. Lungalong (1962) and the version of St Matthew are available. The Zeliangroung have also attempted to speed up translation to Bible.

Textbook Production

The Textbook production branch as a wing of Education Directorate took its inception in 1961-62. Language officers are appointed to write school textbooks in major local languages, to translate certain approved school textbooks in major local languages, to prepare schemes and incur expenditure for printing of textbooks produced departmentally, to distribute such books to the Deputy Inspector of schools for respective areas and to invite private writers for writing textbooks and for contribution of specially selected articles. Textbooks are prepared and procured departmentally.

Textbooks in Angami comprise primers, readers, arithmetic, history and geography for primary and middle standards and vernacular for higher classes, prepared by the recognised local writers. Angami is one of the two major Naga languages in which textbooks are printed. The Aos language has also been adequately developed and besides primers, textbooks of arithmetic, geography, history and supplementary readers are available in Aos language.

In addition there is a state Textbook Committee with 19 members representing different tribes with Director of Education as chairman.

The tens of reference, duties, etc. are:

- to scrutinise all the textbooks written and published by various authors for use in the schools.

- to advise the Director of Education in the selection of textbooks for various classes.

- to delete the names of unsuitable textbooks if such books are in use in any recognised school.

- to advise the Education Department in the preparation of textbooks.

- to keep informing an education library and in maintaining it. The life of the Committee is five years.

Media

A leading Newspaper in the state is the English Weekly entitled 'Citizens Voice'. It is issued every Wednesday. The weekly contains useful local new items and healthy constructive views. It is printed at Kohima Printing Press. Another is Naga Chronicles (news and views: fortnightly). It contains news columns on diverse public affairs; one column contains themes on Naga culture. It is printed from Manipur. There is a Government Press at Kohima.

8

Economy

Nagaland is essentially a tribal state. Like all other tribal regions Nagaland has basically an agricultural economy. Though the proportion of workers directly engaged in agriculture has gone down from 89.36 per cent in 1961 to 78 per cent in 1981, the occupation of agriculture still absorbs an overwhelming majority of the workforce. The tradition-bound superstitious Naga farmers often prays to Gzoang (God) for timely occurrence of rains. He prays for plenty of rice, maize and millets. The taboo prevalent among common Nagas about jobs other than agriculture, hunting, gathering, forestry, fishery, speaks about the predominance of the primary sector. Although steps have already been taken to convert shifting cultivation into sedentary farming, Jhuming (shifting cultivation) is still the dominant agricultural system of the state. In 1960 over 85 per cent of the area under cultivation had been under Jhuming which was reduced to 71 per cent in 1985.

In brief, agriculture is the principal occupation of the Nagas. It is attested by the fact that around 85 per cent of the population is confined to the villages while mixed undertakings connected with contract works, supply, and other small-scale business enterprises have emerged. Technical and non-technical professions have increased for coping with the enforcement of many planned schemes which are supposed to be of benefit at large. Student communities have shown great increase, and education has made notable expansion.

The density of population per sq km is increasing and ranges between 25 persons per sq km in central, areas to 47 persons around Dimapur and Kohima. A pressure of the population to the townships and business centres is an important trend. Forests and lands in their virgin shapes are still abundant on higher altitudes; to the tribes, land is a source of permanent wealth when it is meant to be spared for the use of future generations. In fact, the inheritance of landed property is so devised that the land remains under perpetual ownership of the family or lineage group even though it has to be divided amongst the successors.

The size of the land-holding is the decisive factor in Jhuming cultivation as families have to move from place to place after a plot of land has been affected by the Jhum cycle. Land products such as bamboo, timber, shrub, stone and mineral products are considered to be the most important items of wealth. Because so which value is attached to the soil, it has been found sometimes difficult to work out land acquisition schemes by the administration whatever compensation is offered, because people know that cash value is rather ephemeral.

Technological Patterns

The basic economic problems of Nagaland are poverty, hunger, malnutrition, low yields in Jhuming and depletion of forests. The poverty arises not so much from any iniquitous social system, but mainly from technological backwardness Jhumias and craftsmen which keep their productivity very low. Determined efforts are being made to introduce to the villagers the advantages of using better seeds, fertilizers, and improved agricultural implements through sale of these items at subsidised rates and the implementation of land reclamation, soil conservation and minor irrigation schemes.

The facilities that are being provided for education within the state as well as outside also directly help in making the people technologically more advanced. In majority of schools, training in various trades like blacksmithy, carpentry, etc. is also imparted. Obviously, the transitional trend occurred with coming of independence but apparently, new economic concepts towards a more concrete planning on up-to-date lines have ushered in since the inception of the state of Nagaland. A bulk of machines, engines, tools and implements, electrical fittings, automobiles are brought from outside. The state has only a few standard workshops and factories.

Industry

The development of industries in any state or region is the function of the available resource base, labour, technical skill, capital, market for the manufactured goods, and the overall cultural environment of the people. The natural and cultural environment of Nagaland does not favour the establishment of large-scale and heavy industries. Scarcity of raw material-power, technical skill, capital, transport and market are some of the major barriers in the development of industries in the state. The state, however, offers great potential for the small-scale and village industries.

Spinning and Weaving

Spinning and weaving is a household industry in Nagaland. Weaving is one of the most important duties of females. Weaving of cloths is forbidden for a man to share, with the exception that the spots of dark blue with which white 'Lengta' bands are often decorated are invariably embroidered by man and never by a women.

The method of spinning is almost identical among all the Nagas. The cotton is seeded by rolling a round stick (locally known as Menon grtong of Naktong) over it over a flat stone. This laborious task usually falls to the lot of old women, who being no longer able to go down to the fields, eke out an existence in this way. A little seeding machine consisting of two wooden rollers geared to revolve in opposite direction and turned with a crank is commonly used. Such machines are usually manufactured locally as well as they are imported from the plains of Brahmaputra.

The cotton having been seeded, it is carded by being flicked with a little bow, and rolled into sausages of a convenient size for spinning. The spindle (Pang, Apang) consists of a long pen-shaped piece of wood, with a stone spindle-whorl. The stones are ground to proper shape on other stones and bored with a spear-butt twirled between the hands. To spin the operator places the lower end of the spindle in a broken piece of pot or a little basket covered with a bit of rag, and spins it with a drawing motion against her right thigh, feeding it meanwhile from a sausage of wool held in her left hand. The thread (Ang) collects above the stone until the spindle is full.

It is then taken off, dampened with cold water, and vigorously pounded on a board with a rice pounder, and after being soaked in rice water dried, is rolled into a ball. The Nagaloom is a tension loom of the simple Indonesian type. The women keep the necessary strain by sitting with a belt (Aphi) in the small of her back, attached to a bar from which the warp (Kotong) runs to the beam itself firmly attached either to the well of the house or to two stakes fixed in the ground. The heddle, lease rod, and bar above the lease-rod, round which the wrap is twisted once.

The shuttle is shot through by hand, and the woof beaten up with the sword, which is rubbed either with wax or with a very fine white powder like French chalk, found on the underside of the leaves of a species of wild plantation. The patterns in cloths are obtained by the necessary combinations of different-coloured threads in the warp and woof. Small spots of embroidery and little tufts of red hair are worked in with a porcupine quill while the cloth is being woven. To sew the strips of cloth together for body-cloths or darn holes steel needles from the plains are now commonly used. But the old needle is still to be seen at times. It is simply a thin splinter of cane, or bamboo with a split end on to which the thread is twisted or stuck with little wax.

Weaving specimen from the various districts of Nagaland comprise a wide range and number which display themselves as pieces of the precious art-treasures showing in respect of designing and processing, an accomplishment of great measure. The distinctive costumes and apparels comprise wrappers and shawls, waist-cloths and bodice, girdles (for carrying babies), scarfs, skirts, aprons and lungis resplendent with skilful colour combination in their own fashion and style. In the weaving practices and processing, tribe to tribe variations are noted as occur the divergencies in respect of their dress. Weaving is still the major undertaking as the Nagas of the villages still rely for a great portion of their daily dress upon their own weaving works, particularly women-folk, but in rural places, the dress materials have further been supplemented by mill-made fabrics. The Naga shawls and bags with different textures are highly valued, and have found great demand outside the state irrespective of their high cost price due to the laborious processing and difficulties caused by the dearth of yarn.

The best Naga shawls having different textures are woven of yarn. The shawls on the entire length or borders are striped, each tribe having their own model of geometrical designs, as part of their embroidery. Stripes in all cases are coloured differently from the main background of the cloth.

As stated in preceding para weaving is confined to women folk who, besides shouldering the domestic and cultivation works, weave their apparels, the traditions of weaving being handed from mother to daughter.

In respect of spinning, the Nagas use spindle for spinning cotton while the Semas and Aos have a spindle raised with a flat stone whorl, cotton, jute and even mottle-fibres are woven into cloths. But yarns for the purpose of superior texture, are not locally procurable, a good deal being purchased from outside. The Angami loom is a simple loin loom analogous to Ao, Lothas, and Sema type although petty variations are noted as regards the Angami way of warping and the setting of loom.

Weaving has also been modernised in the hands of the professional weavers who produce the modern designs of shawls, skirts, bags, neckties, tablecloths, bedcovers, curtains and handbags which have had a great deal of demand outside the state.

Dyeing

Nagas have several techniques of dyeing. Dyes are prepared from the leaves of indigo Strobilanthes flaccidifolius which is cultivated for this purpose both in plots in heavy, shady jungles and in the sun, leaves grown in shade and in sun being needed at different stages of the process. The method of preparing and using the blue dye is as follows.

Leaves of plants grown in the shade are pounded up and spread out in the trays to dry. After being kept in the house for a month or two they are for use. They are then put in the cold water and well stirred and left to soak for three days. On the third day wood-ash is stirred in, and in the evening the cloth or thread which is to be dyed is put in and left there till the morning, when it is taken out, rinsed and hung up to dry. If the colour is not considered dark enough it may be soaked again for another night. To finish it off, it is then boiled in water with unpounded leaves from plants grown in the sun.

This process too may be repeated more than once. The best dark blue cloths are made of thread which has been subjected to both cold soaking and boiling before weaving. A

Naga who thinks his white cloth is really getting rather dirty and when he thinks that, it is dirty gets his wife to dye it dark-blue. Cloths dipped in this way are only soaked in the cold dye and are not cooked. While dyeing is going no stranger may watch or the colour will not take, it is believed in the Naga tribes.

The native red dye is now being fast superseded by a red powder sold in Bazaars in the plains. Only old women can die thread or hair red. The colour being that of blood, were a young woman to use red dye she might lose her head in a raid or die a violent death. The dye is obtained from the root of a creeper called *Aozu*. This is thoroughly dried and pounded, and mixed with the dried and pounded leaves of a tree called *Tangshi* and the outer husks of the acid berry of a tree known as *Tangrno*. Water is added to this mixture and the thread or hair which is to be dyed is boiled in it for about half an hour. It is then taken out and dried and brushed clean. Another dye is also used in Longsa for thread, but not apparently for hair, for which it is considered unsuitable.

The process, which is not known is the Mongsem group of Ao Nagas is as follows: The thread is boiled with the seed of the oil-seed plant (Azu), and left soaking in the cold brew for two or three days. When taken out and dried it is pale-brown. Next it is boiled in an infusion of the pounded leaves of the Kotsam tree and bark of the roots of the Chonglong tree. This turns it red. When sufficient colour has been imparted it is taken out, rinsed in cold water, and dried. Apart from dyeing from indigo, tubers, sappers leaves and plants, at present chemical dyes have supplemented those procured locally. In dyeing process, the common system is boiling the yarn or cloth or hair meant for dyeing which gives lasting colouring but variations in the process occur from place to place and from tribe to tribe. Even the goat's hair or human hair dyed red or black or any other colour is used for decorating their weapons or resplendent parts of dress.

Painting on Cloth

Longsa practically holds the monopoly of the decoration of the median bonds of Tsungkotepsu cloths. The pigments is prepared as follows:

> The sap of a tree called *Chengko* is mixed with very strong rice beer and the ash of either its own leaves or of bamboo leaves. The result is a grey fluid which is applied with a pointed piece of bamboo. The operator works free hand, guiding himself by the lines of thread. The pigment dries a dead black and withstands flee ravages of tune and weather well. The same pigment is used in some villages to adorn 'Lengtas' with patterns and roughly draws figures of dogs, cocks and hens and so on.

Pot Making

Pots are made generally by women as it is a taboo for males to make pots. The non-Christians, still observe the old restriction and obtain their cooking pots generally from the Phom District. Among the Nagas the making of pots is as follows:

Red and grey clay are mixed, with a slightly larger proportion of the former and well kneaded with water. A mass large enough to make a pot is then taken and worked on a board into the shape of a large round bun. This is picked up and rammed on to the left fist, the flat bottom being towards the fist. It is then slapped, and worked with the right hand till it forms a sort of cap over the clenched left hand. Next it is put rim upwards on the ground, and further worked with the damped fingers of both hands, first with an upward motion and then with a circular motion round the pot, the left hand being inside and the right outside all the time. When the rough shape of the finished article has been arrived at it is left in the sun to dry for an hour.

Hitherto, the clay being very soft, nothing but the fingers has been used to shape it. After it has hardened a little in the sun the final shaping is begun. For this a mushroom shaped stop of baked clay is held against the inner surface with the left hand and the outside tapped and smoothed with various shaping sticks till the requisite shape and thinners have been obtained. The first shaping stick, which is used for the rough work is a narrow flat piece of wood with a smooth surface. Next a stick with broad ends, like a double paddle, is used.

The four flat surfaces of the paddle-ends of this are deeply grooved in square and lozenges. This gives a rough surface to the pot, and prepares it for the final smoothing stick, which similarly has paddle shaped ends, but with smooth surfaces. After drying for one full day, in the sun, the pot is ready for firing. This is done either before dawn or after sun-set as a rule, the reason being the universal Naga belief that fire is harder to control in the day than at night. To fire the pot they are piled on a very low platform of bamboo, and dry seeds put under and all over them and lighted. There is no restriction as to strangers being present, nor is any particular food barred to the workers at any stage of the proceedings.

The pots when finished are round bottomed, with an overturned rim for lifting them off the fire. No ornamentation of any kind is applied. According to one report the clay in Meluri area of the Kohima district is soft and smooth and it is hoped, it can be used in all types of ceramics. Pots in different sizes and shapes are made. A model of the lauri clay is said to be best for ware moulding and designing. Some of the handmade wares which serve as containers of beer are hanged and have lids. The potters prefer red and black colour for their pots.

Wood and Cane Work

Nagas are pretty skilful in wood cane work. Cane being profuse is largely utilised for works in craft. Picturesque cane crafts comprising bowls, mugs and containers with multi-coloured engravings on them are made by all tribes. Other varieties such as fillets as part of ornamentation have elaborately worked out design. Cane helmets and hot frames are many. Among the Nagas a cane-rain proof hot is also made. Mats woven of cane strings with fine texture have decorative value.

The making of baskets and mats, at which all male Nagas are expert, is a task reserved exclusively for men and boys. Split bamboo is the usual material used for both mats and baskets. A man will make rough open-work basket for temporary use in an incredibly short time, and throw it away when done with. Baskets meant for permanent use are usually of the checker-twilled patterns, or of an open work pattern rather resembling the cane seat of a chair.

The flat-bottomed cylindrical baskets into which rice beer is strained are so closely woven as to be practically water-tight. But to make doubly sure the inside is smeared with the sap of a variety of Ficus called *Akhu*, the only instrument used for basket making. But as the families of the users suffered magically thereby and tended to die out the practice was abandoned.

Baskets are in wide range and number with different shapes and sizes, used for different purposes as containers for crops and other household goods, and as packages for carrying luggage and merchandise. The Japa, a package with lid, hexagonal in form is popularly used all over the state for travelling. There are other kinds of baskets bearing symbolic expression and having numerous engravings. Cane ornaments such as head-hands, bangles, leg-guards, etc. constitute another model of workmanship. A typical haversack is a cane frame, sewn over it by a thick cloth and with the decorations of shells and heads.

The dexterity and skill of Nagas in wood work are exceptional. They carve the figures of men, tiger, hornbills, pythons, Mithuns heads and so on in very high belief with which 'Morung' posts are adorned are excellently done, especially in Aos, and Konyaks. A post which is to be so treated in first roughly squared with a Dao. The outline of the figure desired is then sketched with charcoal and the rest of surface cut away sufficiently to leave it in high relief. Daos are used for most of the work, awkwardly placed pieces of wood being picked out with a Dao blade fastened to a long handle and used as a chisel, when it is called Changba or Uchangba. Any colouring required as a final touch is supplied by pig's blood and soot, while a fiercely striped tiger is often given a pair of 'Goo-Goo eyes' composed of black seeds surrounded by pig's bristles.

Dab is the main tool used for making both the huge xylophone and small dancing drums. Fire is never used to assist in the hallowing process. Dao holders are often ornamented either with a pierced pattern or with carving is low relief of heads, snakes, etc. For this finer work smaller tools are required. A small chisel made from an old Dao tang sharpened down is used to cut out the slits for the Dao and Dao belt. The finer carving is done with sharpened Chabili. Wooden dishes are carved out from the solid and polished with a rough leaf called Poktsok. A cheaper, lighter dish is made of bamboo, and is to be seen in every house. A section of bamboo free of nodes is cut and shaved down till it is very thin. Then it is split down one side and wormed over the fire until it can be opened out flat. Two slits are then cut at each end and the ends folded up like the ends of a paper parcel and laced in place with cane.

Thus, timber has multifarious use. Tree trunks serves as poles, pillars, battens and cross-beams for house construction. A trough used for thrashing paddy is a type of hallowed trunk. The most exquisite manufactures out of wood are dishes (with lags), saucers, platters, cups and other utensils which exhibit in their own fashion a splendid workmanship. A wooden cup may have cane hanks. A mortar, a sort of a big board with three or four holes scooped out, is also made of wood. Smaller mortars have single hole scooped out.

Wood carving has more artistic than commercial value. It was, through its association with its past, connected with head-hunting, as evidenced in the use of the wood carved human skull in imitation of true heads, used generations ago by head-hunters. In the Moung carved animal frames such as Mithun, tiger, elephant, monkey and horn-bill lie scattered about. Wood carving associated with the performance of certain rituals appears to have been undertaken corporately.

By wood carving, dolls, statues, tobacco, pipes and other designs are worked, some of them coloured. Spear shafts are also of wood. By wood carving, they make different figures and furniture for decorating their houses.

Smithery

Local forges where certain agricultural tools and ceremonial weapons are made still exist but their number is dwindling.

In these forges the manufacture of spear-heads, Daos, scrappers, knives, and others, on primitive lines is still going on. The equipment until late years was improvised. Production rates at certain places may have greatly been reduced owing to the availability of the cheaper agricultural tools and implements which are procured from outside. In the forges, the rusted or second-hand iron implements after being melted, are forged into numerous tools and implements. But in the interior places, demand of the indigenous implements has not yet dwindled because the bulk of the village farmers are still acquainted with their age-old tools. It may be worth noting that, at present village blacksmiths have made use of springs and other mechanical devices in place of the old piston bellows for supply of air to the forges. Iron hammers at places have also replaced stone which for so long blacksmiths were using.

In the olden days Rengmas were probably the only Naga tribe who smelted iron by boiling and heating the stone which contained iron-sand. The Rengmas are considered to be among the best Naga blacksmiths. Iron pyrites are abundant on the shales commonly noticed in Lotha Rengma hills.

In the process of smelting, an ore is a form of granite or gneiss moulded cylindraceous was first boiled on a fire as that was a first step to shake sands, clay and other ingredients off a pure ore. This over, the ore was taken and lumped by beating it with a stone hammer. The entire process was repeated for a second time. The ore was boiled in a separate wooden vessel.

The ore had to be washed and its process had to be repeated to remove the sticky stone or sand ingredients or dust. By washing and heating it again during the final stage, they completed a process of extracting a solid metal. A sort of pigeon thus procured was split into two lumps, but to complete the process, it was necessary that they were joined again by means of a red earth, devised in such manner that it gave a necessary plastering and cohesion. It was by means of this first-rate iron that the best implements were manufactured, discernible from those of a second grade or rusted material.

In the system of melting of iron, the Rengmes, Angamis, Lothas and their neighbours use a broken earthen pot by which they keep the ingredients of iron hot by boiling on a fire when they have pasted into a solid mass till the metal becomes red-hot. It is then taken off, laid on a furnace and moulded into a flake by a certain process of hammering. A stone hammer is used in the process of lumping, but at the final stage, a big-sized hammer becomes more necessary. Thus by repeating the process of lumping, the metal becomes ready before it is turned out into different weapons, implements and furniture.

Under the impact of modern technical education a number of smithies have been established all over the state. Bellows, locally known as Misembong of the ordinary Naga type are still used in some villages. Pistons covered with feathers arranged tip downwards to give the necessary vernacular action force air down two bamboo cylinders. At the bottom the two bamboo outlet pipes are embedded in clay and unite at the fire.

All the other tools used are of foreign manufacture. Daos are made in some villages, but are not as a rule considered as good as those imported from the plains or from the Konyaks region. Blades for axes, hoes, and sickles are the articles most commonly made.

Pipes of thick tin or sheet brass obtained from the plains are made at several places. A spade piece of metal is cut out, heated and bent, the 'handle' of the spade forming the stem, and the 'blade' the bowl. A little bamboo mouth-piece bound in with cane completes the pipe. Bracelets, women's head rings and heavy neck rings are cast from broken brass. Stone moulds are used. The inside is smeared with pig's fat and the molten metal poured in. The moulds are straight, and the bars when removed are again heated and bent, and finally finished off with a file. A little ornamentation, more or less of herringbone pattern is put on with a chisel.

Stone Work

Nagas generally neither square nor carve stone, nor make any use of it as a building material. Spindle-whorls are made from certain hard pebbles found in streams. The stone selected is ground flat on other stones, and bored with a spear but twirled between the hands. The edges are then ground until it is circular. Pipe bowls of the kind called *Moyapong* are made in Longmisa and one or two other Chongli villages. The material used is a soft grey stone with a close grain. A conveniently sized piece is scraped down to the shape of a bowl with an old 'Dao' and hollowed out with a little chisel made out of a broken hoe.

The hole in the bottom is made with a finer iron drill twirled between the hands. The outside is then rubbed and smoothed on a stone and, after being smeared with rice water, it is left to be smoked on the bottom try over the fire. Finally it is given - two coatings of the sap of a parasitic tree called *Charak*, which imparts to it a dull black colour. Corundum is found in the district of Mokokchung, where it is used in repairing crystal ear ornaments. Two or three small holes are bored on either side of the break with a fine pump-drill and powdered corundum. The edges are then stuck together with gum, and thread bound tightly through the holes bored to take it.

Manufacture of Salt

From the brine springs, salt is locally excavated and manufactured, by boiling water on the fire over the iron cauldrons or Chungas, especially designed, the lid having been tightly compressed until the water becomes evaporated and turned out into solid salt. Such enterprises are carried in jalukie, Peletkie and Mbaupungwa or Mbangpanlwa (Zeliangroung area), and Akhegwo, Yis, Purr, Molen and Ozeho villages (Chakhesang area). The salt thus manufactured locally sells well in the market as the Nagas prefer it to the imported salt and sometimes make up its deficiency by importing the salt locally produced from the brines of Mao area in the neighbourhood; the local salt being highly valued. In the Zeliangroung area it goes up and sold at a higher price. The salt contains sodium sulphate in great proportion which is admitted to be helpful for digestion.

Fire Making: Long, long ago fire and water fought. Fire could not stand before water, and fled and hid in bamboo and stones, where it is to this day. But someday they will fight again, and fire will put forth all its strength, and the Great Fire (Molomi), which old men talked of long before the missionaries came will sweep up from the banks of the Brahmaputra and burn all that there is upon the earth. Yet water will be the conqueror in the end, and great flood will follow the fire and cover the world for ever. When fire fled from water no one but the grasshopper saw where it had taken refuge. His great staring eyes, however, took in everything and he saw it go and hide in stone and bamboo. In those days men and monkeys alike had hair. And the grass hopper told the monkey where the fire was lying hid, and the monkey made fire come out of a bamboo fire-thong.

But man was watching and stole the fire. So monkeys have no fire and have to keep themselves warm as best they can with their fan. Man, on the other hand, has lost his fun because he has fire and no longer needs it.

It is because fire hid in bamboo and stones that Nagas nowadays make fire both with a bamboo fire-thong, and with hard stone and iron. The fire-thong is of the ordinary Naga type. The end of a dry stick is split and a stone inserted. Tinder consisting of fine shavings or cotton wool or some such things is put on the ground and the fork of the stick held firmly on it with the foot. The operator slips a bamboo thong under the fork and, holding one end in either hand, pulls it rapidly backwards and forwards. In less than half a minute the tinder catches and the thong chars through. When the object is not to make a fire but to make the omens the stick is often not split and tinder is not used.

The thong is simply charred through by being pulled backwards and forwards under the stick, and the fibres at the burnt end of the thong examined and the omens taken from them. The hard stone with which fire is made is found in the various parts of Nagaland. To make fire tinder is held against the stone and the edge of the stone struck a glancing blow with a small piece of iron. For tinder the inner -coating of the bark of a certain palm is used. This, together with the stone and iron, is kept in a little bamboo box. Old men are rarely without one of these boxes, and even for ordinary domestic use prefer stone and iron to the cheap and bad matches sold in the state. For ceremonial, use matches are strictly forbidden to all. For making new fire for a ceremony, the fire-thong is ordinarily used, though some Mongesen villages allow iron and stone to be used on 'Jhums'. For Jhum the fire-thong is de rigueur everywhere.

Other minor enterprises comprise ivory, horn and bone work practised on small domestic scale. They make beads of seeds and from ivory, they made designs such as bracelets and wristlets and other ornamental decorations are moulded. Bone is forged into several ornamental design. Dyed hair is used for decorating spears and sabres and necklaces. Several ornaments are moulded from the beads purchased from the plains.

Collection of honey from the bees warmed orchids is another subsidiary occupation, the local honey fetching good price, although the task is arduous and risky especially at the precipitous terrain. Drying of fish caught from Tizu and its tributaries is practised in and around Mehuri area.

Organised Industries

About the beginning of the present century, mention is made of the Messrs Moole Shuttle and Company, a cotton ginning factory, the first organised industry started at Merapani (Lotha Area). The industry was properly equipped; a pressing machine was installed for extracting oil from the cotton seeds; and cotton flakes prepared at the workshop fetched good prices in the market. The factory consumed a bulk of the locally-grown cotton in the Lotha Rengma, and Ao areas. In 1912, the industry was shifted to Furkating but it continued to consume the locally-grown Naga cotton.

Another private organised industry was saw-mill set up at Rangapahar during the pre-Independence. It was running well, fetching considerable price for the saw timber. Other main manufacturers were packing cases turned out of a soft wood locally known as *Bhelu*. During the Second World War, the mill provided timber to the army establishments in Dimapur. This mill caters to the demands of nearby' plains in both Assam and Nagaland.

Sugar Mills

A sugar factory has been established at Dimapur. The site located at Dimapur commands daily crushing capacity of 120 m tonnes, its installation has cost over 2.5 crore. For the cultivation of sugarcane over 1,000 acres of land has been cleared to feed the Dimapur sugar Factory. For so long the sugarcane from Dimapur was supplied to another sugar mill at Baruabamugaon, about 110 km away. The sugarcane area is to be extended up to 7,000 acres, the cultivation being assigned to the agricultural cooperatives.

The Nagaland Government at the same time constituted the Nagaland Industrial Development Corporation, an autonomous body which have deposited a substantial amount with the sugar schema. The Khandsari sugar plant was entrusted with certain technical works connected with the setting up of the mill. The state Khandsari Sugar Mill was inaugurated in Feb. 1968. This Khandsari mill is in a position to consume the sugarcane grown locally.

Seasoning-cum-Pressure Treatment

A seasoning-cum-Pressure Treatment Plant has been established at Dimapur in 1965. The total cost for 'its establishment involved the sum of Rs. 6 lakh employing at present about 100 persons.

Small Industries

To quote the Industries Revised Annual Plan for 1967-68, the economy of Nagaland was virtually based on agriculture. At present there is no major or medium-sized industries. Weaving and some other handicrafts are practised mostly for domestic and local consumption rather than for any other commercial purpose. Some small scale industries like shoe-making, tailoring, furniture making, printing press, saw mills, rice mills, etc. had sprong up years ago, but their contributions to the economic growth of the state is negligible.

Cottage Industries Training

- *Polytechnic School-cum-Production:* The first technical school was the Fuller Technical School located at Kohima, which provided training in carpentry and blacksmithy (included in the practical part of the curriculum) started in 1908. In 1910 it had an enrolment of fourteen boys trainees. The school provided special scholarships to the meritorious pupils under training.

The workshop's receipts of the school in 1912-13 came to over Rs. 1,177-11-2. The school was one of the most successful of similar institutions in Assam having capable and experienced instructions. In the words of the Chief Commissioner who visited it in 1913. I was very much pleased with my visit to the Fuller Training School at Kohima ....and I was glad that nearly all the boys turned out from here follow the profession which they have been taught in that school. After about fifty years this school became converted the junior Technical School but recently it was again elevated to the Polytechnical School.

In 1962-63 it had five teachers with forty-five trainees under instruction.

The Polytechnic School is so designed that it provides instructions in:

- Blacksmithy.
- Carpentry.
- Paper Making.
- Technical Lines.

At present the school has hosted accommodation for sixty seats, the borders are stipend-holders, worth Rs. 100 per mensem each. The main manufactures are furniture (both household and office), viz. Almirahs, tables, easy chairs, folding tables, tea-pots, etc. A scheme has further been drawn to produce electricians, fitters, and welders from the school.

Ruth's Naga Emporium

An important arts and crafts centre is the Ruth's Naga Emporium, named after (Mrs.) Ruth, the founder, a private organisation, started in Dimapur in 1962 which provides training in weaving. There are about 40 girl trainees at present who receive stipend. It is residential. The main manufactures are as the following:

- Variety bags (small).
- Variety bags (large).
- Neck-tie.
- Striped necktie.
- Lady's coat.
- Lady's coat (with scarf).
- Jacket (for men).
- Scarf (for men).
- Tea-cosy set.
- Dining Table mat.

- Original patterns of Naga shawls.
- Modern pattern of Naga shawls.
- Baby scarf.
- Picture frame (Naga stlye).

A great number of manufactures have been furnished to emporiums at Kolkata, New Delhi, Mumbai, Shimla, Guwahati, and Shillong and good sales have been made locally.

Training Cum Production Centre

Another similar residential institution is the Government Training-cum-production centre also situated in Dimapur at Donkan Basti, started in September 1966. It has an enrolment of twenty trainees. Each of the trainees is given stipend. The course of training is one year. The following articles are produced at this centre.

- Bed cover.
- Shawls.
- Bed Sheets.
- Coating.
- Table cloth.
- Pillow cover.
- Towel.
- Scarfs.
- Shirtings.
- Naga bags.

A scheme is being taken up that the centre would provide demonstration for the use of power-looms during to current plan period, the indent having been made by the Government of India for the supply of one thousand power looms to the entire state. It is expected that the demonstration would create interest for thread procurement on the part of the public.

Besides providing training to the residential trainees, the centre has been distributing threads, yarns and tools to the local weavers.

South Zeliang Weaving Institute

There is in addition at Peren the south Zeliangroung Weaving Institute-cum-production Cooperative Society with 24 members which during this initial stage has two handlooms with one sweater-knitting machine. The Institute produces Zeliang costumes. There are several instructors who impart training to several dozen girls. All these girls are given stipend. The stipend rates varies according to the category of training. The Institute is residential.

Chakhesang Welfare Centre

In the Phek Subdivision, also exist two women Welfare Centres which impart training for tailoring, namely the Women Tailoring cum Production Centre at Pfutsero and Women Welfare Centre at Phek. At the Pfutsero Centre, girls receive training in weaving and spinning, and undertake production of trousers, Naga ties, sweaters, bags and other specimens, the Centre being equipped with 15 machines. The Phek Centre, has not taken up the issue intensively, having only one foot machine and two spinning machines, and has been started only recently. Its main objective is to organise spinning in the area.

Industrial Cooperatives

The cooperatives have a vital role in industrial planning for which the following deserve mention:

- Lulho Weaving Cooperative Society in Kohima.
- Industrial and Multi-purpose Cooperative Society in Kohima.
- Terhase Hand-made Paper Cooperative Society in Kohima.
- Sede Carpentry Cooperative Society, Kohima.
- Terhuja Ivory Cooperative Society in Kohima.
- Naga Dress Weaver Cooperative Society in Kohima.
- Naga Industrial Cooperative Society in Dimapur.

In addition there are at least fifty multi-purpose cooperative Societies in Mokokchung, Phek, Mon, Zenhoboto.

There are a number of schemes for the development of handicrafts in the state

- Extension assistance in carpentry, blacksmithy and sheet metal smithy.
- Setting up of more blacksmithy units to cater to the production of agriculture tools.
- Expansion of assistance in the following enterprise — pottery, beekeeping, gur-making, soap and candle making, hand pounding, etc.
- Making of moulded plastic articles.
- Extension of assistance to the salt makers in Maluri area and steps to boost up production rates.

The Emporium

There is only one Cottage Industries Emporium situated in the capital which stocks with exquisite costumes, manufactures, and handicrafts of Nagaland, the Emporium in addition has transacted sales of handloom and handicraft products in considerable numbers with state's Museums.

Another landmark in the meseulogical development was the proposed construction of Nagaland Industrial Emporium at New Delhi, assigned to the Central Public Works Department, New Delhi, which was to involve an expenditure of almost one and half lakhs of Rupees. It was completed in 1972. The state Emporium is expected to boost up the sales of handloom products and handicrafts of Nagaland, in lines with other State Government scheme in setting up respective Industries Emporium at Delhi.

Exhibition, Demonstration and Melas

To accelerate production rates, it has been decided to display exhibitions in the state. In the exhibition the leading local craftmen are given National Awards. There is special awards for craft in spear making.

The Training

Another scheme towards providing training facilities to local boys and girls in various vocational trades and crafts within and outside the state would be exhibited with an object in view towards accelerating the growth of the large and medium-sized industries. Training facilities have also been provided in the manufacture of sugar, paper and pulp, etc.

Industrial Estate

Survey for establishing the sites for the Industrial Estate at Dimapur as well as its layout has already been expedited and the scheme for building the Small Industries Service Institute Extension Centre has been taken up. By the end of the present Five Year Plan 22 Industrial sheds have been completed.

The state of Nagaland is deficient in coal, petroleum and natural gas. The non-availability of these power resources is coming in the way of industrial development. There is increasing stress on the development of hydel power.

One of the commendable achievements is the installation of the 66 KVA Station at Dimapur on the agreement basis with the Assam Electricity Board for supply of power from other hydro-projects in Assam. The substation at Dimapur when completed with a capacity of over 10,000 KVA would supply electric power to 24 towns.

Schemes for Electrification of Nubza Nullah: Themokedima and Phek are being taken up; schemes at Dimapur and Zubza when expanded would provide power to the offing industrial units. It is important to note that prior to the inception of the interim Government, privately organised power houses existed in Nagaland. In 1963, Electrical Department was bifurcated from PWD and was created into a separate department. It is to be noted that Wokha, the subdivision Headquarters of Lothas north of Tseminyu falls within technical control of a Chief Engineer, Kohima.

Business and Trade

Prior to the British advent, barter (exchange of commodity for commodity) played a dominant role in the local economy. The system was primitive and prevailed among the neighbouring tribes. Its anomaly was that necessity and not value determined the price of a commodity. Merchandise comprising woven goods, yarns, livestock, foodgrains, agricultural implements, house hold furniture, wares were interchanged in a community. There were no market centres. The trade was conducted by peddlers and vendors.

Salt, without which he cannot live, the Naga can only obtain in the plains. To barter for this necessity he, takes down 'pan' cotton, chillies, ginger, gourd, mats and the gum of a tree called *Liyang*. Much of the salt so obtained is sold to Phom and Changs across the Dikhu for pigs, fowls, etc. A Naga selling to trans-frontier tribes in this way expects to make about 300 per cent on the transaction. A small quantity of salt from Naga salt wells reached the people. The distribution system was however not efficient. The local salt was valued more for its medicinal properties than as a condiment. A certain quantity of wild tea seed was taken down to the plains and sold to gardens. Hill 'Pan' is much appreciated by Assamese and Bengalis; large quantities are taken down by Nagas themselves, but some is exported indirectly through Sangtams. Members of Sangtam tribe, who are always hard up, coming to work as casual labourers in the fields of 'Pan' leaves, which they take down to the plains and sell for more than they would have received in cash from their Naga employers. Other 'Pan' goes to Kohima. Lothas from Tsingaki come for it and deliver it fairly fresh in Kohima Bazaar.

Besides salt, large quantities of imperfectly dried fish are brought from the plains. In the villages this dried fish fetches three times the price paid for it on the banks of the Brahmaputra. Only certain villages grow cotton. The surplus is either bartered for salt in the plains or, by villages far in, with other Naga villages for salt. Between Nagas salt is sold for three time, its weight of uncleaned cotton, according to the amount of cotton available.

A Naga usually wears cloths woven by his wife, and if he buys a decorated cloth he must be careful to brush it six times with a bunch of nettles before putting it on, while he utters a prayer that all ill luck there may be in it may depart. Ivory armlets, too, and crystal ear ornaments are considered as dangerous things to buy. The purchaser on his return must sacrifice a fowl and pray that, since the ornaments have not been bought with stolen money but with wealth honestly come by, the wearer may long to enjoy them. Nagas scrape a shaving from a spear or pull a thread from a cloth before selling it.

Trade of cattle is also an important activity in Nagaland. Lothas bring them up in droves and sell them to local people at a flat rate of so much per animal. At first sight the profits made by Naga traders strike one as enormous. But there are certain factors to be taken into consideration. Most Nagas do a little trading, but no one depends on it for his livelihood. There is no one who can wait for a small percentage of profit on a big turn-over. A man whose sole annual commercial venture is a trip to the plains for twenty rupees worth of salt wants a high percentage of profit, or it is not worth going. Out of that profit too he has to feed himself and his assistant while they laboriously carry the salt into the hills, for there are no cart roads or railways in the country. Many Nagas grow rich by agriculture, but few by trade.

The Naga tribes practised also a primitive system of currency. The medium of exchange among the Angami Nagas was a conch-shell equivalent to one cow. They also reckoned value in terms of hoes. Among the Rengmas, one cow was worth fifty baskets of rice. They used also spearheads and Daos for currency. Southern tribes used stones for weighing precious ornaments, one stone being equivalent to a Seer (80 Tolas) of the old Indian system of weights and measures. The practice however, was not common, being applied only to a few dealers who had trade relations with Manipur and Dimapur.

Barter is still confined towards the remote villages which have no regular means of communication with the administrative centres. It is still conducted side by side with currency in the interior areas situated far from the main streams of traffic and commerce. Society therefore ranges from barter to an industrialised stage; the country folk are still prone to practice barter for meeting some of their wants when an emergency has to be tackled with. Regular trade in terms of currency and the present metric standards of weights and measures have replaced barter totally in urban and advanced areas.

There was once an inter-district trade across the hills from Manipur to Sibsagar. Different stories have been preserved of Nagas carrying on trades in the Hats on Dhansiri where Rengmas sold cotton and iron implements in large quantities. Hill products of other Nagas such as honey, wax, ivory, were sold in the plains. Stories still told are of the traders from Zeliangroung and Angami highlands who attended weekly markets hold in the nearby plains. During the middle of the last century the Nagas went to trade as far as Nowgaong but trade had flourished regularly with nearby markets such as Jorhat, Golaghat and Dimapur. The trade again of the southern portion was transacted with Manipur; the trade with Kabui Nagas and other tribes in the present Manipur state was held by Nagas, the immediate neighbours of Angamis to the south of Kohima.

Small Naga agricultural colonies had sprung in the foothills bordering on Sibsagar. Intermediary tribes such as Lothas, Aos conducted trade with southern Nagaland both through the low-lying area along the foothills and the mountain terrain. Salt trade from the plains was the monopoly of Lotha traders who supplied to Rengmas in the hills who were not in possession of brines.

One of the principal imports of Naga Hills was iron and iron-implements but iron-smelting was a one tribe's monopoly. During the pre-British advent iron trade from Rengma hills had considerably diminished. Cotton which the Rengmas had was left but little for trade. Yarn was also considerably purchased from outside. Beads which Nagas much liked for ornamentation were also brought from outside, mainly from Manipur and Assam. Much of the cattle in man's keeping over the highlands were meant for sacrifices during the festivals. Therefore, meat markets had occasionally to be supplemented with livestock purchased in the plains.

At one time before the District was constituted in 1866, Naga Hills were blockaded by the British authorities. Such measures were imposed in order to compel the Nagas to come to terms. It was a failure as many Naga traders in disguise got through the impenetrable jungles to the plain markets. Some traders from North Cachar, Zeliangroung and Angami areas who came openly without permits were confined to Asaloo in the North Cachar Hills.

The settlement of the administration helped to foster trade and commerce. In Government reports, we find a reference to the Zeliang and Angami traders who visited near and distant markets. They went as far as East Bengal, and Kolkata to dispose of merchandise and bring home beads and yarns.

But trade, still rudimentary in organisation, had not yet grown in proportion with the pace of the administrative expansion. Moreover; keen interest had not been taken to encourage trade and commerce on an elaborate 'scale, the entire trade being handled by a small number of merchants. There was a conspicuous absence of markets and whole sale dealers. The newly-opened bridle paths across hills were irregular means of communications, at times disrupted by cracks resulting from gigantic landslides. In other respects, economic transition was caused by the new avenues of employment at the tea estates, road constructions and building works. During the disturbance caused in the hills when the final Anglo-Angami was broken out.

In 1878-79, the Angami merchants numbering about 1,200 went for trade to Golaghat and as far as Guwahatis. They sold ivory, wax and clothes worth Rupees three thousand.

It was the Japanese invasion which brought another land mark in the modern Naga History so that new patterns and industry came into being. The invasion by the great Japanese power, resulted in age-long splendid isolation of the Naga Hills territory. The whole subcontinent became hectic, anticipating the fate of Kohima. Troops from all over India, from Great Britain from the Commonwealth countries came in an unbelievable speed to rescue Kohima, from the grip of the Japanese. With the troops came the supplies, machines and contemporary weapons. Dimapur became the military station and store; local resources were mobalised.

The Naga Hills, hitherto an excluded tract, all of sudden captured the headlines of the international dailies. Kohima became crowded with the multitude of new faces and persons of different complexions. New tastes, new fashions, new styles and new behaviour patterns quickly spread among the indigenous population. Naga dolls, toys, spears, Daos, costumes easily found exit through the soldiers to the different parts of the world. Demand was increased in local building materials and manufactures.

Mechanical Ideas Quickly Spread: stories told are that the local blacksmiths all put to use the condemned parts of machinery when they were forged at the snuthies into new traditional type of weapons and implements, many of which were purchased by soldiers after the war. Moreover, the blacksmiths invented a new device for running the fire into their forges by substituting their piston bellows with a chain which is said to be more economical and less time consuming.

Suppliers who amassed fortune during the war became noted businessmen. Even labourers got anew ideas by coming into contact with the technological operations. After the war electric power projects and piped water supply were started on the private basis by the local men. Communications increased to cover hitherto non-controlled area in Tuensang and Tirap.

Much more progress has been noted after the state was formed. Business has become more mobilised and trade has grown into bigger proportions. New administrative centres have grown into trade and supply stations. These factors coupled with the multifarious developmental projects in agricultural, industrial cooperative, power projects, transport, building and other spheres have set about more patterns of economic activities; ventures on the part of local people, in starting industrial units, stores and shops, cinema Halls, workshops, mills, petrol pumps are worthy of notice to cope with the newly-emerging demands and situations. All the industrial activities are concentrated at Dimapur. But Kohima is not less important as a supply centre to the Nagaland. Dimapur comes first to limelight owing to its railway access with the rest of India.

The main export transacted at Dimapur are cotton, jute, timber, forest produce, chillies, til and mustard seeds. Dimapur is one of the important Naga vegetable markets.

Import are much more varied which comprise groceries and food stuffs, drugs and medicines, textile goods, utensils, furniture and miscellaneous articles and items. In addition, technological, electrical, engineering and mechanical works are concentrated at Dimapur.

Kohima, a motor station which has communications with southern Nagaland and Mokokchung, comes next. Through it, trade, traffic and transport, stock and supplies in increasing volumes, pass to the central and southern Nagaland as well as Manipur. Therefore, it has become another centre. One of the main handicaps is the unhospitable roads and frequent landslides which cause breakdowns of communications during the monsoon. Rice mills, cinematography, furniture, firms, and shopping centres have sprung up; in addition at Kohima, there are many other government institutional centres.

Yet with the present developmental projects came technology and other applied science to the hitherto remote and impenetrable parts of their land. But still the picture ranges from barter to industrialised. Orientalism, modernism, neo-modernism and primitivism are exhibited and combined together. Another development is the growth of the retailed market conducted mainly by the CPOs, which inception dates back to 1957-58 when an Interim Government was formed. Foodstuffs were distributed at the fixed Government rates through the CPOs. About 1962 in the Headquarters only rice was indented and distributed but in Chakesang, other kinds of foodstuffs comprising onion, flower, atta, salt, pulses, sugar, mustard oil, ghee, and tea leaves were catered as domestic trade did not thrive there properly.

In Kohima and Dimapur, registered Ration Shops have replaced the CPOs. Cooperative stores and canteen in compliance with government regulations are selling commodities and goods at company rates. Price restrictions are imposed on the other categories of foodstuffs and goods. But open markets are not retailed. A branch of the State Bank was first set up at Dimapur. Up to 1965, it was the only Banking Institution in the state. In Kohima another branch of the State Bank was established in 1965-66. It settles Government payment and looks after the cash business of the local treasury.

Other cooperative banks are also being constituted which will extend credit facilities to the rural communities.

Agriculture

Agriculture on which men, animals and plants depend for their sustenance, is being influenced continuously by a set of physical and cultural factors. The physical factors influencing agriculture include topography, slopes, soils and climate.

Soils

Data based on scientific classification of soils of the Nagaland state is not adequately available. Even in the District Gazetteers and settlement reports there is scanty description of soils. In these government reports the soils have been briefly described in which texture, colour and level of land have been taken as the basis of soil classification.

In general, the soil cover in Nagaland, excepting the Valleys and along the foothills is quite thin. On the steeper slopes, torrential rains result in quick leaching of soils. The soil material washed is deposited in the valleys and along the foothills. The levelled flood plains which cover less than five per cent of the total area of the state are covered by clayey loams. These soils are rich in humus content and therefore well known for their fertility.

The hilly and mountainous slopes of Nagaland are covered by laterites and ferruginous red soil. Laterites found near Sibsagar District of Assam are deficient in organic matter and consequently of little importance from the agricultural point of view. Jhuming is normally practised in the ferruginous red soils. These soils have light texture and porous as well as friable structure. The Kaolinitic structure of soil is largely due to the higher proportion of clay.

The torrential rains during summer season lead to rapid soil erosion on the steep slopes. The problem of soil erosion has been accentuated by shifting cultivation which is the main mode of soil utilisation over the greater parts of the mountainous region.

In the southern parts of Nagaland, especially the territory occupied by Angamis, Chakhesang and Zelliangs, the rock strata being weak, landslides are frequent and occur almost annually during the monsoon and post-monsoon periods, causing disruption to communications and transportations. The Manipur National Highway and Kohima road which have been carved out in the soft clayey sedimentary rocks are often damaged by landslides resulting into transport disruption.

The Farming

Nagaland is essentially an agrarian state of the country. About 80 per cent of its total population is directly dependent on agriculture. In some of the tribes of Nagas, working in jobs other than farming, hunting, forestry and gathering is considered as a taboo. Although sedentary agriculture is practised but it is insignificant and confined to terraces around Kohima and in the arrow river terraces and alluvial fans. Shifting cultivation is the dominant agricultural system. It is therefore imperative to discuss the salient features of the shifting cultivation known as Jhuming in North East India.

Jhuming also known as 'Slash and Burn' is widely practised in the Hills of Nagaland. It covers over 73 per cent of the total arable area of the state. In Jhuming agricultural system the slopes of the hills are cultivated as long as they retain sufficient productivity to support the farmers. A field is sown usually for two to three years. When the fertility declines, the Jhumias shift their cultivation to new locations and establish new fields. The former field is abandoned to lie fallow long enough to regain fertility.

The key variable in the system is the fertility of the soil. Giving the nature of the system, vast tracts of land are required to support the dependent population at a reasonable standard of nutrition. It is said that Jhuming destroys vegetation and damages the resilient characteristics of the ecosystems. For these reasons it is considered to be the most uneconomic and primitive form of land resource utilisation. Nevertheless it is the material base for Naga tribes. Whatsoever the merits and demerits of shifting cultivation may be, most of the Naga tribes draw their livelihood partly from the natural ecosystem (collection and gathering) as well as from the manipulated ecosystem' in the form of Jhuming. Their economy is subsistence in character. The exploited of natural endowment is, labour-intensive, which is also aimed at producing crops form the family consumption.

According to one definition "Jhuming has been described as" any continuing agricultural system in which impermanent clearings are cropped for shorter period in years than they are allowed to remain fallow." As the nomenclature suggests a piece of land is cleared of its vegetative cover. The cut trees and undergrowth are allowed to dry at the spot and later on put fire. The ashes thus collected are spread on the entire patch before the onset of rains. Thereafter seeds are dibbled in the soil with the help of pointed digging sticks or other rudimentary implements.

The crops raised are protected against the ravages of wild birds and animals. On this land crops are raised for one to three years and thereafter when the soil is unable to support any crop further the field is abandoned to get recouped naturally. Cultivation is shifted to another patch and returns to the original plot after the completion of a cycle during which all favourable plots are cultivated from one to three years. Thus the cultivation moves in a circle, around the settlement which forms a permanent nucleus.

Shifting cultivation is subsistence in character. The subsistence character of Jhuming may be appreciated from the fact that a Jhuming plants specific crops to provide subsistence to the family at different times over the greater parts of the year and to ensure that each distinctive microclimatic and soil regime will be utilised by the crop that can best use its nutrients and moisture. The banana, pineapple and ginger are planted on the most fertile soils; pumpkin, beans and sweet potatoes in areas with high ash contents; potatoes in well-drained fertile patches; Yams in moist depressions; climbers along the fences and grains on the drier areas of Jhum field.

The crops grown, the agricultural operations done in an agricultural year differ from latitude to latitude and meso to micro agro-climatic regions. Nevertheless, the major agricultural activities and Jhuming operations may be broadly classified under the following headings.

- Search for Jhum land.
- Felling of trees and clearing of Jungles.
- Burning of trees and dried vegetation.
- Allotment of land.
- Sowing and plantation of crops.
- Digging and hoeing of fields.
- Plantation of vegetables, dibbling and sowing of seeds.
- Weeding and harvesting of vegetables.
- Harvest of main crops.
- Fallowing.
- Collection of ratoon crops.

In order to understand the cultural ethos of Naga tribes and Jhuming as their material base, it is essential to examine these operations in detail.

Search for Jhum land: The usual process of shifting cultivation demands the selection of a patch of land on hill slope. The selection of land is normally done in winter months

(December of January). The auspicious task of selection of field and delineation of its boundary is the function of the village headman, who normally take the advice of the village priest and other elderly persons of the village. The selection of a tract to be brought under cultivation in a given year is done on the basis of colour, texture and structure of the soils about which the elderly Jhuming have empirical experience and expertise.

Usually a whole village cultivates in one tract though in the case of very big village each Khel (an exogamous group which indicates the unit or subdivision of a village) may select a different area for cultivation of crops. The gregarious method has several advantages. It is easier to fence in a big block than a lot of small fields, birds are not as destructive to cereal crops as they would be in small isolated patches in the Jungle; the access and approach paths can be prepared and maintained easily; and friends can conveniently help each other in sowing, planting, hoeing, weeding and harvesting operations.

The day when the village headman alongwith his advisors goes in the forest for the identification and selection of suitable patch to be brought under cultivation, the village must remain Genna (chaste) the night before and must refrain from eating the meat of anything killed. It is believed that any violation of this may bring hardship to the village in the shape of crop failure and epidemics.

Once the area to be brought under cultivation is determined the villagers cut small footpath to make easy access to the field.

Clearing of Jungles and falling of trees is an arduous operation and therefore usually done by male workforce. The clearing of vegetation is done with the help of Daon, bush knives and axes with great manual energy. Slashing and lopping of trees commences in the early hours of the day and continues till sunset with a rest period in the midday in the field. This operation takes six to ten days, depending on the nature of forest and the infested undergrowth.

In some of the Naga tribes, clearing of Jungle is a joint responsibility of the entire village or Khel, while in others it is the task of individual families. February is the month for slashing and fields development. Bushes, shrubs and small trees with this stems are cut, but big trees and those which are at suitable places for use as climbing poles for Yams, beans, gourds, pumpkins are after left standing. Trees with well-grown thick stems are merely lopped, and in some villages rich men leave a few branches unlopped at the top of trees. There is apparently no idea of leaving a place of refuge for supernatural Jungle spirits. Leaving a few branches is considered as a symbol of status and wealth.

The slope selected for Jhuming, being a community land is allotted to each household. At the time of allotment of land, the size of family and workforce available are the standard norms taken into consideration. The area allotted per family varies on an average between 0.5 to 2 acres. More area is given to large-sized families or to the households who is allotted steep sloppy land.

March is the month of clear skies in Nagaland in which the day temperature reads up to 32°C. After slashing the twigs, branches, straw, grasses and logs are spread over the field and allowed to dry under the scorching heat. The drying period may last for three to four weeks. Though the Nagas can lit a fire even with very wet wood, nevertheless they prefer to wait until the slashed material is reasonably dry, otherwise they say, the firing will be too tiring and the results unsatisfactory. After slashing and lopping comes the burning stage of Jhum land. Depending on the prevailing conditions, the dried growth as well as the uncut trees standing in the clearance are set on fire. The objective of burning is to add more nitrates to the soil to enhance its fertility and to remove weed tree for a longer period. In fact, the burning process raises the ground temperature up to 64°C. Consequently, seeds of weed are reduced to ashes.

Burning of fields may last one day to one week, depending on the weather, winds, man power available and the size of field. Proper burning of fields requires a good deal of knowledge, skill and expertise. The fire must be neither too intense damaging the soil nor too weak. If the fire is weak the soil is left black with too much of charcoal and unburnt wood. On the contrary, well-burnt land has a greyish white colour with ashes is proper place and with all the remaining large trees dead.

Superstition is a part of tribal cultural ethos. Even in the case of sowing and plantation operations they strongly believe in auspicious and bad omen dates and days. For example, the most auspicious time for burning of Jhum field is the seventh and ninth days after the full moon. The Jhum tract occupied by dry grasses, stems and twigs is lighted from the bottom with a fire-Thong, match sticks and match box must on no occasion be used. Initially, the forest is lit by the village priest after performing certain rituals and religious ceremonies. The experienced Jhumias taking advantage of the wind will fire the field from the windward side which makes it look as the work goes on by itself.

Learners have a hand time as their Jhum field fire tends to go out. At the time of burning operation, care is taken so that the fire does not spread into forest. After the burning is complete, the unburnt or partly burnt rubbish are collected at once along the boundary of the field especially on the downward slope to check soil erosion. When the burning is over, the ashes are scattered over the ground to increase the phosphate and nitrogen contents in the soil. A prolonged period of dry-weather may render the land useless for Yams and some other crops in such case only maize, pulses, millets and vegetables are grown.

After the burning and allotment of Jhum field, each household selects a site for his field house, locally known as Aluchen, Alute. Selection of site is a crucial decision and cannot be done in haste, for on that site will be his place of sacrifices, his thrashing floor, and the little house where he and his family will eat their midday meal on the working day — obviously a spot where every precaution must be taken against evil spirit. He must therefore remain chaste the night before and refrain from eating the meat of anything killed at a ceremony for sickness.

The Jhuming goes down early in the morning and clears a little space. Then he takes the omen with a fire-Thong. He also notes his dreams of that night and if they indicate that all is well he goes down alone again the subsequent day and offers an egg or a fowl with a prayer that he may have good crops and be preserved from sickness. He eats the fowl himself, and if he does not finish it he must not bring the what is left over into house but must eat it in the Morung (Bachelor's dormitory).

Dibbling and broadcast of seeds take place in the old fields in the later part of April or in the first week of May, depending on the availability of soil moisture, while the newly-established Jhum field is generally sown in the last week of May or the first week of June.

Before the commencement of sowing and dibbling of seeds, in all the Naga tribes, the village priest is invited to initiate the formal sowing. The village priest goes about half way down to the new fields with a fowl of either sex and some seeds or rice. He clears a little space and sows the rice seeds and fences it round. Then he kills the fowl by cutting his throat with a sharp bamboo and takes the omens. The fowl he cooks and eats except for one leg which he puts in his basket and carries home. This leg will be required later. As he goes towards the village he complains of the weight of his load (presumably to induce heavy loads at the ensuing harvest) and custom ordains that he should sit down and rest at least once on the way. This ceremony is called *Tenten* and the next day is Tentenmung.

Sowing can be done at any time after the tenth day from the new moon, but the period from full moon to the end of the new moon is the best. Others, say that the best day on which the moon is half way to ill and that the next best day is the seventh day from this date. These ceremonies are known to result into good crop and overall prosperity to the family.

The day of general sowing is a ceremonial occasion for the whole village. On this day it is interesting to observe that the male members of each family on reaching the Jhum field in the morning engages themselves in the preparation of digging sticks. The seeds are sown either by broadcast or by dibbling. The dibbling and planting off seed is an exclusive job of the female workers. The male workers broadcast seeds of crops like maize, millets, pulses, cotton, and sesamum while vegetables are dibbled by females.

In the process of dibbling the seeds, the females walk over the field with a digging stick or bill-hook in hand, make hole in the ground, sow a few seeds and cover it over with earth by pressing it down with her toe. At the occurrence of showers, the seed began to sprout. In general the entire field is never dug and no irrigation is made. While sowing, care is taken to dibble the seeds of climbers along the outer boundary of the field or near the stems of lopped trees or at the place where the ash deposits had been maximum. This practice economise on land and gives better agricultural returns.

Once the crop is sown, the Jhumias pay cursory attention to the crop. He however, removes weeds and the crops are protected from stray cattle and wild animals by erecting bamboo fences at the vulnerable sides. Moreover, weeds are removed from the crops. In case weeding is not done, they would grow up faster and choke the crops sown.

Weeding of crops is done with the help of hoe, locally known as Alulem or Aya. The hoe is usually a small hoop of iron with two pieces of bamboo attached to either end crossing to form a handle. A further development of primitive form consists of a bamboo handle branching out into a bark to the limbs of which the half circle of iron is attached. The bamboo hoe is however, still in use in many Lotha, Ao, Rengma, Angami and Sema villages. Usually weeding is done after about three weeks from the date of sowing, while hoeing of vegetables is a must for after every ten to fifteen days. Millets, rice, cotton, maize and pulses sown mixed together are not hoed more than once.

Under the warm and moist conditions the crops grow rapidly, but this agro-climatic condition is conducive for the fast growth of insects and pests also. These insects and pests damage the crops. Insecticides and pesticides, the costly inputs, are not being applied by the shifting cultivators. They however perform certain ceremonies to protect their crops from pests and disease, which they believe occur because of the ill effects of bad spirits. For example, when peddy is a few inches in height every villager observes one day's Anmng called *Mosurnung*. This is supposed to prevent the young plants from withering. When the rice is about a foot and half in height they observe another Amung Called rice plant insect catching ceremony. The Misenis a little brown beetle which is very destructive to young rice plants. The day on which the elders give notice call in the village catch and kill a few of these pests and throw the dawn outside the village fence as they come home in the evening. The next day, they clear the paths. The insect catching is done with the help of indigenous net traps.

About one and a half months after the date of sowings beans, gourds, cucumbers, turnips and pumpkins are ready for harvest and the shifting cultivators start their harvesting after performing certain rituals. From thence onwards there is adequate availability of fresh vegetables. The surplus vegetables are given as gifts to the neighbours or bartered with them when the vegetables are in abundance, they are supplied to the markets of neighbouring towns to fetch some amount, out of which kerosene, oil, spices, salt, utensils are purchased. Thus from June to September the shifting cultivators regularly get fresh vegetables to eat and also some money for their families.

Harvesting is continuous process which last for about six months, i.e. June to September. Vegetable, cotton, etc. are the crops which demand regular harvesting. But the main crops of cereals are harvested in September and October.

Crops grown in the old fields are harvested first as they are sown earlier (August, September) as compared to the sowings of newly-established Jhum fields. The main crops of new Jhum fields are normally harvested between the middle of September and October. Maize, millets, and pulses are harvested simultaneously (September). Paddy is however, the last to be harvested.

Before the cereal crops are harvested a pig of either sex is sacrificed by the village priest. First of all the senior priest of the village reaps a few ears of paddy and puts them into his basket. He struggles home complaining of the weight and his wife helps him to put down his load and remarks how exhausted he is with his heavy work and what a fine crop there is. He and his wife eat a little of this rice in the evening.

Sickle and sharp indigenous knives are the tools used in ripening the crops. The reapers cut the ears with a very short stalk (stalk is not needed for fodder as cattle-keeping is rare in Nagas), gathering a bunch in the left hand and cutting with a small sickle thrown over the shoulder into the reaping basket on the back. Families combine at the time of harvest and help each other to get their crops quickly. Women, girls, and elderly men reap, while sturdy young men go round with baskets into which they empty the contents of each reaper's basket, taking what they have collected to the threshing floor.

The harvested paddy is thrashed by being beating on a wooden log and winnowed with a fan of bamboo matting. The grains thus obtained are measured in measuring baskets and carried up to the granary.

Once the complete crop is harvested in the month of October, the Jhum land usually has a well-developed cover of weeds. The weeds, however, do not develop in the sweat potatoes fields and the vegetable beds as there crops are repeatedly hoed and weeding operations are frequently done in them. From the fallow lands the shifting cultivators gather ratoon vegetables and cereals for one year and then finally leave the field to recoup fertility.

Seasons of the Main Crops

Generally the sowing season for terraced rice-fields is April-May. The grain ripens towards October. The Jhum paddy seed is sown during the spring time; in many cases the plant sprouts in May, followed in July by weeding, the grain ripens in July but sometimes the ripening season may go as late as September.

Millets do not take a long stage to ripen. The seed is usually sown in January and the grains ripens in April or May; the harvest soon follows.

In the case of maize, the seed is sown during March and harvested in July. In many places millets are grown mixed with maize. Kachu is grown during March but takes quite long to ripen for it is harvested towards the close of the year.

Pulses are planted in May, harvest comes is December, Soya beans are also grown during the same season with pulses while Til Sesamum is grown in April and harvested in November. Ginger is sown in March and harvested in December and January. Sugarcane is planted in January and February and harvested after ten months in December. Potato is grown in March, the harvest following after about two and a half months. The sowing and harvesting periods also depend on the attitude of a place above the sea level. Thus a uniform crop calendar is not feasible. Cropping practices and agricultural operation also vary in the valleys and slopes, in the Jhuming and terraced fields.

Some vegetable crops such as brinjal, potato, tomato, mustard have two seasons of growth in one year, conforming to the summer and winter. Mustard both leaf and seeds are grown in October or November which harvest in February. Brinjals do not take a long stage to ripen. The seeds being sown in March, while the harvest follows just after a couple of months. Tomato is grown in October but fruiting is caused till February. Most of the beans are sown in March, yielding the harvest in May. Gourds are generally grown in February while harvesting is done in July.

Mixed Cropping

Mixed cropping is a common practice in the Jhuni lands of Nagaland. Cash crops like pineapple, and bananas are however, grown as monocrops which are perennial in character. Usually, different crops are sown together in Jhum land. This is also known as irregular planting.

Mixed cropping has been adopted by the Nagas as it has several advantages. A mixed of plants may grow more efficiently than single species because different species may create a local milieu and exploit it better. This practice gives additional yields of vegetables and root crops without much extra work. The shifting cultivators on the basis of their empirical experience mix the soil exhausting crops with the soil-enriching crops. Rice, maize, millets, Til (sesamum) and cotton, the soil exhausting crops are mixed with lagumes (Green-gram, black-gram, red-gram, etc.) which increase the fertility of soil. Moreover, through the practice of mixed cropping, the vegetables and cereals harvest at different periods, thereby providing the Jhuming with varied foods for nearly nine months in a year. In a year of adverse weather conditions also they get something as the high moisture requiring crops are mixed with draught-resistant crops.

Selection of crops to be inter-planted depends on the general slope of the field, depth and quality of soil, the overall milieu of the main crop and the time needed for the full growth and life-cycle of the main crop. Owing to variations in geo-ecological conditions a uniform inter-planting of crops is not possible. Consequently, what applies to Angamis may not be fit to Lothas, Konyaks, Semas and Chang tribes.

When rice is the main crop, tapioca, ginger, jute, hemp are mixed and inter planted. In maize area, Arum, tobacco, potatoes, turnips, cotton and beans are inter planted, while a Yam field is mixed with Kiri (small-millet), topioca, beans, sesamum and vegetables. In a Taro field, bananas, and vegetables are grown. These mixtures are highly diversified and therefore generalisation is difficult as the decision-making about crops to be sown differs from family to family depending on its requirements and inputs available.

Calendar

The Jhuming follow a definite schedule in their agricultural activities. In fact, Jhuming is a way of life, evolved as a reflex to the special ecosystem and the sociocultural milieu. There are cogent reasons behind the customs and agricultural practices of the Naga tribes. The climate, the terrain, the food habits, and their self reliance, all have a say in shifting operations. The whole gamut of primitive society is inter-woven with the means of food production. Unless the weather conditions force, they try to follow the traditional schedules (based on empirical experience) in the sowing, harvesting, and other agricultural operations. They know by experience that the success or failure of Jhum crops largely depends on timely sowing and weeding. The inputs need to be applied at the right time.

In the agricultural operations the Naga tribes follow a lunar month. No one can say off-hand how many months are there in a year. Only a few months have names, the nameless ones being reckoned as so many months after a named month or describing according to the agricultural operations carried on in them or after the festival celebrated in them.

In shifting agricultural system, agricultural operations are largely confined from February to November, though December and January are the months in which reconnaissance of slopes to be brought under cultivation is done. The Nagas who depend on shifting cultivation remain busy throughout the year, doing various agricultural activities, though the work load is maximum during the slashing off forests, sowing and harvesting of crops. Mid-November to the end of January is the period in which very little work is done in the Jhum field. This is the period when they collect ratoon crops and gather fruits nuts and other edible from forests. During this period of less work Naga youths go for hunting in the nearby forests and hunt indiscriminately birds, fowls, dear, crow, hornbill while the females remain busy in weaving and handicrafts.

Jhum Cycle

Slopes and tracts for Jhuming are not selected and cleared in any given sequence. There is always room for choice. The period of consecutive cropping and fallowing differs from tribe to tribe and altitude to altitude. It cannot be said with authenticity after what length of time the primitive inventor of shifting cultivation had to come back to the same plot in Nagaland because he had vast areas to move about. But at present, the tremendous increase in population, decrease in death rate, depletion in soil fertility of Jhum and have staked down the Jhumias to smaller areas. The shifting cultivators have not got much choice left to shift about. This world has become small which is becoming increasingly smaller and he has been forced to move about in a narrow circle. In the forties and fifties of the last century, the period before which the Jhuming had to return to cultivate the same field was about fifteen to twenty-five years. This long Jhum cycle was partly due to small size of population and partly due to better fertility of soil which used to be rested for about twenty to thirty years.

Now Jhum cycle in various tribes of Nagaland varies from five to fifteen years. The longer Jhum cycle has been recorded in Konyaks, Changs, and Sangtams who live in sparsely-populated and less accessible hilly areas.

Rotation of Crops

In general, rotation of crops is very much constrained by the geo-ecological, agro-climatic and socio-economic conditions. The rotation of crops followed by the Naga tribes is traditionally, exclusively designed to fulfil the essential needs of the family, there is more stress on cereals, pulses and vegetables. In fact, they always mix legumes with maize and millets to maintain the fertility of soil, even then the new seeds of these crops which may provide higher returns have not been developed and diffused.

The cold and relatively long dry spells of rabi (winter) season do not encourage the Jhumias to grow a second crop in the field in winter. It was however, observed in the Jhum lands of Lotha territories that they grow in small patches oil-seeds in winter. Large-scale adoption of dry-weather resistant rape-seeds if developed and diffused may bring additional incomes to the Jhumias which demand investigation and experiments.

Labour Requirements

To ascertain the labour requirements in shifting cultivation is a tedious job. The jhum fields show large individual variations in requirements of work per acre and there is absence of monoculture. Further great care had to be taken in estimating the areas of Jhum fields because of their irregular shapes and even more difficult indistinct boundaries. Another serious problem remained to be solved is that the Jhum fields are not harvested within a definite period. Food and vegetables are taken from them over a period of seven to eight months.

Nagaland:Rotation of Crops

First year	-	Second year	
Kharif (Summer Season)	*Rabi* (Winter Season)	*Kharif* (Summer Season)	*Rabi* (Winter Season)
(a) Paddy, Kachu, Sesamum, vegetables, ginger, Mejack, jute, hemp, tapioca	- - -	(a) Short duration paddy or maize or small millets	- - -
(b) Maize mixed with Nagdal, cotton	Rapeseeds'	(b) Kiri (small millets)	-
(c) Paddy, lentil, Nagdal.	-	(c) Kiri mixed with Nagdal	-
(d) Jobster, maize, pulses,	-	(d) Potatoes or millets	-
(e) Potatoes	-	(e) Potatoes	-
(f) Sweat-potatoes, tobacco, vegetables, maize	- -	(f) Early paddy or millets or vegetables	- -

Source: Field work by the author '

Only the innovators which constitute an insignificant minority sow oil-seeds (rape seeds) in the rabi (winter) season.

An acre of average Jhum field with moderate vegetation and average slope selected for Jhuming requires about 32 hours for slashing and lopping, 24 hours for burning, 26 hours for digging and removal of unburnt logs. Digging of fields is not a usual practice which is done normally in the cash crops (Yam, Taro, potatoes, ginger, pineapple). Sowing is a short duration operation to be finished within two to three days. When several crops are sown mixed, hoeing is rarely done but in the case of vegetables, potatoes maize, and cotton, it is required in the infancy stage of growth of the crop. Since crops are grown mixed all the crops are not harvested simultaneously and the period of their harvesting and threshing or processing also very for crop to crop, it is difficult to ascertain the working hours required for the cultivation of individual crops.

In Nagaland cultivation of perennial crops demands more working hours as compared to tubers, Taro, potato, Yam and sweet-potatoes. The labour required for gathering and collecting of food from the abandoned fields is hardly assessable. Under these conditions, assessment of actual labour input in Jhuming is difficult as the situation is altogether different from that of other agricultural systems.

Abuse of Jhuming

There are divergent opinions about the evils and adverse effects of shifting cultivation on the natural resources, ecosystems and ecology of the state. Many of the environmentalists, geographers and social scientists hold that it is primitive and unprofitable. It causes serious problems of soil erosion, soil depletion, forests, wildlife and water resources. It also disturbs ecosystems causing great ecological imbalances and therefore shifting cultivation should be stopped completely.

The opposite view supporting the continuance of shifting cultivation with necessary and effective reforms are of the opinion that it does little damage to soil in the form of soil erosion as the high humidity and heavy rainfall in the region does not permit the soil to remain exposed and uncovered by grasses for a longer period. Some form of vegetation immediately covers the top soil which contain it from further leaching and erosion. During the agricultural operations also as no ploughing, hoeing and pulverisation of soil is done, the soil remains compact and gets eroded at a relatively very slow pace. Moreover, Jhuming lands are generally steep slopes on which sedentary cultivation cannot be developed easily. In fact, Jhuming is a way of life, evolved as a reflex to the physiographical character of land under the special ecosystems. It is practised for livelihood and not without the knowledge of its adverse effects. The system, in spite of planning efforts, therefore, cannot be transformed easily.

Assessing the fact that Jhuming system cannot be stopped altogether, it is necessary to make the process more productive so that it may sustain the growing pressure of

Jhumia's population at a reasonably good standard of nutrition. For a change in Jhuming typology it is essential that the Jhumias are provided with land where they can cultivate and derive profits permanently. Once the retainability of soil is ensured, then the question of augmenting the soil fertility through the addition of manures and fertilizers could be meaningful. Measures should be taken to see that the Jhumias are trained in other types of occupations.

They should be given training in raising trees and plant protection, cottage and small industries, and indigenous handicrafts. Moreover, they should be trained in the development of dairying, piggery, sheep rearing, poultry, duck-keeping, fisheries, beekeeping and sericulture. For the effective implementation of these programmes, extension service, cooperative and marketing facilities are essential. The establishment of forest-based-small-scale industries may also help in boosting up the economy of the tribes and ultimately that of the state.

New crops of economic importance have to be searched and their diffusion should be extended in the isolated hilly tracts. In fact, a cropping pattern with higher inputs will enable the farmers to obtain greater yields per unit area and that will help in detracting the shifting cultivators from the uncertain way of life. The Jhumias should be provided inputs at a subsidised rates. The extension service units of the Agricultural Department should see that the amount advanced to the Jhumias is judiciously utilised for the productive purposes. The main approach to overcome the evil effects of shifting cultivation should be to change the Jhuming lands into sedentary farms or terraced fields.

In the Hilly areas, one of the most common measures that has been adopted in many small tracts with success is the construction and development of terraces. The area around Kohima inhabited by the Angamis has excellent terraced fields. Different types of terraces can be adopted to fit in with a particular type of ecosystem. These terraces have a definite advantage towards achieving sedentary farming in the areas of shifting cultivation. It has been accepted by most of the planners that terracing has to play a major role if agricultural land use in the hilly tracts is to be permanent.

There are however, many techno-economic problems in the development of terraces. Terracing, apart from being a costly measure, requires adequate irrigation facilities within the mountainous areas cannot be provided easily. It therefore, may not be feasible to go for large-scale terracing. The human energy input used in the Jhuming however, can be used, for the development of small terraced fields. In the Angami areas terraces have been developed with the help of local human energy, involving very little direct monetary input. Small demonstration centres in various pockets, providing technical helps, development of road connections and taking the farm community leaders on field visits to terrace cultivation areas may probably help in avoiding huge capital expenditure for large-scale terracing. This would provide productive use of human energy for land resource development.

So far as the slope limit for the development of terraces is concerned, it is difficult to prescribe any slope limit unless detailed evaluation for the existing terrace system in the region is made and other technical details are experimentally examined. A slope of 30° can be terraced and in the areas of steep slopes partial terracing may be developed. Once soil is properly developed with the help of manures and crop rotation practices the shifting typology will gradually get transformed into sedentary system.

Apart from terracing other soil conservation measures like bunding, trenching, gully plugging, etc. can be adopted according to the need of the area. Equally important is the development of protective cover like the development of orchards, suitable cash crops, grasses and leguminous crops especially on steep slopes. In short land use planning and practices should be based according to land capability and suitability.

The shifting cultivation is a way of life and there are cogent reasons behind the customs and practices of the tribal people. The climate, the terrain, their food habits, their families needs, their self reliance, all have a say in shifting cultivation. The whole gamut of the Naga society is interwoven with the means of food production. In other words, their way of life, training of youths, social and political systems, festivals, and beliefs, their philosophy of life are the products of Jhuming system of economy. This is why many of the new methods of cultivation recently introduced in the tribal areas, are yet to generate the process of cultural acceptability. Transformation of shifting cultivation into sedentary farming therefore, should be gradual and smooth, causing the least disturbance and human ecological imbalances to the Jhumias who are still in the relatively primitive stage of culture.

In view of the tradition-bound character of the society, the Jhum fields should be converted into permanent ones to secure (i) social acceptability from the tribes, (ii) full protection from deforestation as well as soil erosion, and (iii) the optional and judicious use of land resources.

As stated in the proceeding paras one of the ways of utilising the existing agricultural land without creating danger of large-scale erosion is to convert the gentle slopes into terraced fields in a phased manner. The Government of Nagaland has undertaken this formidable task of building the terraces. Besides granting subsidies and loans the government is also extending technical assistance. As a result the terraced average has increased from 21,363 hectares in 1962-63 to about 45,000 hectares in 1985-86. Keeping in view the time taken and monetary resources spent the achievements are far from satisfactory. Some of the bottlenecks have impeded the desired progress of the scheme. So as to overpower these hurdles it is desired that an effective and massive programme of educating the people about the abuses of the system nourished and enriched by their ancestors and merits of the proposed system be launched vigorously. It would be in the fitness of things to start at least one demonstrative form in each village.

Terraced cultivation needs adequate irrigation facilities. It is of no use to expand terraced average if there are no steps to irrigate the terraced fields artificially. To keep up the fertility of the soil it is essential that chemical fertilizers are used in required amount and the use of chemical fertilizers demand adequate irrigation facilities. In Nagaland three methods are employed for irrigating land. Contour channels like Kukals are taken out of the streams to irrigate fields located at higher, elevations. There are contour channels also taken out of the small reservoirs constructed by damming the streams. In some valleys a crude form of lift irrigation using mainly manual power is also used. It is to be noted that irrigation till about three decades ago was practised only by the Angami and Chakhe-sang Nagas, who have terraced fields.

Nonetheless, the first method is by far the most common and likely to remain the most important device even in future. There are many sites potentially suitable for the construction of small dams and weirs across the streams but a close as well as intensive study of the flow patterns of the streams is required. All such schemes need to be planned carefully so that the diversion of water may not affect other areas already depending upon the water of those streams. If cheap power is made available in the state steps can be taken to accelerate the lift irrigation scheme, so far limited to some valleys only. Currently there is a provision of extending subsidy to the farmers for building contour channels. This subsidy of course at enhanced rate should be continued. Apart from that the government should own the responsibility of constructing dams and weirs. The efforts of the state in this field have so far been quite satisfactory. Moreover, gully plugging and trenching, etc. apart from terracing can go a long way in arresting soil erosion and its conservation.

The success of these soil conservation measures would, nontheless, depend upon the extent the Nagas move from their present settlements located on steeper slopes to gentle gradient areas. Traditionally in view of strategic reasons in this region, an area of internecine warfare, the Naga groups have in the past always chosen hill tops, i.e. areas of steeper slopes for their settlements. In those days Naga village had to defend itself against the periodic raids of other tribes. Thus the vantage point of hill-top definitely had significant value. But this led to the non-cultivation of gentle gradient and valley flat areas located away from the settlements. Today when the dangers of raids have almost disappeared and head-hunting traditions abandoned, settlements can move to the more hospitable gentler slopes with much to gain and little to lose. Once again for this uphill task to be achieved in a tradition-bond society Herculean persuasive as well as demonstrative efforts are needed. Once a good number of Naga settlements are moved to gentler slopes, the menace of Jhuming is likely to disappear in a phased manner. At present the current fallow period on the Jhum land is wasted. Only secondary growth of shrubs, grasses and tree species appear on the fallow land. Besides offering some resistance of erosion the only other benefit rendered by this secondary growth is of providing manure when scorched into the soil at the time of second crop. If during this period plantation crops with shorter maturity period (wattle, bluegum, etc.) than the Jhum cycle are grown it would yield far greater benefits. These crops would add to the protective cover against soil erosion. The grasses can be put to some better use. Moreover, the plantation crops would provide an additional source of income.

After having a good crop from Jhum field it can be converted into fruit orchard. Since currently jhum fields are located at a height ranging from 900 metres to 1,500 metres above the Sea Level, the climate is suitable for the temperate and citrus fruits. Oranges, lemons, pears, peaches, apples, apricots, pineapple, bananas and beverages (tea and coffee) can be easily grown on these slopes. The experimental plantation of apple orchards in some areas have already met success. The orchards would not only provide extra but accelerated source of income. It has however, to be observed that like an ordinary lay farmer, a Naga also gives top priority to the production of cereals. This overriding consideration with a Naga cultivator stands in the way of expansion of horticulture. Moreover, in this remote and secluded corner of the country there can be a problem of market for the produce. To overcome this handicap following suggestions can be examined.

- In orchards inter-culture (maize, millets, barley, busk-wheat) can be obtained. To some extent such a practice would minimise the danger of food shortage.

- Now when keeping in view the sensitive and strategic location, military and paramilitary forces are stationed there, a ready market is available in the state. Forces which at present mostly depend upon the canned fruit or imported fruit would gladly go for the fresh fruit produced in the state itself.

- Now when means of transport are being developed, the villages are being interlinked by way of all-weather roads and there are good chances of exporting fruits to the other areas of the country. The state has already started drawing plans for the industrial development of the state and it would be good to start mini fruit-based factories. Juice, sausages, tinned fruits, vinegar, alcohol and even wines can be produced locally. The market for all these products as well as fresh fruits is likely to expand in view of natural population growth and in migration of technical as well as non-technical staff required for carrying on the socio-economic development of the state.

- Once a common Naga is convinced about the efficacy as well as authenticity of monitised market, he can be persuaded to trade the fruits for cereals outside the state also. So far it has been observed that a Naga is only in entering this sort of trade. But now when many of the stuffs to the people are being supplied by outside agencies he has shown favourable inclination and it in worthwhile to launch a programme of expanding horticulture.

On the whole it must be remembered that all suggestions given above involve a lot of expenditure and human efforts. The organisation of collective jhuming should be exploited to the maximum as individual families can never achieve fruitful results in this field. On the other hand it is to be kept in mind that economic and social growth is a function of time. "Any attempt to telescope the growth process is fraught with danger. A quick transformation of a poor and stagnant economy into a complex and sophisticated one carries with it grave risks.

But to refuse to take to these risks is to abdicate responsibilities. There will be some kind of shocks, but if advanced action is taken to absorb the shock, then there need not be much apprehension. Such action would mean the establishment of responsive administrative machinery to protect the tribals against exploitation of all kinds, to promote educational programme with a view to condition them for a changed way of life and to carry out constant research for adopting modern methods of production to their social and cultural patterns. So far as the government fails to provide all the assistance, incentive and means of bringing about fruitful socio-economic changes it would be futile to make peace-meal efforts as that would badly disturb the ecological balance and create more problems than it solves.

It is of interest to note that according to the prevailing standards of cereal consumption an average Naga village is self-reliant in food grains. Land being not evenly distributed create some problems to the small farmers. However, the big and well of Jhuming have always surplus foodstuffs with them. But it is a very good practice among the Nagas that those hold surplus stocks part with it for the needy.

Traditionally it is the duty of a Naga community to ensure a minimum sustenance to each dweller of the village. Viewed from another angle such a responsibility of the village has never left any incentive with the people (most of the have-nots) to put in strenuous labour and look for alternative means of livelihood. Feasts are an important status symbol and the families with surplus stock after distributing to the needy at 'square meals standards' gain credit through feasting the entire village on auspicious occasions.

Some villagers have also the tradition of building a buffer stock against possible crop failures. Earlier such families had also to part with some stock and give the same for the upkeep of the hostile element. Failure to oblige the demands of hostiles caused complete devastation of many prosperous Naga families. Now Nagaland has started receiving huge imports of cereals needed for the military, paramilitary and urban population. However, there are still such people, who would prefer to starve, rather than to rely on government rations. Such people many a time, make their both ends meet with the help of Taro (Yam) which is a tuber and can be grown under any adverse weather conditions. A number of roots and wild fruits are also used during such food shortages.

Agricultural Farms and Research Stations: The most important agricultural farms of the state are at Jharnapani, the Horticultural Farm at Pfutsero and Mokokchung, the Integrated Extension Training centre at Medziphema, the Agricultural Research and Extension Centres of Wokha and Zunheboto.

At the horticultural farm at Pfutsero more than 25,000 apple plants procured from Kashmir, Shimla and Ranikhet have been introduced. Apple orchards though slowly but with commendable success are being diffused in the conducive slopes of Nagaland.

The Integrated Extension Training Centre at Medzhiphema was started in April 1966. Similar centres have been established at Mokokchung, Wokha and Zunheboto. The centre imparts training to village-level workers. Over 150 trainees are trained at these centres every year. The scheme, on experimental basis covers an area of over 4,500 acres. Fishery, soil conservation, horticulture and farming are the other areas in which youths are trained.

Irrigation: Agricultural is the dominant economic activity of Nagaland. The input of water is very vital for realising the full potential of this sector. The optimum development and efficient utilisation of water resources, therefore, assumes great significance.

The agrarian economy of Nagaland is largely characterised by shifting cultivation. Since shifting cultivation is done under rain-fed conditions, irrigation of crops is a rare phenomenon. In the terraced fields around Kohima, especially in the Angami and Chakhesang areas irrigation is essentially required. Elaborate arrangements have been made in the terraced fields of artificial irrigation.

There are several minor irrigation projects in Nagaland. The two foremost irrigation projects hitherto undertaken are located at Zudga (Zubza) and Khupanala. These projects were inaugurated in the middle of 1969. The Zudga Project is scheduled to serve an area of about 500 acres for which 200 acres have already been covered by terraced cultivation. Another Project Khupanala near Dimapur will cover an area of about 1,000 acres. In taking up the above project the government has been receiving valuable assistance from the local people in respect of labour and material.

To popularise sprinkle irrigation in the Jhum lands several plans have been prepared. Around Mokokchung efforts are being made to develop sprinkle irrigation.

Animal Husbandry

In a mountainous state like Nagaland animal husbandry provides additional income to the cultivators. The animals provide the stock of wealth for Nagas. The principal domesticated animals are cattle, Mithun, pigs, and poultry. The climate of Nagaland is congenial, there being good pasture grounds, all over the state, with plenty of grass where cattle can thrive on. Owing to the pasture grounds which abound, the land therefore has bright prospects for the development of dairying industries. The animals though lean and small are quite sturdy and strong.

In the past, cattle, pigs, poultry and dogs were reared in larger numbers but the best in the stock were killed during the village sacrifices and festivals. In the olden days Bisons were also kept in many villages but now the trade in them has been dwindled. In the plains buffaloes and cart-horses are used as draught animals.

Among all the animals, perhaps pigs are attended with more care as special fodders prepared of crops are given to them. The Nagas have more of pigs than poultry and cattle. One disadvantage is that special piggery or pigsty is not raised. Generally cows are kept for milk and beef. The Angamis and Rengmas rear the herds of cattle in large number with Khutis, where cattle are shut and sheltered at night. They are cattle dealers. They make profit not only from the sale of cattle but from the cow-dung as well. The Rengmas are said to have supplied cattle to Lotha and Sema pastoral communities in the past. In other places, during slack agricultural seasons, cattle are let loose. Elsewhere a porch during the rainy season serves as a cowshed. It is the traditional way of keeping the Mithuns in semi-wild condition. The animals are sometimes counted as the media of exchange on the occasions when fines are paid and disputes settled.

The people do not raise special pens for poultry birds but keep them inside the house. A few Nepalese have started Khutis near the headquarters and have made income out of the sale of milk. Herds of sheep have been noticed grazing along the grass-lands on the National Highway. Meat markets in certain places have been supplemented with supplies brought from Dinapur and areas nearby.

Almost each family keeps pigs. An average Naga family owns two to four pigs who occupy the front portion of the Naga house. Excepting the occasional feed of paddy husk of maize, the pigs are left to roam and hunt their own food. "In this process, they perform the important function of scavenging Pork is a delicacy for Nagas and in his diet comes next only to rice and its products. Pigs reared in this fashion undoubtedly carry worms and are one of the main sources of the relatively common complaint of tapeworms among the people."

Poultry birds roam about in the village surroundings and find their food. During nights the birds are kept under a cane basket in the front portion of the dwelling. Chicken and eggs are consumed locally and not sent to the market. Indigenous cattle are small in stature and light in weight. They are made to graze on nutritiously inadequate grass, bushes, shrubs, etc. They are not fed on fodder or hay. Consequently, these cattle yield very inferior quality of beef. In some of the villages buffaloes have also been seen. Normally a Naga settlement has about 250 animals but prosperous villages may contain more.

In recent years steps have been taken to replace the indigenous cattle by better breeds. Moreover, facilities are being extended to the people to rear sheep and goats (which are otherwise rarely found in Nagaland). The Piggery. Farms at Tuensang, Tijit, Mokokchung Wokho, Phom and Zhenobata have been provided with 100 sows each. Under the North Eastern Council (NEC) Scheme a Brown Swiss Cattle Breeding Farm at Jaluke have been set up. The Rural Dairy Centre at Dinapur has been provided with all up-to-date equipment. The centre now supplies about 1,200 litres of fresh milk daily to the towns of Dinapur, Kohima, Mokochung, Wokha and Zhenoboato.

For upgrading the indigenous stock, breeding-bulls have been provided to the rural areas on subsidy. Piggery units consisting of three sows each have also been provided on to the poor rural householders. Under a centrally-sponsored project (Pig Production and Heifers Rearing) piggery units consisting of three rows each have been supplied free of cost to the rural cultivators of selected compact areas. Concentrated feeds were also supplied to such farmers who own cross-bred calves and heifers. The aim has been to increase the milk production. In order to provide veterinary aid in the villages treatment centres have been established in some of the villages of Kohima, Tuensang, Wokha, Mokokchung, Phom and Zhenoboto Districts.

Finding unsatisfactory functioning of some of the units and misuse of loans and subsidies the present government decided to non-proliferate such farms and to revamp the entire system. In order to provide healthy meat to the citizens three modern slaughter houses are being set up. The cattle being brought into Nagaland are being properly examined. Selected number of unemployed graduates are being trained in piggery and dairy farming. So far as the veterinary are concerned a number of veterinaries have been established in the various parts of the state. Previously Animal Husbandry and Veterinary Units were under the control of the Directorate of Agriculture. But a separate Veterinary Department was created with a Deputy Director in 1964, who in 1967, was designated Director. There is also a separate District Veterinary Officer.

The Department has the following centres — the Feed Manufacturing Centre, the State Duck Farm, The State Poultry Farm and the Tractor unit located at Dimapur. Dimapur has now a complete upgrading unit and a food factory for feeding poultry units. In addition there is a State Dairy Farm at Jharnapani, there are State Piggery and Poultry Farms at Medziphema (Ghaspani). In Kohima town are located the following centres — the Rinderpest Eradication (Scheme) Centre, the Poultry Upgrading Centre, the Small Scale Dairy Farm and the Dairy Upgrading Centre.

In addition there are the pig breeding centre at Chazouba and the sheep breeding centre at Hainuki. There are veterinary hospitals at Kohima, Dimapur, Wokha, Mookchung, Zhonobota and Phom towns, and dispensaries at Peren, Phek, Aliba, Chungtia. Kohima and Mokokcung are the Headquarters of District Veterinary Officer, dairy poultry, piggery and sheep upgrading centres are also assigned to the charge of respective veterinary field assistants or managers.

Animal husbandry has been taken up in almost all the upgrading farms. The breeds comprises of red Sindhi-bulls, Jersy-bulls and Australian-bulls. Special fodder plants have been grown and steps have been taken to increase the daily dairying capacity.

Fisheries

In the field of pisiculture the state possesses seven fish farms, three fish culture units, four induced breeding units, one riverine fishery unit, three paddy cum fish culture units.

A high altitude fish seed multiplication farm at Thizama is fast coming up. During the year 1981-82 about 250 lakhs of fingerlings, both of major crops species and common species have been produced in the Induced Breeding Farms at Dimapur.

The breeder fish farm at Dimapur, Wokha, and Tijit have only recently started functioning. The paddy-cum-fish culture programme is being propagated among the paddy cultivators by way of distributing free fingerlings. Once the Jhuming fields are terraced this scheme would bring out wonderful results.

About three hundred tanks built around Dimapur, if properly maintained are potentially very good centres for protein-rich food fish. A scheme of constructing and maintaining fish tanks in all the villages of Nagaland can also bring fruitful returns. In some of the villages the inhabitants have impounded river water to provide as reservoir both for irrigation and fish culture. Hero fish production can be increased manifold by the application of standard fingerlings and modern methods of handling the fish. Alongwith these schemes, an attempt should also be made to introduce trout and Mahaseer in the hill streams. The main object of stocking the streams with these varieties is eventually to offer an attraction for tourists. Hill streams stocked with these fish offer excellent opportunity for angling and are a good draw for tourists.

Hunting

Nagas keep dogs for hunting and little enthusiasm is shown for this sport. The method of catching deer is (or rather was, till the government stopped it) to dig pit-falls at likely places, such as where the animals are in the habit of crossing a saddle, or near a salt lick. Long bamboo spikes were fixed at the bottom in order to impale any animal which fell in.

For elephant iron 'Punjis' were used. Little holes were dug in their path, and at the path, and at the bottom of each a flat stone or block of wood was placed. On this was set an iron spike, usually a spear but, and the hole lightly filled in with soft earth. If an elephant trod on one of these iron spikes, the iron, with the resistance of the stone or block of wood to help it, would go right through the sole of its foot. With such a wound an elephant stands still for a long time and then only travels very slowly. A poor beast could thus be dispatched at each with spears. Cases of this cruel practice, though it is strictly forbidden still crop up from time to time.

Another way of dealing with the elephants was to hang a weighted spear over the path. In passing the animal touched a string which released the spear. This rarely did more than give the elephant a slight wound and a bad enough fright to prevent its coming that way again to damage the crops. Solitary tusker boars are tracked down and killed with spears. In some villages each hunter has his own boar, which he knows by the tracks. He gives to the other hunters bits of bamboo, the length of the footprint of his particular boar, and each goes after his own only.

Sometimes a man will take two or three years to kill his animal, going out into the jungle on any day when he feels so inclined and animal, going out into the jungle on any day when he feels so inclined and picking up the tracks in the hope of a lucky meeting. The best days are wet days in the summer. At such times solitary boars make themselves nests of sticks and rubbish in which they sleep snug and dry throughout the day. They snore loudly and can be approached quite near.

The hunter who is lucky enough to come on one of these nests creeps up as close as he can and hurls his spear through it. Then without a moment's hesitation he and the one or two men he has with him (for no Naga ever hunts alone) draw their Daos and rush the nest and jump on it. It is believed that, though a boar which gets away wounded in very dangerous, a man will never be killed or injured in this first rush, "because the bore will not defile its house." Probably it is too bewildered by its rude awakening from sleep to do anything.

It is in ringing herds of pigs, however, rather than in the pursuit of solitary animals, that the Naga really excels. In the summer months the pigs move about in big herds, consisting of sows, three quarters — grown, young and a few mature boars. If there is a herd in the neighbourhood the young men of the village go out under a leader chosen before hand, who must come of a long line of warriors.

Once on the track they get as close to the herd as they can without alarming it — it is usually lying up or moving slowly about in the jungle during the day and cut a narrow strip of jungle in a wide circle round it. Should the herd move it will not generally cross this ring, as the small of man turns it back at every point. Then a smaller circle is cut, and so on till the herd is enclosed in an area small enough to be fenced round. The herd soon gets suspicious, but hearing voices all round, it does not know which way to break and usually keeps quite still, in the hope that it will be overlooked. When all the men are at their stations the leader puts on the pigs' tracks a little coil of creeper "to entangle their feet," and upright in the middle a little sausage of mud, with the prayer that the animals may be blind and deaf and unable to get away.

If the sausage topples over towards the hunters it is a good omen. Word is then sent to the village and all the hunters set to work to build a stout fence, each man working where he stands and using the brushwood and stakes ready to his hand. When the messenger reaches the village all get ready to come down, men with spears and 'Daos' and woman with supplies of rice beer. An egg is first required. A 'medicine man' taken the omens to see who will supply a lucky one.

An Ao man then goes to the house selected and holds out his cloth to receive the egg. When it is put into his cloth he wraps it up quickly and says:" I have shut it up. It cannot escape." He then goes down with the rest and puts the egg on the tracks of the herd at the point where they enter the enclosure, with the usual prayer that the animals may be blind and so on. All is then ready for the drive to begin. The enclosure is, of course, on 'z' slope, like all ground in the Naga Hills, and care is taken to leave uncut the jungle in that direction and will not come up to the fence if there is a clear space to cross. Little platforms are built jutting out over the fence on the lower side, and on these the older men take their stand.

The pigs, as a rule, do not charge straight at the fence — if they do nothing can stop them- but rush along, hugging it and trying to find a way out. The men of the platforms spear them — and jump down with Daos to finish them. For first blood counts for nothing. Extra shares of meat go to the men near whose platform the dead pig lies. So you must stop your animal. The scene is one of wild excitement — men shouting, pigs squealing, and women at the back excitedly pouring out drinks ready for their thirsty champions.

That is when the drive is a success, of course. Very often things go wrong; sometimes the pigs pluck up courage and change out before the fence is ready; sometimes a pig piece of jungle is enclosed only to find that the quarry has slipped away and it is empty; quite often the bag is only a small one. But on a lucky day a whole herd will be wiped cut and not only much pork gained for the village but the ravaging of the crops stopped.

Many villages ring tiger and leopard with the same preliminaries. For these the fence is prolonged into a V. The jungle is cleared inside and the ground studded with 'Pinjis' The young men, all carrying shields, drive slowly down from the top, half of them cutting the jungle as they go and half advancing with speared poised. The idea is to make the animal charge down the V, where it is met with showers of spears from the men waiting for it.

Aos are wonderfully expert at this sport, and no tiger or leopard survives long on their land. When a village is outringing a leopard or tiger all 'medicine men' Who of course have these animals as familiars, must remain shut up in their houses. If they go out of their houses the animal will get out of the ring. Sometimes, they rather object to having to aid and abet the death of their own familiars. But their scruples have to give way before custom.

Leopards, and more rarely tigers, are also trapped. A long, low shed is made by fixing stakes firmly into the ground and lashing them together at the top. One end is closed with stakes and the other a very heavy wooden door is suspended. Inside there are two compartments; in the back one of which a goat is placed for bait. The leopard enters the front compartment in an attempt to get through to the goat, releases a catch, and drops the heavy door behind him.

The killing of a leopard or tiger is celebrated as the death of an enemy and the chant which announces it is that which proclaims the taking of the head. The carcase, lashed to supports on a bier in a standing position, with the tail straight up in the air and the mouth wedged open with a piece of wood, is carried in triumph to the village, where the warriors dance round it. It is then carried out, accompanied by a crowd of man and boys, and deposited on a platform in the place assigned by tradition to this purpose, usually near the cemetery. On the way back a row of little peeled stick is stuck up along the path. The more there are the better, for the spirit of the tiger seeing them will think that each was put there by a separate warrior, and refrain from troubling such a powerful village. The village observes the next day as Amung.

Small box-traps with falling doors are often made for monkeys in the fields, and are baited with a cucumber or some such thing. Big bags of stump-tailed macaques are sometimes made by driving them, as many as forty or fifty being killed in a day. This species of monkey climbs badly and for choice travels along the ground. If a band is located in a convenient piece of jungle a long, narrow, roofed tunnel, with the far end closed is constructed in a gully with steep sides. The monkeys are driven towards it and take shelter in it. Finding the end closed they completely lose their heads and cling to each other jibbering till they are dispatched.

The Semas, Lothas, Cliangs, Angamis and Aos also use triangular traps. A miniature fence is made, with gaps at intervals, at each of which a trap is set for any birds or small animals which may try to run through. More usually nooses to catch birds' feat are set at gaps in fences. Baited nooses are also set for ground-feeding birds and around flowers very fine nooses are arranged for little birds which are attracted by the insects and honey.

Birdlime is much used. It is prepared as follows: Sap of the Ficus elastica is collected and stirred till it becomes thick. Then it is heated in a bamboo 'chunga' and allowed to cool again. Fresh sap of another Ficus is finally stirred in till the lime is of the desired consistency.

Horticulture

In the mountainous and hilly areas of the world, especially with mild and temperate climates, horticulture is coming up very strongly. Horticulture has great productive and protective utility. It has been increasingly realised the utility of fruit farming in the context of soil conservation as well as supplementation of farmers' income. Since 1978 a well coordinated horticulture development plan has been undertaken. The plan envisaged new orchards covering an area of about 5,000 hectares and rejuvenation of existing about 1,500 hectarage orchards. All Government run 16 nurseries and orchards were in a miserable condition.

The lack of proper supervision, paucity of staff, non-availability of organisational facilities, fencing and funds had made those places a liability on the government. The paucity of trained technical staff is a problem with almost every scheme. Positive steps should be taken to make up this deficiency.

There is a great potential for the development of almost all kinds of fruits, vegetables, cash crops, coffee, tea and aromatic plants. Most of the area outside the valleys carries a slope of more than 45 degrees. Such an area is comparatively more suitable for orchards and plantation crops (excluding sugarcane and cotton) than cereals. No doubt the government granted a subsidy of Rs. 2,500 to every deserving private person for developing one hectare of land into orchards, but it has been observed that for want of expert supervision the survival rate was extremely very poor. The experimental apple plantations have shown very good success. Even otherwise, as already stated a good part of the Nagaland landscape enjoys temperate climate and fruits like apples, apricots, peaches, oranges, lemons, almonds, etc., can be planted at appropriate slopes.

Sericulture

There is only one sericulture farm with headquarters at Dhansiripar and six demonstration units located. The local people have received seri-seeds from the farm. At present it is equipped with 25 machines. The farm has distributed spinning machines to the weavers at the rates. An appreciable cocoons are further available with the demonstration units. There is in addition another sericulture demonstration garden at Peren.

On the recommendations of the National Council of Applied Economics and Research a paper-cum-pulp mill at Tuli was established. Three farm were producing citronella set up at Lizumi, Kontsunyis and Mongsenyimti: A pineapple fibre plant has also come up at Bhagti. The plant went into operation in August 1976. A spinning mill had also been established that initiated production in 1978. A hand made paper unit had also been set up at Dimapur.

With a view to give fillip to small-scale industries six District Industries offices have been created at Wokha, Phek, Mon, Mokokchung, Kohima and Zunhaboto. In 1984-85, as many as 51 small scale units were provided with power and easy instalment loans on low interest were sanctioned. Thirty five knitting machines and sewing machines were given at subsidised rates to local artisans in Kohima and Mokokchung Districts.

Thirty weavers were provided with tools and implements under promotional activities schemes. Three weaving centres were been completed at Chaizami, Khonoma, and Phesachaduma villages under Intensive Handloom Development Projects. Under North Eastern Hill Council Programmes new Oak Tsar composite centres opened at Akiguo, Lasami, Chizami and Meluri village.

In the words of S. C. Jamir, "Our villagers are normally good in handicrafts and they do it at their leisure. If we properly organise, there is a great possibility for supply of handicrafts. In big cities and towns tastes and fashions are changing and now the people are gradually returning to indigenous material rather than machine-made goods. Baskets, pipes, bamboo plates, wooden spoons, lamp stands and such other decorative pieces will be in great demand. I wish that every household in Nagaland becomes a centre of cottage industry by itself ...It will be source of income for the villagers. These facilities are too near to us and we are determined to apply our mind to derive its economic benefits."

Weaving training cum production centres have been set up at Mokokchung, and Dimapur. A cottage industries cum training cum production centre come at Mon and a cottage industries training centre at Aghunato was established. Industries like soap making, candle making and bee-keeping are being developed. The existing two bee-keeping farms are better equipped for enhanced production. The Industrial Estate at Dimapur is a landmark in the economy of the state of Nagaland.

Forestry

The people of this mountainous state, covered with humid tropical deciduous and evergreen forests, obtain several benefits from the natural vegetation. In fact, out of the total work-force dependent on primary activities, about 8 per cent are dependent on forestry. Thus forests have a great economic value and form the principal source of revenue.

The forests of Nagaland provide fuel-wood, building materials, in addition to barks and leaves, highly priced by the local people during the manufacture of dyes and drugs. Forests give direct income-Agar-wood, teak, and rubber have been exploited at local scale for trade purpose which fetch good income.

Forest produce are grouped as follows:

- timber, charcoal, caoutchouc, catechu, wood-oils, resin, natural varnish, bark, lac, myrobalans, rhinoceros horns;
- trees, leaves and fruits;
- plants-viz., creepers, grass, reed and moss;
- animal wealth, with species such as wild animal, birds, butterflies, insects, and skins, horn and bones, silk, cocoons, wax and honey;
- peat, surface oil, rocks and minerals (limestone, laterite, mineral oil and other items of mineral wealth).

Up to 1957, the whole of Nagaland was one Forest Division of Assam. From 1961 to 1963, forests of Nagaland were in the charge of the Chief Forest Officer. It was on February 1, 1963 that the Directorate of Forests came into existence, under which arrangement, the District of Kohima has been assigned to charge of the Divisional Forest Officer with Headquarters at Dimapur. In Nagaland forests are graded into three classes — private forest which belong to the village people, whole protected and reserved, the other two categories, are placed in the charge of the government.

Transportation and Communication

The history of the development of modern means of transport and communications is quite recent. In the olden days, paths and tracks were the connecting routes of various tribes. A brief emphasis may be laid on the importance and service of the age-old bridle paths and the trans-district tracks which connect Nagaland with Cachar, Sibsagar, Manipur and eastern regions before a review of the growth and development of the modern means of transportation and communications. Those old time tracks hitherto were in the use by groups of tribal immigrants as well as the traders, warriors, and ambassadors. Across the Saramati Range of Tuensang bordering on the east and along the course of Barak river in the southwest, the tracks lose themselves in the rugged steeps of the difficult mountain terrain, sometimes almost impassable.

The first landmark constituted in the existing means of communications in the last century was the cutting of a road (Golaghat-Chumukedima) running a distance of 67 miles, the greater part of the road being situated in the plains, the road was fit at foothills for wheel traffic. When this line opened, part of the government transport was brought by boats along the Dhansiri (which navigation opened from April to September) to Dimapur, while elephants were engaged to remove the transport again from Dimapur to the station; wheel traffic also plied from Dimapur to Chumkedima.

Before 1880 the construction of more bridle-paths was undertaken which connected Nowgong, Manipur and North Cachar with the region of Nagaland, while an access road which linked the Golaghat plains with the first subdivisional headquarters was being constructed. Later on the headquarters at Mokokchung (Subdivision) was also connected with Wokha. Another road was provided afterwards with an outpost located northwardly of the subdivisional headquarters. But only Golaghat-Chumukedima road was fair weather, the rest were mere tracks. In course of time three bridle paths were opened for Tuensang. By 1909 the region of Nagaland had a total of 821 miles (bridle path).

One of the greatest contributions to the resumption of road surveys and constructions since the inception of Naga Hills District was the occurrence of frequent landslides which held up transport, the problems which are still formidable irrespective of equipments and tools which the age has invented. The cart-road which has become a double-traffic national highway was reported as early as 1909 to have been impassable as soon as the rains set in. This state of things still continues. The occurrence of landslides near Kohima in 1966, 1967, 1979, 1980, 1981, 1985 and 1987 are the instances, in consequence of which traffic was blocked at a stretch of weeks necessitating transhipment. It took time also to clear the slide. Bridging on rivers was also difficult as many bridges were washed away by the swollen rivers.

The Second World War gave more impetus, there were military undertakings for the construction of additional motor roads and tracks which were of great benefit to the public as 200 miles of motorable roads were added to the existing one; the roads led to the expansion of administration in the hitherto unadministered area.

But enormous progress has resulted out of the formation of Nagaland when all the potential resources were tapped under the Third, Fourth, Fifth and Sixth Five Year Plans.

The expansion of roads has greatly assisted in boosting up production rates, enhancing trade and the speedy expedition of the developmental projects.

Before 1957, i.e. prior to the constitution of Naga Hill Tuesang Area, the position of the communications in Nagaland was not very satisfactory. Only two roads were fair weather. A great difference was noted in April 1966 when the surfaced roads were prolonged by 20 miles while the unsurfaced sector, 470 miles were added, and 80 miles being newly widened over porter tracks and mule paths and the roads were converted to all weather lines of communications. At present Nagaland has 745 km of state Highway, 840 km of major district roads, 650 km of other district roads and 1,575 km of village roads.

In all the state in 1985 had 4,464 kilometres of all types of roads. Out of it 103 km were National Highway, 1,114 km. State Highway (metalled 1,065 and unmetalled 768 km), 882 district roads, (metalled 114 km and unmetalled 49 km) and village roads 2,368 km. Besides there were 11 km and 24 km long industrial roads in Kohima and Mokokchung districts respectively. The road density in Nagaland compares favourably with other mountainous states of India.

The roads constructed by the Border Roads Organisation between Akhegwo and Tuensang, Kohima and Mehiri, and Mokokchung and Tuensang are the real feats of engineering skill. These roads piercing the breasts of the proud mountains, girdling their way in a serpentine curve, negotiating heights and going down the valleys, have given a new sense of unity and purpose to the Naga people. No doubt the romantic silence of the hills has been destroyed in the process and the chirping of birds and music of streams are today drowned in the rumblings of bulldozers and the explosions of rocks caused by the engineers of Border Roads, but these arteries of exchange are surely going to import a new life, for the hitherto backwards as well as traditional people.

National Highways

The only road classed as National Highway traverses from Dimapur to Khuzarna, from where it prolongs itself to Imphal, the capital of Manipur. It is a double traffic National Highway.

State Highways

Kohima-Phek: Part of the road as much as Pfutsro from Kohima is considered to be one of the best roads in the state of Nagaland.

Kohima-Mokokchung: It connects Kohima with the District Headquarters of Mokokchung. It runs through the territory of Lotha tribe and joins Wokha with Kohima in the south and Mokokchung in the worth.

Local Roads

After Independence enough stress has been laid on the development of infrastructural facilities, especially the metalled and unmetalled-roads. Consequently, there are a number of short distance roads built by Community Project Blocks and the Forest Department of the State.

The task in cutting roads is insurmountable against the precipitous heights, cliffs and crags and the vast mountain terrain especially in Chakesang and Zeliang areas, roads taking largely hazardous and zigzag course.

The construction of roads is mainly the task of the Border Road Organisation. Their maintenance is largely the responsibility of the Public Works Department (PWD). Despite several years of planning, many of the villages of Nagaland are accessible only by mule tracks and paths. It is therefore necessary that the development of metalled and unmetalled roads is done on a priority basis. This effort should continue till every settlement is linked with the outside world by way of all, weather roads.

Railways

The state of Nagaland is on the Railway Map of the country. The state has railway connection through Dimapur on the North-East Frontier Railway Line with Assam. The railway line covers only five miles of the Dimapur Mauza. The Dimapur Railway station has been expanded and renovated. The station Buildings at Dimapur station including parcel room, ticket collectors' and counters room, waiting room and restaurant are built.

There are cooperative workshop, railway police office, school and small colony for the railway employees. There are the Manipur and Nagaland State Transport stations at Dimapur which arrange transport and traffic with Imphal and Kohima respectively. Dimapur is also known as Manipur-Road owing to the motor road link with Imphal.

There are other transport arrangement with Assam and neighbouring states.

An enormous increase of traffic with both the state and Manipur has been another important development. Dimapur has become a great supply centre added to the impetus laid down by the Second World War, while government undertakings have grown outside by side with the commercial and industrial firms.

Undoubtedly, there has been an increase in the number of privately-owned vehicles and public carriers to cater for movement of transport and traffic on the highways and the local roads. In the plains, rickshaws and cycles are used in large number for short distance transport, while horse-carts help to supplement the movement of some small-scale local traffic. Hundreds of privately-owned vehicles laden with the merchandise ply daily on the double traffic National Highway. More than forty private vehicles ply daily on the Kohima-Pfutsero.

Transport Service

In 1962, data were collected on the possibility, income and expenditure on the feasibility of introducing daily transport services in the state. The proposal was put up for the sanction of 45 buses which involved an estimated cost of Rupees twenty lakhs. On the Republic Day 1964, Nagaland State Transport was inaugurated, planned scheme being drawn up to introduce transport services on the following roads.

- Kohima-Dimapur, taken then over.
- Kohima-Wokha, opened in 1966.
- Kohima-Mao (in Manipur).
- Kohima-Pfutsero, starting first up to Charkhabama, then to Pfutsero in 1967.
- Pfutsero-Chizami, 1968.
- Dimapur-Jorhat, 1968.
- Mokokchung-Mon.
- Mokokchung-Zunheboto
- Akhegwo-Tuensang
- Zunheboto-Tuensang

Two bus services in 1964-65 for sometime were provided in Dimapur and Kohima towns, and daily taxi services were also introduced on Kohima-Imphal Road. Further the goods services were also arranged daily on the national and state highways. But town bus service became suspended very soon, i.e. in 1965. But in 1967-68 bus services were reopened in both Kohima and Dimapur towns.

Postal Service

At the beginning of the 20th century, postal services were instituted in five administrative centres of Nagaland while before 1910 telegraphic services were being opened in two Headquarters, i.e. Kohima and Dimapur. After about 53 years the district of Nagaland had only eleven post offices and 199 letter boxes in 1963 but in 1965 they had increased to 12 and 20 respectively. In 1964-65, a scheme was drawn up to provide 12 hanging letter boxes inside Kohima until they were replaced by the pillar letter boxes.

In 1965, automatic telephone exchanges were instituted at Kohima and Dimapur by replacing the old and out of date centre Battery Manual System. At present all the district headquarters, i.e. Kohima, Phek, Wokha, Zunheboto, Mokokchung, Tuensang and Mon have telephonic facilities. Telephones exchanges have also been installed in the major Tehsils of Kohima and Mokok-chung Districts.

9

Polity

India, a union of states, is Sovereign Socialist Secular Democratic Republic with a parliamentary system of Government. The Republic is governed in terms' of Constitution, which was adopted by the Constituent Assembly on 26 November, 1946 and came into force on 26th January, 1950. The Constitution which envisages a parliamentary form of Government is federal in structure with unitary features. The President of India is the Constitutional head of the executive of the union. The real executive power vests in the Council of Ministers with the Prime Minister as the head.

The Constitution distributes the legislative power between the Union Legislature and the State Legislature and provides for vesting of residual powers in Parliament. The power to amend the Constitution also vests in Parliament. The Constitution has provisions of independence of Judiciary, the Controller and Auditor General of India, the Public Service Commission and the Chief Election Commissioner. The judiciary has been separated from the executive at all levels throughout the country. After many years of demand and rebellion, the Naga people of Northeastern India were delighted to have their own state in the year 1963. P. Shilo Ao was the first Chief Minister of Nagaland. The major political parties in Nagaland are the Naga National Democratic Party, Nagaland People's Front and Nagaland Democratic Party. National parties like the Indian National Congress, Bharatiya Janata Part and Janata Dal (Secular) are also present in the state.

Administration

The Governor of Nagaland is the constitutional head of state, representative of the President of India. He possesses largely ceremonial responsibilities. The Vidhan Sabha is a 60-member House elected by the people. Leader of the majority party/coalition parties is appointed Chief Minister by the Governor. Other ministers of the council are also appointed by the Governor on the recommendation of Chief Minister. Unlike most Indian states, Nagaland has been granted a great degree of state autonomy, as well as special powers and autonomy for Naga tribes to conduct their own affairs. Each tribe has a hierarchy of councils — at the village, range and tribal levels dealing with local disputes. There is a special regional council for the Tuensang District, elected by the tribes of the area. The state is divided into eleven districts.

Area, Population and Headquarters of Districts

S.No.	District	Area (sq km)	Population	Headquarters
1	Kohima	3,144	3,14,366	Kohima
2.	Mokokchung	1,615	2,27,320	Mokokchung
3.	Mon	1,876	2,59,604	Mon
4.	Tuensang	4,228	4,14,801	Phek
5.	Zunheboto	1,255	1,54,909	Tuensang
6.	Wokha	1,628	1,61,098	Wokha
7.	Dimapur	927	3,08,382	Dimapur
8.	Phek	2,026	1,48,246	Phek
9.	Kiphire	1,255	1,06,136	Kiphire
10.	Longleng	885	1,58,300	Longleng
11.	Peren	2,300	96,825	Peren Town

(Based on latest available data)

The Governance

The system of government in the states closely resembles that of the union.

The Executive

The state executive consists of the Governor and Council of Ministers with the Chief Minister as its head. The Governor of the State is appointed by the President of India for a term of five years and holds office during his pleasure. At present General K. Y. Krishna Rao (Rtd.) is the Governor of Nagaland.

The Council of Ministers, with the Chief Minister as the head aids and advises the Governor in the exercise of his functions except in so far as he is by or under the Constitution required to exercise his functions or any of them in his discretion.

In respect of Nagaland, the Governor has special responsibility under Article 371 of the Constitution with respect to law and order in Nagaland and even though it is necessary for him to consult the Council of Ministers in matters relating to law and order, he can exercise his individual judgement as the action to be taken. He also enjoys his discretion on all matters relating to the Tuensang District of Nagaland.

The Chief Minister is appointed by the Governor, who also appoints other Ministers on the advice of the Chief Minister. The Council of Ministers is collectively responsible to the legislative assembly of the state. After the 1982 Assembly Election Shri S. C. Jamir is the Chief Minister of Nagaland.

In the state of Nagaland there is only one house known as the Vidhan Sabha or the Legislative Assembly. The total number of seats of the State Assembly is sixty, out of which 36 were won by the Indian National Congress (I) and the remaining 24 went to Nagaland Peoples Conference (NPC). In fact Congress (I) and the National Peoples Conference (NPC) are the main political parties of the state.

The State Legislature has exclusive powers the subjects enumerated in List II of the Seventh Schedule to the Constitution and concurrent powers over those enumerated in List III. The financial powers of the legislature include authorisation of all expenditure, taxation and borrowing by the State Government. The Legislative Assembly alone has the power to originate money bills.

The Legislative Assembly controls the executive. It uses all the parliamentary devices like questions, discussions, debates, adjournment and no-confidence motion and resolutions to keep a watch over the' day-to-day work of the executive. The Vidhan Sabha also has its committees on Estimates and Public Accounts to ensure that grants sanctioned by the Legislature are properly utilised.

Moreover, for the administration of the district headquarters and towns (Kohima, Mokochung, Wokha, Phek, Zunheboto, Tuensang, Mon, Dimapur), there are local self government in the form of municipalities. The functions of the municipalities include public safety, health, education and other convenience of citizens as well as construction and maintenance of waterworks and sewage, streets and bridges, parks and recreation grounds, markets and shopping centres and so on.

Kohima being the seat of Government, all the Heads of Departments are therefore located at Kohima. The following Heads of the Departments have a vital role in the administration:

- The Secretariat with the Chief Secretary to the Government of Nagaland.
- Commissioner of Transport.
- Commissioner of Taxes.
- Development Commissioner.

- Director of Education.
- Director of Agriculture.
- Director of Health Services
- Director of Industries
- Conservator of Forest.
- Director of Information and Publicity.
- Director of the Veterinary and Animal Husbandry.
- Director of Supply.
- Chief Engineer PWD.
- The Chief Electoral Officer.
- Superintending Engineer, Electricity
- The General Manager, Nagaland State Transport.
- Registrar of Cooperative Societies.

At the Secretariat level the following departments are mentioned with the nature of business assigned to them.

Legislature

The Legislature of Nagaland is controlled by the Legislative Assembly of the state and plays a monumental role. The speaker presides over the proceedings of the Legislative Assembly. The speaker is assisted by the Deputy Speaker. The constitutional head is the Governor. The Members of legislative Assembly are the elected representatives from various constituencies of Nagaland.

The Taxation

House Tax

An important source of Government income during the beginning of the British administration in the District was the house tax; but there were variations in taxation assessment in view of the fact that Angami Nagas were levied Rs. 3 later on reduced to Rs. 2 per house, non-Angami Nagas paying Rs. 2 while outsiders were levied Rs. 5 each.

The village headman performed collectorate duties receiving 12.5 per cent of the amount collected as commission. The first assessment was enforced as early as between 1874 and 1976, but Chmukendima had started paying house tax in 1867, just after the inception of the District.

Land Tax

In 1869-70, a few proprietors paid a land tax. The tenants being classed as the modest-Rayatwari type, being hereditary and transferable. The assessment rates were as follows:

> Busti (homestead) and Pharingati (dry land) which returned Rs. 2.50 per acre. Rupti or lowland (moist soil) which yielded about Rs. 3 per acre. Pharingati or dryland returned the same amount as Busti. House Tax was exempted from those who paid up land tax; the quality of the soil being the major factor which determined the rate of assessment. But this tax was very meagre.

Forest Royalty

In 1910-11, the total forest revenue was classified as follows:

- Licence fee for Elephant Mahal.

No.1 (as paid to Jorhat Treasury was Rs. 2,249) and royalty paid on elephants captured (as deposited with the Golaghat Treasury amounting to Rs. 800).

- Licence fee of rubber, Cane and Agar Mahal No. l, paid into Kohima Treasury Rs. 400. Licence fee of rubber, Cane and Agar Mahal No. II, paid into Kohima Treasury Rs. 1,600.

- Licence fee of rubber and Agar Cane Mahal No.I, and II paid into Sibagar Treasury amounting to Rs. 375 and Rs. 1,600 respectively.

Rule of Law

When the Naga Hills District was formed in 1866-67, the Deputy Commissioner was empowered to deal with all cases, except death sentence and more than seven years imprisonment for which all appeals against such decision lay to judicial Commissioner. The Deputy Commissioner was assisted by the Assistant Commissioner whose rank was that of a First Class Magistrate (as defined in the criminal Procedure Code). In the disposal of cases, great importance was attached to the local customary laws, for which a body of Naga Assessors was appointed.

When the District became the Political Agency in 1872, criminal justice was administered by the Deputy Commissioner, his assistant and the Village Chief. According to the Act V of 1861, the Deputy Commissioner was competent to pass and serve sentence for less than seven years' imprisonment and fine upto any amount, but sentences which exceeded seven years had to be concurred with the Chief Commissioner who in turn could enhance or cancel any sentence or remand the case for retrial against such sentences passed by his subordinates but no offence could be punished by sentence exceeding that awardable under the provisions of the Indian Panel Code. Village authorities in turn were empowered to dispose of cases of persons charged with any of the offences relating to damage to property not exceeding Rs. 50, injury to persons not endangering loss of life or limb, house-trespass and affronted of whatever kind. They could levy trivial fines upto Rs. 50, award restitution and compensate to the extent of the injury sustained, and enforce it by distraint of the property of the offender and report to the Deputy Commissioner in case of non-payment of fines. Each village chief was to receive a Sunnad on appointment from the Deputy Commissioner.

The above rules for the administration of justice and police in the Naga Hills District still remain in force with amendments made from time to time.

When the Interim Government was formed, it was agreed that no act or law passed by the Union Parliament affecting the following would have any legal form in Nagaland unless specifically applied to it by a majority vote of the Nagaland Legislative Assembly — " (i) religious or social practice, (ii) Customary Naga Law and procedure, and (iii) civil and criminal justice (so far these would concern decisions according to Naga Customary Law)." The existing laws relating to administration of civil and criminal justice as provided for in the rules for the administration of justice and police in the Naga Hills District would remain to be in force.

But the regulation 1954 (Regulation No. 1 of 1954), an important provision has been that appeals shall be to the High Court from any order of conviction passed by the Deputy Commissioner, awarding a sentence of imprisonment for six months or more, of a fine of Rs. 1,000 or more: that case shall be so settled according to the tribal customary law prevailing at the time, provided such settlements were not at variance with ordinary criminal law. An important provision is that no appeal against the unanimous decision involving the breach of customary law of the village court shall lie. Village court is advised to put on record all cases settled but it is not compulsory in each and every case.

Police Force: Its Organisation: by the Act V of 1861, a regular police was constituted for the District but it was supplemented by the rural police vested in the village authorities as cognisable by the Deputy Commissioner. The control of the entire police force evolved on the Deputy Commissioner, who worked under the orders of the Chief Commissioner of Assam. The Act provided that misconduct on 'he part of the regular police was punishable in accordance with the provisions of the Act and the Panel Code, or any special law thereof as could be extended to the Naga Hills.

Misconduct on the part of the rural police was punishable by a fine up to Rs. 500 or by imprisonment to an extent exerciseable under the Panel code for a like offence. In lieu of imprisonment, punishment by fines could be enforced as might be prescribed by the Deputy Commissioner or any other officer duly recognised. An appeal for all orders against decision of the village heads in police matters lay to the Deputy Commissioner subject to the approval or modification of the Chief Commissioner.

According to this provision, the Chief Commissioner exercised his powers as the Inspector-General of Police as defined by section 5, section (B.G.) of 1869. Village heads were delegated the powers to arrest all criminal and repress all disorders within their respective jurisdictions. They had been specially authorised to report to the Deputy Commissioner all crimes, violent deaths, or serious accidents likely to affect the public peace, to deliver up offenders, and bring to the notice of the administration such occurrences as promptly as possible.

Under the Act, heinous crimes include rebellion, riot, counterfeit, murder, rape, theft, robbery, dacoity, cattle stealing, arson, house breaking and forgery. Occurrences of such offences were to be prepared at once to the Deputy Commissioner or his commissioned assistants. Movements 6f the offenders were immediately to be traced to areas even beyond their jurisdiction but within the administrative control with the co-operation of the localities where the offenders had gone; but if they failed, the aid of the regular police had to be called in. The village chiefs in particular were to arrest gamblers, illegal hawkers and drunkards. The village authorities were expected to succeed in the performance of such duties to them and to obtain public co-operation in respect of such functions. Failing that, they were liable to be held responsible and punishable with fines upon themselves or the community which was apathetic to performing such works. During the inception of administration, the work in the restoration of law and order was done by a military police side by side with civil police.

In 1884-85, the Frontier Police Force comprised one Commandant, 4 Subedars, 9 Jamadars, 43 Havildars and 502 Sepoys and Buglers. From that year the Frontier Police Force was reorganised and important police methods for training were introduced on physical side including drill, exercise, battalion parade, musketeers and skirmishes.

Before the First World War, only one police station existed at Kohima, but outposts along the cart road existed on Nichuguguard, Piphema, Zubza, and Viswema. The Civil Police were chiefly concerned with the supervision of traffic on the cart road, and were not allowed to enter the Naga villages or take up a Naga case except under special orders from the Deputy Commissioner.

Important changes were enforced in 1937, the police was restituted on the lines prescribed both by the Act V of 1861 and the Assam Rifle Act, 1920. The Governor of Assam taking off the powers from the Commissioner. The Act provided that the Regular Police acted when required to do so by the Inspector General of Police or the Deputy Commissioner. The Village Authorities were deemed necessary to exercise the ordinary duties of police. All the inhabitants under clause 14 were urged to aid the regular and the village police in the maintenance of order or 'the performance of ordinary duties for public security, and liable to penalties if they refused.

During the years which marked political disturbances (at their pitch), 1957-64, Village Guards were constituted to assist the police in the restoration of order and in the prevention of further occurrences of crimes and offences resulting from subversive works and operations. The guards were armed and played the part of police vide section 5(1) of the

Assam Frontier (Administration of justice) Regulation, 1945 (Regulation I of 1948) and rule 2(b) of the rules for the administration of justice and Police in the Naga Hills District along with the Assam Rifles (hitherto Frontier Police) whose existence dates back to the last century, and other security forces who also made notable exertions of maintaining public security, although their functions in certain respects were discernible from the police. From 1957 until the appointment of the Inspector General of Police, the Superintendent was in overall charge of the police strength. In 1965, the Inspector General was appointed. But the most effective measure was setting up of the police training school at Chumukedima in 1965-66, so designed for furthering the task in imparting necessary training to the Nagaland Police at the state level. In the same year, the village guards were absorbed into the Nagaland Armed Police.

The Police Training, School was started in 1961 hitherto without sufficiently organised staff to cope with, that time training being imparted to recruits by a few' Havildars and Sub-Inspectors only while law classes were conducted by an Inspector and Sub Inspector. In August 1965 the school was taken charge by a Deputy Superintendent of Police at Kohima assisted by an Assistant Inspector. The school became full-fledged when it was shifted to Chumukedima with permanent buildings in November 1966. The principal responsible for its running at present comprise a Principal, a Chief Law Inspector, a Chief Drill Inspector, seven Sub-Inspectors and six Havildars. The course of training covers six months. In addition four Nagaland Armed Police Battalions have been constituted in the state since April 1964. The battalions play a role to assist civil Administration in the enforcement of Law and Order and to act as second line of defence of country. The first and the fourth are located at the District, the second is located at Alichan (Mokochung) and the third at Tuensang, the Bahalions in the District are situated at Chumukedima near the Police Training School. The Fourth Battalion however is proposed to be shifted to Kohima before the end of 1969.

For enlistment the following approach generally is adopted, "wide publicity is given in all areas prior to the date of recruitment and all candidates are grouped at a specific place and the Commandant of the Unit after checking the persons physically select the eligible candidates who are appointed after medical examination."

Gazetted Officers in the Armed Police Battalion are recruited through the State Public Service Commission; there is also a promotion system upto Inspectors' level. In some cases ex-army personnels' service is accepted on contract basis, some officers are deputed from other states. Recruits receive intensive training in drills, parades and weapons for a month at the Headquarters. They, will later on go to the respective Units for advanced training. Gazetted Officers undergo 14 months, training at the Police Training Colleges outside the state or other training centres set up with the Central Government.

Normally Deputy Commissioner requisitions the services of Nagaland Armed Police for deployment in his district to P. Headquarters. On orders of Police Headquarters the

Unit concerned place the services of armed police wing at the disposal for the local civil Administration. But in case of emergency the local civil authority's requisition of services of Nagaland Armed Police to the Section Commanders or Commandants has also to be ratified by the armed police authorities.

This issues out of the reorganisation of the Police Force after the Nagaland Act 5 of 1965, (the Nagaland Police Enhanced Disciplinary Power Act) which vested the superintendence and control of the Nagaland Armed Police Battalion in a person or an authority designated as Commandant of Nagaland Armed Police Battalion when so appointed by the State Government, the rules relating to the degree of disciplinary action or punishment upon the ranks and files who deserve it having been enjoined in the Act.

Crime and Punishment: Indigenous Settlement

Although there are tribe to tribe variations, the mode of assessing crimes and punishment is almost the same over the entire territory of Nagaland the most common system of punishment being the imposition of fines which however, vary according to crimes and offences.

In Angami system a thief is punished by recovering from the thief seven times worth the price of the thing stolen, but the condition of payment might have been adjusted so, to fit in the circumstances, if the thief was so impoverished. Otherwise he might have simply been beaten by the victim's party or the more lenient terms may have just been imposed. If the murder by accident was committed and in the event the offender was not paid back in his coins, he was retributed by deporting from the village for a seven years' term, on the completion of which he was allowed to return. The same terms apply to punishment of homicide caused by a duel. If death resulted of any act of treason or kidnap, the murderer and his relatives were exiled. Adultery leads to divorce the wife relinquishing any claims.

The Zeliangroung customary law is more severe because the murderer is liable to exile for a period of seven years along with his close relatives. Their houses and property are to be destroyed and their fields will be abandoned. On completion of the term, the relations of the deceased are obliged to call back those exiled to their original village. In case of adultery the wife is to leave her husband empty-handed and she has no right to claim any property.

If divorce occurs as amongst the Pochuri, the property is equally divided between the husband and the wife, but if the latter takes the initiative and leaves him, she is deprived of the share.' In case of murder, if it is not intentionally committed, the man who is responsible, is to pay with some moveable property and ornaments, but now it is in terms of cash. The terms relating to adultery are more relaxable, because the wife is just divorced if she has committed such thing, while the other man is just fined.

Among the Rengmas, fines imposed upon theft are taken with thirty baskets of rice (now they reckon the value in terms of cash). Sometimes habitual thieves are exposed to the public bound with ropes. Fines for adultery and robbery may have been paid in instalments for which adultery, the wife refunds the bride-price but pays the fine, while milder terms are imposed in case of men. For acts of homicide and arson, it is the, exile of the culprit and dismantling of his house.

Among all the tribes, rape results in punishment, acts of murder lead to excommunication of the offender (as in the case of Rengma) from the society for a definite period of one year. Now in advanced areas, time factor for the offender's exclusion from society might have gone far less.

10

Tourism

Nagaland, the land of the hospitable and warm Nagas, lies in the corner of India's North-East-bordering Myanmar. It has always evoked a sense of awe and wonder in the minds of people including the visitors. Although most of the Nagas have now become Christians, they still preserve the remnants of their early animist culture and ancient traditions. Historically, the Nagas have always been brave warriors. They consider the safety and security of their guests as an honour and prestige and will never allow any harm to be done to any of their guests/visitors.

Topographically, Nagaland is mostly a hilly region with a pleasant and salubrious climate throughout the year, except for a small region in the foothills. Nagas are by race of the Mongoloid stock and speak Tibeto-Burman group of languages. But English and Hindi are widely spoken and language is no problem in Nagaland. Colourful life and culture are an integral part of the 16 officially recognised Naga tribes of Nagaland. These 16 tribes are different and unique in their customs and traditions. These customs and traditions are further translated into festivals which revolve around their agricultural cycle. Songs and dances form the soul of these festivals through which their oral history has been passed down the generations.

Nature has been kind to the Nagas and their land. Though by virtue of her natural beauty, the whole of Nagaland is a tourist hotspot, yet certain exceptionally charming places have been identified and developed by the government to promote tourism in the state, some of which are highlighted in the website. This focused approach helps in providing easy access to travellers of all categories — tourists, researchers, backpackers, ecologists, etc. Since this little explored state is still developing and many more places remain 'unmarked' — making them even more exclusive and fascinating to explore.

Floureshing Tourism

Tourism is one of the fast growing sectors in Nagaland. The breathtaking natural beauty and rich culture draws thousands of domestic and international travellers every year. Dotted with undulating mountains, thundering rivers, and lush green forests, Nagaland tourism has lot to offer to adventure enthusiasts and nature lovers. One can indulge in trekking, rock climbing, camping, and river rafting, angling and other exhilarating adventure activities. Nagaland tourism Department conducts exciting long treks and tours within and outside state. Nagaland tourism also provides various adventure equipments on loan on nominal payment. The Tourism Guide available at Nagaland tourism reception centre has all details about Nagaland travel destinations, famous treks, and many other important travel related information.

Tourist Attractions

Nagaland attractions are known for their natural scenic beauty. The various places of tourist interests bear relics to the rich cultural heritage and traditional legacy of the place. The ideal time to visit is from October to May.

Khonoma, Gate of Nagaland, reflects the courageous nature of the local indigenous inhabitants of Khonoma village who had built the huge gate to protect themselves from the British intruders. Endowed with natural splendour, Khonoma Gate draws several visitors from far and wide.

Dzukou Valley offers the tourists with a wonderful opportunity to experience the bounty of nature. Located at a height of 2,438.4 metres, the Dzukou Valley provides breathtaking view of the picturesque landscape.

The Japfu Peak is ideal for scaling and trekking the steep slopes of the high hills of the region. Tuli town is known for its unique natural splendour. Located in the district of Mokokchung the serene surrounding of the Tuli Town rejuvenates the visitors with renewed energy and vigour.

Naganimora offers the tourists with a scope to explore their inherent sporting zeal and sportsman spirit through the various adventure sports of the region. Blessed with natural beauty, Naganimora attracts several tourists who are thrilled with the bewitching sight. Changtongya and Meluri are prominent tourist destinations of Nagaland that are endowed with rich natural splendour. The tourist places of Nagaland are easily accessible from all parts of the state by well built roads.

Below is the list of Nagaland Attractions:

* Khonoma Gate;
* Dzukou;
* Japfu Peak;
* Tuli Town;

- Naganimora;
- Changtongya;
- Meluri;
- Wildlife in Nagaland;
- Nagaland Museums;
- Shopping in Nagaland.

Variety of Tourism

The enchanting state of Nagaland is dotted with picturesque sceneries and lush green fields and is indeed a traveller's delight. Nagaland is one of the seven sisters' states of North Eastern India. The virgin terrains of the state are breathtakingly enthralling. A home to as many as sixteen tribes, the state has much to discover. The capital of Nagaland is Kohima and the largest city of the state is Dimapur. In this beautiful state people of almost 20 different dialects dwell happily together. Kohima is the home to the beautiful rocky Naga Hills. It has one of the most magnificent panoramic views. The travellers should make it a point to visit this capital city. Nagaland is a paradise for the lovers of nature. The adventurous land of Nagaland offers plentiful trekking opportunities.

Pilgrimage Tourism

With the promising number of cathedral and churches pilgrimage tours in Nagaland has a great value. The Catholic Cathedral in Kohima is a landmark of the place. It is said to be one of the biggest Cathedrals in the whole north east India. It also possesses the biggest cross in India carved out of wood. The roofs of it are coloured red and it is situated at Aradura hill. On the UN's day of Reconciliation, this Cathedral was inaugurated. This is one of the most peaceful places where prayer and worship can be performed in tranquility. This is a must visit place of Nagaland, which is a combination of aboriginal architecture.

Nature Tourism

If one wishes to enjoy the natural glory of Nagaland he or she should visit Dzulekie, an exquisite place adjacent to Kohima. Here, the domesticated bisons roam freely in pastoral ambience. The green hills surrounding the area and the little waterfalls present a fully packaged natural beauty. Another natural glory here is the 'Triple Falls' located in Seithekima village area near Dimapur. This fall is pouring from a height of 280 feet into an inviting natural pool. Zoological park of Nagaland is another interesting place to visit. The glimpses of the fauna of Nagaland can be seen here. One can see the rare Blythe's Tragopan in this zoological park of Nagaland, which is in the verge of extinction. The beautiful and rare species of orchids can also be seen here. Intanki Wildlife Sanctuary is another place to visit in Nagaland. It is situated just thirty seven kilometres away from Dimapur. Various animals and rare species of birds can be seen inhabiting here. An exotic Intanki Wildlife Sanctuary is home to Hoolock Gibbon, the only Gibbon found in India; other wildlife includes Elephant, Barking Deer, Flying Squirrel, Mithun, Sambar, Wild Dog, Tiger, and Sloth Bear. Among Birds are Kaleej and common pheasant, Hornbill and Black Stor. There are two other sanctuaries in Nagaland, which can be ventured by the tourists. One of them is the Fakim sanctuary, near the Myanmar border and famous for tigers and Hoolock gibbons. The other is the Pulie Bazde sanctuary, which is situated near Kohima. This sanctuary is a nature lover's delight because it if rich in wildlife. The sanctuary is situated in a attractive spot surrounded by green hills and streams. The sanctuary is well-known for the wide diversity of birds. Tragopan Blythii and White-naped Yuhina are among the exceptional variety of birds which can be perceived here.

Leisure Tourism

With a series of natural wonder Nagaland is one of the best places to experience the wonder of leisure tourism. Kohima war cemetery of Nagaland is a place where one can go with friends and family and enjoy an introspective leisurely walk. This is an emblematic memorial. It was built in the memory of those officers and men of the allied forces who sacrificed their lives to stop the Japanese attack during the Second World War. This was said to be their last post. The Commonwealth War Graves Commission has maintained this cemetery very carefully and nicely. The state museum of Kohima in Nagaland is another must visit place for the tourists. One can see the historical artifacts, log drums, tools and implements, old Naga currencies, attire of warriors, dresses as well as costumes, which are preserved here very carefully. Here, one can also see the collection of rare artifacts of the colourful tribes in close quarters. Ruzaphema is one more ideal place for leisure and recreation. Its bazaars are very colourful for the wide range of beautiful tribal handicrafts.

Adventure Tourism

Surrounded by rivulets and laced by the peaks and mountains Nagaland is the most sought after destination to experience adventure tourism. Japfu peak is a peak of Nagaland, which is situated at 3,048 metres above sea level. One can reach there by trekking. It is very tiresome to reach the place but if one can once reach there, the natural scenery from here is very thrilling. It is an ideal haunt for adventure lovers and trekkers. From the top of the peak, one can get magnificent vista of the sunrise and sunset and the panoramic view of the hills below. It is perfectly suited for trekking and scaling from the months of November to March when visibility is at its best. The total area is covered by mist during the break of dawn, which glorifies more this mystic beauty. Dzukou Valley is another interesting place surrounded by hills, natural caves and rocks. This valley is situated at 2,438 metres above the sea level and is perfect for camping. The entire valley gets bloomed with a carpet of wild flowers during the month of June to September. The Dzukou Valley is one of the most idyllic places for harmony and nature lovers. This is one of the best trekking spots in the Northeastern Region. A few tourist rest houses are constructed for trekkers.

Village Tourism

One must visit the Khonoma to see the village lifestyle of the people of Nagaland. This village has historical importance and its ecological propriety is also very rich. One can hear various fascinating stories of folklore here from the villagers. The Kohima village of Nagaland is considered one of the largest in Asia and the visitors of the village are greeted by a large gate at the entrance. In the Kohima village of Nagaland, the stones of different sizes and shapes can be seen, which are implanted within the compound or skulls of buffaloes and mithuns adorning the portico. From this, the glory of the great ancestors of them can be imagined.

Tribal Tourism

The tribal villages situated on the hilltops tell about the legendary tales of the brave Naga tribes who were fierce headhunters in the olden days. The tour of the beautiful Dzakou Valley, Touphema village, Wokha, Phek, Zunheloto, Mon and Twensang can give an idea about the tribals living here. Here, one can also see the attractive tribal crafts of Nagaland. The items made by these Naga people with bamboo and forest wood are very gorgeous. The works of the tribal potteries here are also noteworthy. The Zeliang dance performances here are very talented musicians, who perform with folk instruments such as Petu, Theku, flutes and trumpets. The war dances performed by the Naga tribes are very enthralling.

Tourism Potentials

Nagaland today is in a situation where many other famous tourist destinations were some decades back. However, the potentials and diversity it holds are perhaps more than a lot of existing popular destinations. Over the years, the state has been through a lot of ups and downs – but this has been a blessing in disguise for it has preserved the beauty, natural wealth and the overall sanity of the place.

Today, as India's northeast is making rapid economic progress and carving out a corridor into South East Asia, Nagaland is standing on the threshold of an economic boom. Among all other industries that the central and State Governments are trying to promote, substantial tourism is gaining the upper hand, for it is the only way for progress and eco-friendliness to walk hand-in-hand.

If, for the traveller, there are so many spots to discover and so much culture and exoticism to experience, for the investor there is an imminent 'gold rush' waiting to happen with Nagaland's tourism potentials; all it needs is a bit of vision on the part of the entrepreneur, and the Directorate of Tourism is waiting with open arms to provide all the support to them.

Cultural, ethnic, Adventure, nature, Tourism, etc. are the areas where the government is working on currently. They also have plans to develop amusement parks, ropeways, large resorts and hotels in order to prepare the right infrastructure for all types of tourists.

The Govt. of Nagaland has designed a unique model, whereby villagers generate their own income through communitisation of assets. Under the guidance of the Village Tourism Board, the villagers sustain their own villages and generate revenue through tourism. The threefold objectives of this model is to conserve and promote the natural resources of Nagaland, promote its cultural heritage and promote eco and adventure tourism. All this is achieved through senimars/workshops and various human resources development efforts. Once he enters a village, the tribal code of honour provides hospitality and protection to the tourist, who by default turns into a guest and friend of the whole village. Warmth and the neighbour fraternity ensure that no harm to hurdle befalls the guest. In fact, the guest can even participate in the cultural/traditional activities of the villagers and cooking using local produces, besides enjoying the culinary skills of the hosts.

Wildlife Tourism

Nagaland is a state which is completely hilly. Nagaland is a state which is situated on the border in the northeast India on Indo-Mayanmarese. The main hilly areas are Patkai and Barail. The state consists of a total area of 16,626 sq km.

The wildlife sanctuaries are in large area which has protected the large number of species of birds and animals. People can visit the wild sanctuaries by paying a very small amount of fees. When you visit national parks and sanctuaries they create a good adventure for the visitors. It offers unique and exciting scene of wildlife.

Ghosu Bird Sanctuary

The peculiarity of this bird sanctuary is the maintenance of the sanctuary by the village community itself. Located at a distance for about 8 km from Zunheboto district headquarters, this is home to more than twenty species of endangered birds. Anyone interested in bird-seeing can watch from the month of June.

Intangki Wildlife Sanctuary

About 37 km drive from Dimapur, Intangki Wildlife Sanctuary is home to the hoolock baboon which is the only gibbon found in India. The sanctuary has an area of 202 sq km and is 677 metres above sea level. It is habitat to a number of elephants, tigers, sambhar, wild dog, goral, sloth bear and a quite a number of rare species of bird. It is preserved by the Forest Wildlife Department. Any person caring to stay a night can be provided a forest rest house managed by Government Tourist Department.

Satoi Range

Located in Zunherboto district, this is the only remaining virgin forest in the region. Blythi Tragopan, an endangered species of bird, is also found in this forest. It is an ideal place for camping and trekking. People come to see the rare rhododendrons which adorn the hills during the months of April and May.

Tourist Spots

Nagaland, essentially a mountainous state passed through a political chaos during the last few hundred years. Consequently, it could develop as a tourist place and the process of urbanisation also remained very slow. Even at present only about one sixth of the total population is living in the urban places and towns.

After the restructuring and recarving of the district Headquarters, some new towns are growing fast and it is hoped that the process of urbanisation will accelerate in the years to come. Some of the important towns and places of interest have been discussed in the following paras.

Kohima

Kohima is the capital of Nagaland. It has enormous floral wealth, war cemetery, museum and parks.

Kohima is situated on a saddle and has a charming landscape. Kohima captured the headlines of the world dailies during April 1944 when the Japanese invaded the Naga Hills and many soldiers along with the local persons had laid down their lives during its defence. The Second World War cemetery situated in the heart of the town commemorates the grim story of the war and of those engaged in its defence. In Kohima, there is a Museum attached to the Directorate of Art and Culture.

Kohima is not a very old and historical town. In 1850, Kohima joined Khonoma, Jotsoma, and Kikrima in fighting against British expeditions. During Angami uprising against the British in 1878-79, it became the battlefield when the Angamis rose against the government. It has been the District Headquarters since 1878 and until Independence (1947) it was the only town in Naga Hills District. In 1878, when Kohima achieved the status of District Headquarters, it had the following institutions: a court-house, a block comprising a magazine, treasury and records, two small lockups, hospital ground, quarter-guard, Government Staff Buildings and lines for scouts and peons and bazar.

Kohima presents a contrast today when after Nagaland was formed, large-scale buildings-offices, government institutions and residential quarters were raised on an intensive scale and along with these, trade and traffic in and around the town have become more and more enhanced. The town has a network of communications with the nearby and distant interior places over the whole State now. Transport has become fast and cheap.

Consequently, the ridges and mountain slopes which remained hitherto desolate in Kohima have been full of buildings. Constructing works are increasing and new sites for the administrative headquarters are emerging along with the cooperative stores, canteens, and other installations.

The important localities of Nagaland are:

Local name	English name
Mechozue	High School, Road
Mission Compound	Rivenburg Road
Soninu	Cemetery
Kakaie	PWD
Terbunyuike	Kuki Picquet
Dzudouzou	Chandmari
Kharuzou	Below Assam Rifles
Pezeliestsie	Veterinary Compound
Zienuobadze	High School Site
Seruzouna	Hospital Area

Kohima was a large village situated on the highest summit on the northeastern direction and opposite the Japoo and Kapamedzu ridges on southeast, is a big village said to contain more than 10,000 inhabitants. It had the following Khels.

T - Khel or Tsutuonoma.

L - Khel or Lhisema.

D - Khel or Dapfutsuma.

P - Khel or Pfuchatsuma.

The population of Kohima has crossed one lakh. It is growing at a faster paces.

Wokha

Wokha situated about 103 km to the north of Kohima is the district headquarters of Wokha District. The dominant tribe in Wokha tribe is Lotha. Its total population is around 15 thousand. There is a Government Degree college, a District Hospital and several Government offices.

Apart from above towns and district headquarters, there are several important historical and cultural places which are mainly situated in the southern parts of Nagaland. A brief description of these places has been given in the following paras.

Peren is situated at a distance of about one hundred kilometres from Kohima. The Subdivisional officers headquarters which was emerged in the heart of Zeliang tribe's territory. Peren is of great economic importance as a supply centre to the Zeliang-Kuki area with direct road communications with Dimapur. Its old village name is Birema. Till the time of the British administration, it had but only a primary school institution. Recently, parts of the government buildings with the offices of the SDO have shifted to Jalukie, the headquarters for Zeliangroung area.

Tseminyu is situated about 50 Kilometres from the capital of Nagaland. It was started as the headquarters of the civil liaison officer in 1956 in the Rengma area, which was however, replaced by an Assistant Commissioner when Naga Hills Tuensang area was constituted in the year 1957. Afterwards the Extra-Assistant Commissioner was placed In-charge. The Tseminya Subdivision comprises of 18 villages, almost all Rengma with Pughoboto circle of 16 Sema villages. Tseminyu with its characteristic feature as an administrative centre has buildings such as Public Works Departments (PWD), the block, hospital, court and schools. A new township is now under construction and when ready the new headquarters will shift there.

Meluri

Meluri first came into limelight in 1909 when an outpost was raised to check the incursions of the neighbouring war-like tribes. But it was in 1923 that the vast portion of eastern Chakhesang country was incorporated in the administration. A regular administration was started in 1955, but it was in 1960 that a Circle officer was given the charge of Meluri. In 1962 an Extra-Assistant Commissioner was posted attached to the Additional Deputy Commissioner at Phek.

Pfutsero

Its increasing importance is more as business than administrative headquarters in the heart of the chakhesang mountain terrain, where many shops and miscellaneous patterns of business have sprung up. There are horticultural gardens, weaving cooperatives, hospital and school institutions. The circle is attached to Phek District. It is also a Chakhesang Christian Centre with some noted Baptist institutions.

Khanoma

Khanoma is a historical place in the District of Kohima. Khanoma undertook warfare operations with the British explorers on numerous occasions. The first import war occurred in 1850 during the Lt. Vincent's engagement when this village with its confederates with held British advent for many months. But the most famous freedom struggle was in 1878-79, when it obstructed the troops' entry into the village for six months. The Government records point out that this village remained belligerent and impregnable despite overwhelming counter attack of the troops.

Mezoma

Mezoma is another war-like village. In 1840 with Piphema and jotsoma, the village obstructed Grange's survey operation. For 25 years, from 1840-65, it was renowned for its raids in the North Cachar and Mikir Hills. In 1850 with Khonoma, it offered stubborn resistance to the British advent in their land. In 1877, a strong punitive expedition was taken against Mezoma after its raids in North Cachar, but against severe odds, it protracted the warfare till January 1878. Mezoma next organised the Angami liberation war which broke out in September 1878.

Chumukedima

Chumukedima is an important centre in the southern parts of Nagaland. It attained foremost importance during the inception of the Naga Hills District when it was made the first Deputy Commissioner's Headquarters in 1866. It is situated in the foothills near the Diphu-Khukhi confluence at the part where these two rivers debouch the hills upon the plains. It is also known as Nichuguard or Samaguting (after mispronunciation of Chumukedima). The dominant vegetation around Chumukedima is mainly tropical. Some of the forests have however, been damaged by the shifting cultivators.

Ao the district headquarters, many expeditions and campaigns were sent out to the interior places and rudimentary steps were adopted to consolidate the administration in the neighbourhood from this district headquarters. The roads built by the earliest Deputy Commissioners such as John Gregory and Butler still survive which connect it Zeliang, Angami and Lotha areas. Chumukedima had the privilege of having the first school, hospital and other administrative buildings and the first mission centre, before they shifted to Kohima in 1878-80.

Chumukedima lies on the Dimapur-Imphal National Highway. There are a botanical park, a police training centre, water work and police station.

The original inhabitants are believed to have belonged to the Khonoma Angami group who migrated and settled at Chumukedima some generations ago.

Ghaspani or Medziphema

Situated at the foothills of Kohima Dimapur National Highway, with its tropical feature of weather and vegetation, it has grown as pineapple plantation centre and road-side station. There is an integrated extension training centre which conducts agricultural research and which imparts training to the village-level workers. At Ghaspani an Agricultural College has been established which is under the jurisdiction of the North Eastern Hill University, Shillong. This college has a beautiful campus and the students have been provided the residential facilities in hostels.

In brief Nagaland abounds in aesthetic beauty. Many villages raised over spurs of hills are not tiny but are big enough for accommodating hundreds of houses. Villages unadulterated yet in some remote interior places furnish sights of old marks of culture with rows of stone monuments, gate system and Morung. Road access are available with all the emerging townships in the Mate of Nagaland.

The ideal season for visiting the state of Nagaland is from November to March. Entry permit from the State Government is however, necessary. The festival of Sekrenyi, held in February attracts a large number of people. Christmas is another important festival in Nagaland.

It may be summarised that although for hundreds of years the Nagas resented the visits of strangers, their former attitude was probably was due to a rather natural suspicion and fear; today they are most open-hearted and generous of people, and the spirit of hospitality, which was always one of the most treasured virtues as among themselves, is now extended to their visitors. The traditional Naga attitude to property is very fascinating. The Feasts of Merit, in fact, is the distribution of wealth rather than its possession that was important. And this distribution includes everyone, not merely one's own relations and rich friends, but the poorest and the least important. Women hold a high and respectable position. They work on equal terms with the men in the field. The educated are among the most graceful and charming of India's womanhood. A belief in the importance of loyalty, a hardness of moral and physical fibre, courage before impossible living conditions, the love for adventure and explorations, a fresh, candid, simple attitude to life's problem are among the other qualities that the Nagas, alongwith many other hill people, have to give the world. If Nagaland can realise that Angami and Sema, Konyak and Ao, rebel and liberal, hillman and plainsman are 'but alternate beats of the same hearts', it will have a great and happy future.

As Nagaland realises its position in the great country of which it is so precious a part, it will share in the fulfilment of this ideal.

Dimapur

Originally a kachhari word Dimasa after the rivers which flow through it and was the renowned headquarters of the old kachhari kingdom, before it was shifted to Maibong; hitherto prior to its shifting, it was described to be a great city with large-scale undertaking in pottery and sericulture. The stone memorials and tanks which still survive point out to its ancient greatness.

Dimapur was the renowned Naga centre in the past while other supplementary petty markets have grown on the Dhansiri in its vicinity. Traditions point out to ancient Rengma inhabitation at Dimapur and along the Zubzar, a tributary of Doyang which they call Rengmapani. Later on they migrated northwardly to Borpathor and Rengmapahar near Golaghat where their colonies still survive.

According to traditions, the Rengmas left at Dimapur a rock inscription of arrow while all the other stone monuments constructed by Kacharis are believed to have been raised on the Rengma Naga rituals. Before the arrival of the British, the Rengmas supplied iron implements to the plains. Later on, the Angami and Zeliang in close proximity preponderated. For administrative convenience, Dimapur was bifurcated from Assam and incorporated in Naga Hill District.

Dimapur started to gain economic significance shortly after the railway line and Imphal road were constructed. More impetus was laid during the Japanese invasion when it was made military strategic camp. After Nagaland was formed, Dimapur has become a principal supply centre and an active subdivisional headquarters. There are SDO's office, State Bank, Forest and PWD colonies, Nagaland and Manipur State Transport stations, and other branch offices of the important directorates. Among educational institutions there is a high school with a spacious hostel compound, a college and cottage training centres (both government and private).

There are the industrial estate of Nagaland and the Khandsari Sugar Plant and other minor industries. Among the hotels mention may be made of Deluxe, Hotel Mandira, Punjab Hotel and Manipuri Hotels. The circuit house is presumably one of the best in the state. Many workshops and mills, shops and stores are growing out. Merchant classes from outside the district get special permits. The population is mixed. A great portion of the wasteland has been distributed to deserving Naga persons for construction of houses and cultivation purpose.

The following are the important localities of Dimapur:

- Kusiaribil, Darogajan, Puranabazar, Nahabari, Padumpukhuri, Bamun-pukhuri, Disagophu, Dhansiripar, Amaluma, Doyapur, Goneshnagar, Haladisa and Mangzumukh. All these are the Kachhari colonies which existed from time immemorial.

- Hatimora, Dobagaon, and Samaguri-Garo — another Basti-Dorago Pathar is a mixed Gao and Kachhari Busti (settlement).

- Kashiram - Mikir Busti (settlement).

- Nagorjan — mixed Zeliangroung and Angami settlement.

- Fafijung — kuki Busti (settlement).

- Kacharigaon-Nepalese — Nepalese are also scattered at Lengrijan, Nepaligaon, Nutan Busti, Singrijan, and Dhopanala.

- Doncan after Mr. S. J. Duncan, Deputy commissioner — mixed Ao and Lotha Busti (settlement).

- Colliery Colony — mainly a Bengali locality in addition to other mixed communities.

- Diphupar — having a mixed population.

- Rangapahar Side — inhabited by Sangtam-Sila and Aos.

- Singrijan — known as Christian Busti (settlement) inhabited by Munda, ex-tea estate labourers.

- Signal — mixed sema, Nepali and Angami, originally known as Oriya Bengali-Gaon (village).

- Naga New Model Mixed Tribes.

- Thaehahekhu (Thehekhum) — a sema Busti (settlement).

- Erabil — a new Ao colony.

The population in Dimapur town is heterogeneous owing to the important business, traffic, industrial and other establishments, thus exhibiting diverse culturable aspects. Dimapur is growing at a faster pace, though there is not much qualitative change in the process and pattern of Dimapur's growth and development.

Mokokchung

Situated in the territory of Ao tribe about 160 km to the north of Kohima, Mokokchung is the third largest town of Nagaland after Kohima and Dimapur. Its population is around twenty thousand. Being the administrative centre is has many social and educational institutions. Owing to these amenities, Mokokchung in working as the pull factor and attracting more population from the neighbouring villages and other small towns of the region. The Fazle Ali Govt. Degree College is one of the prestigious colleges of the state. Mokokchung has numerous orchids and is famous for oranges.

Phek

Situated about 120 km from Kohima, Phek is the District Headquarters of the Phek District. It is situated in the territory of Phek tribe. Before achieving the status of the District, Phek was having dispensary, and High School. Now, for the administrative offices a new township site has been selected in which modern structures are coming up. The District Headquarters have shifted to the new site.

Mon

Mon is the district headquarters of Mon district. The dominant tribe in this district is Konyak. The town of Mon is situated about 165 km. Its total population is around ten thousand (1981) and the town has a -mixed population of primary, secondary and tertiary sectors. The town is in the evolutionary stages.

Tuensang

Tuensang is the district headquarters of Tuensang district. It is situated about 40 km to the east of Mokokchung town. It is a very small town which has not gone under much transformation. Now several administrative building are being constructed to accommodate the government offices.

Zinheboto

Zinheboto is an emerging town and the administrative headquarters of zinheboto District. It is situated at a distance of about 62 km from Kohima — the state capital of Nagaland. It has a degree college and several government offices, circuit house, parks and play grounds.

Bibliography

Abbi, A. and Ahum, V.: *Expressive Morphology as Manner Adverbs in Khas, Tangkhul-Naga and Kuki-Chin languages*, Abb, 1997.

Ahum, V.: *A Grammatical Study of Expressives and Echo Formations in Tangkhul-Naga. M. Phil. Dissertation*, J.N.U., New Delhi, 1992.

Allen, B. C.: *Gazetteer of Naga Hills and Manipur*, Mittal Publications, New Delhi, 1905.

Anand, V.K.: *Nagaland in Transition*, Associated Publishing House, New Delhi, 1969.

Avery, John.: *The Hill Tribes of India*, American Antiquarium, New York, 1884.

Bareh, H.: *Naga Institute of Culture: The Art and Crafts of Nagaland*, Rohi Pub., Kolkata, 1970.

Bhat, D.N.S.: *Tangkhul-Naga Vocabulary*, Deccan College, Poona, 1969.

Bhaumik, Subir: *Insurgent Cross Fire: North-East India*, Lancer Publishers, New Delhi, 1996.

Bhuyan, B. C.: *Political Development of the North East*, Omsons Publications, New Delhi, 1989.

Bor, N.L. & Hutton, J.H.: *The Use of Tones in Sema Naga*, J.R.A.S., Nagaland, 1927.

Bronson, M.: *Phrases in English and Naga*, A.B.M. Press, Jaipur, 1867.

Brown, R.: *Statistical Account of the Native State of Manipur and the Hill Territory under its Rule*, Govt. Printing, Kolkata, 1873.

Butler, J.: *Rough Notes on the Angam Nagas*, J.A.S.B., Nagaland, 1875.

Butler, Major: *Sketch of Nagaland*, MacMillan, London, 1847.

Chasie, Charles: *The Naga Imbroglio: A Personal Perspective*, Standard Printers & Publishers, Kohima, 1999.

Chaube, S. K.: *Hill Politics in Northeast India*, Orient Longman Limited, Patna, 1973.

Clark, E.W.: *Naga Dictionary*, Baptist Mission Press, Kolkata, 1911.

Clarke, C.B.: *On the Plants of Kohima and Muneypor*, London, 1889.

Crawford, C.G.: *A Handbook of Kuki Custom*, State Printing Press, Imphal, 1927.

Damant, G.H.: *The Story of Khamba and Thoibi: A Manipuri Tale*, Indian Antiquary, Manipur, 1877.

Das, Gurudas and Purkayastha, R. K.: *Border Trade: North-East India and Neighbouring Countries*, Akansha Publishing House, New Delhi, 2000.

Das, Gurudas: *Research Priorities in North-East India: With Special Reference to Arunachal Pradesh*, Regency Publications, New Delhi, 2002.

Das, N.K. and Imechen, C.L.: *People of India*, Nagaland, 1994.

Datta, P.S.: *North East and the Indian State: Paradoxes of a Periphery*, Vikas Publishing House, New Delhi, 1995.

—————: *Northeast: A Study of Mobility and Political Behaviour*, Omsons Publications, Guwahati, 1991.

Deorani, S.C. and Sharma, G.D. Bishen Singh Mahendra Pal Singh: *Medicinal Plants of Nagaland*, Nagaland, 2007.

Devender Kumar Sikri: *Census of India 2001: Nagaland Administrative Atlas*, Controller of Pub, 2006.

Dutta, N.C.: *Politics of Identity and Nation Building in North-East India*, South Asian Press, New Delhi, 1997.

Elles, A.S.: *Chin Lushai Land*, Thacker & Spink, Kolkata, 1892.

Elwin, Verrier: *The Nagas in the Nineteenth Century*, Oxford University Press, London, 1969.

Fuchs, Stephen: *The Aboriginal Tribes of India*, St. Martin's Press, New York, 1973.

Furer-Haimendorf, Christoph von: *Return to the Naked Nagas*, Vikas Publishing House, New Delhi, 1976.

Furness, W.H.: *Ethnography of the Nagas of Eastern Assam*, J.R.A.I., Nagaland, 1902.

Gaite, A.E.: *History of Nagaland*, MacMillan, London, 1907.

Ganguli, Milada: *A Pilgrimage to the Nagas*, Oxford and IBH Publishing Co., New Delhi, 1984.

Gassah, L. S.: *Regional Political Parties in North East India*, Omsons Publications, New Delhi, 1992.

Ghosh, Subir: *Frontier Travails: Northeast: The Politics of a Mess*, MacMillan, New Delhi, 2001.

Giridhar, P.P.: *On the Word in Angami Naga*, Linguistics of Tibeto-Burman Area, Spring, 1991.

Givon, T.: *Syntax: A Functional-Typological Introduction*, John Benjamins, 1984.

Gopalakrishnan, R. and Joshua Thomas, C.: *Conflict to Reconstruction: Some Observations on Nagaland and Manipur*, Regency Pub, 2005.

Gopalkrishnan, R.: *Research Priorities in North-East India: With Special Reference to Assam*, Regency Publication, New Delhi, 2001.

Gowda, K.S.G.: *Ao Grammar*, CIIL Grammar Series, 1975.

Grang, G.R.: *Narrative of an Expedition into the Naga Territory of Assam*, J.A.S.B., Nagaland, 1939.

Grierson, G.A.: *Linguistic Survey of Indian*, Naga Group, Tibeto-Burman, 1928.

Griffith, F.L.: Travels in Assam, Burma and Nagaland, Bishop's College Press, Kolkata, 1847.

Hargovind Joshi: *Nagaland: Past and Present*, Akansha, 2001.

Horam, M.: *Social and Cultural Life of Nagas*, B.R. Publishing Corp., New Delhi, 1977.

Howkins, P.: *Introducing Phonology*, Hutchinson, 1984.

Husain, V.: *Nagaland Habitat Society and Shifting Cultivation*, Rima Pub., New Delhi, 1988.

Hutton, John Henry: *The Angami Nagas*, Oxford University Press, London, 1921.

Hyman, L.M.: *The Great Igbo Tone Shift: Third Annual Conference of African Linguistics*, Indiana University, Erhard Voeltz, 1974.

Hynniewta, T.M. Kataki S.K. and Wadhwa, B.M.: *Orchids of Nagaland*, Botanical Survey of India, India, 2000.

Iralu, Kaka D.: *How Then Shall We Live: Reflections on the Political, Economic and Religious Implications of Naga Nationhood*, Kaka D. Iralu, Kohima, 2001.

Jamir, N.S. and Rao, B.R.: *The Ferns of Nagaland*, 1988.

Jamir, S. C.: *Chief Ministers of Nagaland*, Nagaland, 1999.

Jenkins Capt.: *The Nagas of Assam*, J.A.S.B., Nagaland, 1936.

Jenkins, Major: *A Sketch of our Relations with the Angami Nagas*, Oxford, New York, 1994.

Johnstone, K.C.: *My EXperience in Manipur and the Naga Hills, Simpson Low*, Marston and Co., London, 1896.

Joshua, C. Thomas and Gurudas Das: *Dimensions of Development in Nagaland*, Regency Pub, Nagaland, 2002.

Kuhoi K Zhimomi: *Politics and Militancy in Nagaland*, Deep and Deep, 2004.

Kumar, Nikhilesh: *Survey of Research in Sociology and Social Anthropology in North-East India, 1970-1990*, Regency Publications, New Delhi, 1999.

Kunz, Richard and Vibha Joshi: *Naga – A Forgotten Mountain Region Rediscovered*, Merian, Basel, 2008.

Lanunungsang A.: *The Naga National Question in North-East India*, Mittal Publications, New Delhi, 2002.

LeBar, Frank M.: *Ethnic Groups of Mainland Southeast Asia*, HRAF Press, New Haven, 1964.

Mackenzie, A.: *A History of the Relations of Government with the Hill Tribes of the Nagaland*, Nagaland, 1884.

Maitra, Kiranshankar: *The Noxious Web: Insurgency in the Northeast*, Kanishka Publishers, Distributors, New Delhi, 2002.

Majumdar, D.N.: *Races and Cultures of India*, Asia Publishing House, New York, 1944.

Maloney, Clarence: *Peoples of South Asia*, Rinehart & Winston, New York, 1974.

Mattisoff, J.A.: *Review of Tangkhul-Naga Vocabulary*, Language, 1972.

Maxwell, Neville George Anthony: *India and the Nagas*, The Nagas and the North-East, India, 1980.

McChulloch, W.: *Account of the Valley of Munnipore and the Hill Tribes with a Comparative Vocabulary*, Nengal Printing Co., Kolkata, 1859.

McCulloch, Major W.: *Account of the Valley of Munnipore*, Sopvomâ, Mao Naga, 1859.

Mey, J.L.: *Pragmatics: An Introduction*, Blackwell, Oxford, 1993.

Mills, J.P.: *The Rengma Nagas*, MacMillan, London, 1937.

—————: *The Ao Nagas*, Oxford University Press, London, 1926.

Nag, Sajal: *India and North-East India: Mind, Politics and the Process of Integration 1946-1950*, Regency Publications, New Delhi, 1998.

Namo, Dalle: *The Prisoner From Nagaland*, United Publisher, Nagaland, 1987.

Neufville, Capt.: *On the Geography and Population of Nagaland*, Asiatic Researches, Nagaland, 1995.

Nibedita Sen and Rosamma Mathew: *Studies on Lower Vertebrates of Nagaland*, Zoological Survey of India, ZSI, 2008.

Nibedon, Nirmal: *Nagaland the Night of the Guerrillas*, Lancers Publishers, New Delhi, 1978.

Nuh, V. K.: *Crusade on Naga Morality*, Council of Naga Baptist Churches, Kohima, 1996.

Oppitz, Michael, Thomas Kaiser, Alban von Stockhausen and Marion Wettstein: *Naga Identities: Changing Local Cultures in the Northeast of India*, Snoeck Publishers, Gent, 2008.

Owen, J.: *Notes on the Naga Tribes in Communication with Nagaland*, W.H. Carey & Co., Kolkata, 1844.

Pakem, B.: *Insurgency in North-East India*, Om Sons Publications, New Delhi, 1997.

Pettigrew, Rev. Fr. W.: *Tangkhul-Naga Grammar and Dictionary*, The Tangkhul-Naga Baptist Convention, Ukhrul, 1979.

Philip, P. T.: *The Growth of Baptist Churches in Nahgaland*, Christian Literature Centre, Guwahati, 1976.

Phukon, Girin: *Politics of Regionalism in Northeast India*, Spectrum Publications, Guwahati, 1996.

Pike, K.L. and Pike, E.G.: *Text and Tagmeme*, Frances Printer, London, 1983.

Rahman, S.A.: *The Beautiful India: Nagaland*, Reference Press, 2006.

Rahul Karmakar: *Where Warriors Waltz: Festivals of Nagaland*, Photographs by Merimvu Doulo, Red River an Imprint of LBS, 2008.

Rawlins, J.: *On the Manners, Religion and Laws of the Cucis, or Mountaineers of Tipra*, Asiatic Researches, Nagaland, 1792.

S.K. Khanna: *Encyclopaedia of North-East India: Arunachal Pradesh, Assam, Manipur, Meghalaya, Tripura, Sikkim, Mizoram and Nagaland Tripura Sikkim*, Indian Pub, New York, 1999.

Sachdeva, Gulshan: *Economy of the North-East: Policy, Present Conditions and Future Possibilities*, Konark Publishers, Delhi, 2000.

Sachdeva, Rajesh: *Language Education in Nagaland: Sociolinguistic Dimensions*, Regency Publications, New Delhi, 2001.

Sema, Piketo: *British Policy and Administration in Nagaland 1881-1947*, Scholar Publishing House, New Delhi, 1992.

Shukla, R.P. and Buno Zetsuvi, Manas: *Education Development in Nagaland*, 2006.

Singh, H.B.: *Current Trends in Life Sciences-XIX: Recent Trends in Plant Disease Control: Proceedings of the National Symposium on Recent Trends in Plant Disease Control, April 12-14, 1989*, Nagaland, India, 1993.

Singh, K. S.: *People of India: Nagaland*, Seagull Books, Calcutta, 1994.

Singh, K.P. and Sinha, G.P.: *Lichen Flora of Nagaland*, 1994.

Sinha, A.C.: *Youth Movements in North-East India: Structural Imperatives and Aspects of Change*, Indus Publishing Company, New Delhi, 1994.

Smith, William C.: *The Ao-Naga Tribe of Assam*, Mittal, New Delhi, 2002.

Srivastav, Nirankar: *Survey of Research in Economics on North East India 1970-1990*, Regency Publications, New Delhi, 2000.

Stracly, P.D.: *Nagaland Nightmare*, Popular Prakashan, Bombay, 1958.

Syiemlieh, R. David: *Survey of Research in History on North-East India 1970-1990,* Regency Publication, New Delhi, 2000.

Thakur, G. C. Sharma: *The Plains of Tribes of Lakhimpur, Dibrugargh, Sibsagar and Nowgong,* Tribal Research Institute, Assam, 1972.

Thomas, C. Joshua and Das Gurudas: *Dimensions of Development in Nagaland,* Regency Publications, New Delhi, 2002.

Triveni Goswami: *Gender and Conflict Transformation,* Nagaland and Egypt, Akansha Pub, Nagaland, 2007.

Udayon Misra: *The Periphery Strikes Back: Challenges to the Nation-State in Assam and Nagaland,* Indian Institute of Advanced Study, New York, 2000.

Vachaspati, J.: *Nagaland (Hindi)*, Publication Division, New Delhi, 1969.

Varman, S. B. K. Dev: *Young, Gavin, Indo-Naga War: A Journalist Account (1961),* Gase Publications, Viphuora, 2001.

Verghese, B.G.: *India's North East Resurgent: Ethnicity, Insurgency, Governance, and Development,* Konark Publishers, New Delhi, 1997.

Woodthrope, R.G.: *Report of the Survey Operations in the Naga Hills,* Secretariat Press, Shillong, 1876.

Index

❑❑❑❑

www.ingramcontent.com/pod-product-compliance
Lightning Source LLC
Chambersburg PA
CBHW080759300326

41914CB00055B/947